21850
35.00

Fort Pitt
Rochester
Kent
ME1 1DZ

Tel: 01634 888734

E-mail:
gatewayrochester@uca.ac.uk

POLITICAL VIRTUE AND SHOPPING
INDIVIDUALS, CONSUMERISM, AND COLLECTIVE ACTION

Michele Micheletti

First published 2003 by
PALGRAVE MACMILLAN™
175 Fifth Avenue, New York, N.Y. 10010 and
Houndmills, Basingstoke, Hampshire, England RG21 6XS.
Companies and representatives throughout the world.

PALGRAVE MACMILLAN is the global academic imprint of the Palgrave Macmillan division of St. Martin's Press, LLC and of Palgrave Macmillan Ltd. Macmillan® is a registered trademark in the United States, United Kingdom and other countries. Palgrave is a registered trademark in the European Union and other countries.

ISBN 1–4039–6133–6 hardback

Library of Congress Cataloging-in-Publication Data
Micheletti, Michele.
    Political virtue and shopping: individuals, consumerism, and collective action/by Michele Micheletti.
        p. cm.
    Includes bibliographical references and index.
    ISBN 1–4039–6133–6
        1. Consumption (Economics)—Social aspects. 2. Consumption (Economics)—Political aspects. 3. Consumption (Economics)—Moral and ethical aspects. 4. Consumer protection—Citizen participation. 5. Political participation. 6. Individualism. 7. Consumers—Sweden—Political activity—Case studies. I. Title.

HC79.C6M53 2003
306.3—dc21   2003051726

A catalogue record for this book is available from the British Library.

Design by Newgen Imaging Systems (P) Ltd., Chennai, India.

First edition: September, 2003
10 9 8 7 6 5 4 3 2 1

Printed in the United States of America.

TABLE OF CONTENTS

FOREWORD

This book is part of a large research program that was administered by City University of Stockholm entitled "Ethics, Virtues, and Social Capital in Sweden." Its coordinator was Emil Uddhammar. The Axel och Margaret Ax:son Johnson Foundation generously funded the program and my project. Their funding allowed for course release for research, an international seminar on political consumerism in May/June 2001, and even facilitated my stay as a visiting scholar in the United States in the first months of winter 2000. The International Seminar on Political Consumerism resulted in an anthology on political consumerism, *Politics, Products, and Markets: Exploring Political Consumerism Past and Present* (Transaction Publishers) and consolidated a research network. Many of the seminar participants have offered good comments on my work, and I want to thank them collectively. One participant, Bente Halkier from Roskilde University, sent me written comments on the first draft of this book from March 2001. I also want to thank everyone at City University for making my time there both productive and enjoyable. Joel Aberbach at the Department of Political Science, UCLA, helped me greatly with my stay as a visiting scholar at his university. Time away at another university gave me occasion to think and discuss my research ideas in a new and different surrounding. The talk I gave there helped me craft my research agenda more clearly. Then I moved east. Bert Rockman, at that time at the Department of Political Science, University of Pittsburgh, gave me the opportunity to hold a seminar on my research. I received good feedback in Pittsburgh and met people with common research interests. Versions of chapters 1, 2, and 4 were presented at different conferences in Europe and the United States between 1999 and 2002. The comments I received helped me to understand the importance of the phenomenon of political consumerism more fully. Political consumerism has been a topic in a number of different courses in Stockholm and elsewhere. Students who attended my lectures gave me valuable comments. My home department, the Department of Political Science, Stockholm University, gave and continues to give me the opportunity to develop courses around political consumerism and new forms of political participation. These courses have been golden opportunities for me to discuss a first draft of my completed book manuscript with under-graduate and graduate students. The Swedish Society for the Conservation of Nature, the subject of the case study in chapter 4, had a very open attitude to researchers and provided me with exten-sive internal material. Four officials gave of their time to discuss green political consumerism with me. Eva Eiderström and Helena Norin at the eco-label Good Environmental Choice unit and Lars Vaste and Anders Friström at the SNF central headquarters deserve special thanks.

This book was researched and written within a two-year period on a half-time basis. It was revised in fall 2002. During this time, I found that political consumerism is a much richer area for scholarly study than I envisioned at first. Scholars need to do much more work in this field. And I can say that this book is far from my final encounter with the fascinating phenomenon of political consumerism. I hope it is the same for you.

Michele Micheletti
Stockholm
December 2002

Preface

If you think about it, daily trips to the market to buy food and clothing for our families and more substantive shopping events like purchasing a car, a boat, or furniture for the living room involve many more aspects than just deciding if you like the product and can afford it. We may consider where we want to purchase the product. Some stores may be more appealing than others because of their location, their look, the way they deal with customers, or even how they treat their employees. Maybe we are concerned about where and how the product is made. Does it include chemicals harmful to our health, to the people that made it, or for the environment? Another set of shopping considerations may be the people behind the product. Who are they, and how are they treated? Is child labor involved?

Shopping involves more than just economic considerations like the relationship between material quality and price. There are social, ethical, and political issues embedded in shopping decisions as well. Yet most of us do not give a lot of conscious thought to what can be called the politics of a product. We take for granted that the products we buy are made according to our own ethical standards. Or perhaps we do not really care. Most of the time the politics of a product are latent or invisible, but they become visible when citizens give them public significance and begin to see how they compare with their philosophy of life and political persuasion. When citizens act on these considerations they behave as *political consumers.*

Political consumerist considerations play an increasingly important role in the world today. Growing numbers of university students question university policy on the procurement of sports equipment and they give serious thought to the kind of coffee they drink on campus and elsewhere. Groups like the European Clean Clothes Campaign and North American anti-sweatshop movement (or No Sweat as it is called) as well as campaigns like Responsible Coffee and institutions like Forest Stewardship Certification and eco-labeling schemes encourage people from all walks of life to reflect on the role that their consumer choices play in the world today.

But why these concerns now? At least part of the answer is globalization and free trade, which bring people around the world closer together in interesting and new ways. Globalization is also making it more difficult for companies to hide the politics of products. An increasing number of labeling institutions and consumer-oriented campaigns are bringing the politics behind products to the fore. Internet campaigns have been started to inform consumers about the politics of specific products; books are written on how to shop for a better world; consumers are mobilized in boycotts and "buycotts" to choose products in a more politically conscious way; labeling schemes that evaluate the politics of a product are institutionalized, and companies are encouraged to change their policies and develop codes of conduct so that their products reflect ethical, political, environmental, and social concerns. Politics is, therefore, entering the marketplace through the pocketbooks of consumers and organizations that serve them.

Concepts such as the citizen-consumer, business ethics, corporate citizenship, social responsible investing, and political consumerism among others have been created to identify this development. The phenomenon of political consumerism is the focus of this book. Although the phenomenon itself is not at all new, the term "political consumerism" is of recent origin. It was first used in Denmark in the mid-1990s to understand the boycott of Shell Oil.[1] In Danish it is "politiske forbruger" and was an attempt by its authors to capture the sense of social and political global responsibility that consumers can exercise in understanding material products as more than just objects of material use and consumption. Political consumerism concerns the politics of products, which in a nutshell can be defined as power relations among people and choices about how resources should be used and allocated globally. Political consumers choose products, producers, and services more on the basis of the politics of the product than the product as material object per se. Their choices are informed by political values, virtues, and ethics. They differ from economic consumers who are just looking for a good buy, that is, a satisfactory relationship between material quality and economic costs. Political consumers also tend to differ from lifestyle consumers who shop for products with the sole aim of helping to define and enhance their self-identity.

The phenomenon of political consumerism has, as discussed in chapter 2, long historical roots. And it is surprising that scholars have not studied it to any great degree. This aim of this book is to offer a comprehensive overview of the phenomenon and to understand why people engage in political consumerist acts. With this book, I want to place political consumerism more securely on the social science research agenda.

There are several different ways of studying political consumerism, and they all depend on the disciplinary perspective of the scholar. Market researchers stress the impact of political consumer choice on market actors. They measure its effectiveness by its market share and effect on the thinking and behavior of companies. Sociologists find the phenomenon fascinating because it allows them to penetrate theories of late capitalism, postmodernism, and self-reflexivity. Economists study its outcomes, that is, whether political consumer choice can redistribute resources globally. Students of the history of ideas ponder whether political consumerism is a break from the past in our thinking on the separation of the political from the economic sphere. For political scientists, the fascination concerns the market as an arena for politics. This is by no way uncontroversial for a discipline that has its roots in the study of states, governments, public policy, and political participation in the political system. In political science, my own discipline, we study the phenomenon of political consumerism in two basic ways: as an example of governance, soft laws, and new regulatory tools and as a form of citizen involvement in politics. We investigate the development of new institutions to assess whether they fill regulatory vacuums and curb responsibility-floating.[2] My focus is the second approach. Political consumerism is studied as a form of citizen engagement in politics, though I do discuss its institutional framing and regulatory character in chapter 3.

Chapter 1 focuses on why political consumerism has developed as a form of political participation and why it is perceived by many people as a controversial phenomenon. This is done in a discussion on how it can be understood theoretically. Emphasis is placed on political consumerism as a new form of political participation, by which I mean that it conceptualizes itself differently than most other forms of citizen involvement in politics. The chapter discusses how changes in the political landscape have politicized consumption and why our everyday life as consumers is increasingly intertwined with global politics. A new concept, *individualized collective action*, is introduced to understand how this interconnection becomes political activity. Theoretical attention is also focused on the empowering force of political consumerism and on how private concerns have public meaning by analyzing the relationship between private interest and public virtue. Here I discuss two sources of political consumer activism, the private virtue and public virtue tradition.

Chapter 2 penetrates the historical roots of political consumerism. It analyzes a collection of examples mainly from secondary literature and historical sources, interpreted and discussed through the political consumerism lens. I have chosen to interpret the material in this fashion because the authors referenced in the chapter have in most cases not discussed their examples and cases as illustrations of political consumerist participation. The chapter emphasizes how women, ethnic groups, civil society associations, and revolutionary movements have used consumption and "private" consumer choices as a tool for change. Most of the material concerns the United States, and I have made an effort to include European examples known to me. The problematic nature of political consumerism historically and currently is stressed in a section dealing with the dilemmas of market-based collective action for politics and democracy. This chapter is important because it helps me to develop research questions about the similarities and differences between earlier and current forms of political consumerism.

Contemporary forms of political consumerism are the focus of chapter 3, which discusses its scope, variety, institutionalization, and importance for politics today. The different categories that are explained and analyzed are consumer boycotts, labeling schemes, stewardship certification, and socially responsible investing. The institutionalization of political consumerism is contrasted with other market-based regulatory tools and the characteristics of contemporary political consumerism are systematized. One interesting finding discussed in some detail is trends toward mainstreaming.

Chapter 4 takes a closer look at why people engage in political consumerism. What motivates them to get involved in this fashion? Who are political consumers? And how are current forms of political consumerism similar and different from the past? These are broad, encompassing questions that require a variety of research methods and approaches to be answered successfully. My answers come from a case study of green political consumerist activities in Sweden. Sweden was chosen because one would assume that it is an unlikely place for political activism in the marketplace. It is an unlikely setting because the Swedish state is strong, social democratic, and with a good record on environmental policymaking. Following the understanding of political consumerism developed in chapter 1, one would easily assume that Sweden does not need to use the market as a site for politics because it does not have governability problems: the political system works effectively; Swedish citizens have trust in it, and collectivistic rather than individualized collective action tends to characterize their

political involvements. Its presence in Sweden is explained by the
effects of globalization and postmodernization, which are opening
up new opportunities for different kinds of political engagements
and individualized collective action. Results from the case study are
related back to the discussion in chapter 1, which emphasize the
importance of such political landscape changes as globalization,
individualization, postmodernization, ecological modernization, risk
society, and even governance as catalysts for current political consumerist endeavors. A new research finding from the case study is
the similarities between the historical and contemporary forms of
political consumerism. Three significant underlying ones are the role
played by women as political consumers, the creation of social capital
as a necessary condition for political consumerism to be successful,
and the importance of the private virtue tradition or focusing on
everyday problems of satisfying self-oriented interests for mobilizing
citizens politically. Contrary to many other studies of political participation and social capital, my findings also show how political action
in the form of political consumerism creates new social capital and
broad societal trust. Thus, the causal link is reversed: participation is
shown to create social capital in the case study. The role of women
as everyday green political shoppers and activists has been instrumental here.

Another important research finding is the changing role of
government for political consumerism and political action in general.
When compared to history and the discussion in chapter 2, the contemporary examples from chapter 3 and case study from chapter 4
show how political consumers tend to appeal to government as a large
institutional consumer. This appeal differs considerably from the traditional relationship between citizen and government, which takes its
point of departure in government as the maker of public policy. This
book discusses how government procurement policy—that is its consumer choices—interests political consumers. Results from the case
study in chapter 4 show how political consumer activists successfully
lobbied municipal governments to choose a more environmentally
friendly office paper and how this change in government purchasing
practices quickly altered the production methods of Swedish paper
mills. Swedish green political activists are not alone in noting the
impact that large consumers like governments, universities, and businesses can have on corporate policy and behavior. Institutional
procurement policy is presently a contentious issue on American
university campuses, and it will most likely be an extremely important
political battlefield in the future.

Chapter 5 asks why we are increasingly concerned with applying virtues in the marketplace, presents and addresses the main criticisms of political consumerism, discusses the relationship between political consumerism and trust and social capital, and ends by pondering whether the new actor categories created from viewing the market as a site for politics—citizen-consumers, corporate citizenship, and socially responsible investors, and others—represent a new great transformation that is carving a new sphere of action now that we are reshaping responsibility-taking globally and individualizing its causes and effects. It shows how virtues work as generic benchmarks in times of redistribution of responsibility-taking among actors and spheres and discusses the role of bonding and bridging social capital in reshaping responsibility-taking. The chapter also identifies the main criticisms against political consumerism and relates them to the findings in this book. A criticism that is given particular attention is the claim that political consumerism is not effective. This chapter begins a discussion on how effectiveness should be measured that is continued in the appendix, which outlines a research agenda for the study of political consumerism. The discussion shows that effectiveness must be measured in at least five different and interrelated ways that begin with the wording of problem formulations and end with an evaluation of outcomes and problem solutions. Claims of greenwash, bluewash, and sweatwash do not consider the process-orientation of political consumerism and need to be modified.

1

WHY POLITICAL CONSUMERISM?

WHEN PRODUCTS BECOME POLITICAL

How should we understand the impact of an E-mail exchange between an individual consumer requesting that the word sweatshop be put on his customized shoes and a multinational corporation in the global garment industry? This now classic Nike Email Exchange reached millions of people worldwide and turned its initiator, a university student, into a global media celebrity. Some people reacted by considering the exchange an important new way of making political statements and influencing powerful global actors. Others were either outraged by it or saw it as a childish and silly way of dealing with the serious problem of offshore employment policy and the effects of economic globalization on developing countries. Yet it appears that everyone who knew about it was affected, including Nike who decided to debate its labor practices in offshore factories with this young man on American national television.[1]

What explains public interest in this event and public reaction to it? Why are consumer campaigns like Responsible Coffee, Clean Clothes, and No Sweat and institutions called Forest Stewardship Certification and Good Environmental Choice being established? The short answer is that these endeavors have been initiated to influence the commodity chain of products. Their mission is to ensure that goods produced domestically and globally are traded on the basis of fairness, good labor practices, and sustainable development.[2]

A more penetrating answer is the subject of this book, which understands the examples and the questions they raise as representing more profound changes in how we think about politics and economics and the relationship between our public and private lives. I begin to answer these questions in this chapter, which takes its theoretical point of departure in changes in our political landscape and challenges to our conventional view of politics and political participation.

Most of us have been taught to participate in politics by voting in elections and by becoming involved in political parties and civic associations.[3] The E-mail exchange as well as the consumer campaigns and institutions mentioned above imply a different view of citizen engagement in politics. They show that there is a political connection between our daily consumer choices and important global issues of environmentalism, labor rights, human rights, and sustainable development. There is, in other words, a politics of consumer products, which for growing numbers of people implies the need to think politically privately. This politicizes what we have traditionally conceived as private consumer choice and erases the division between the political and economic spheres.

People who view consumer choice in this fashion see no border between the political and economic spheres. For them, the market is an arena for politics. They also believe that their private choices have political consequences. They see an interconnectedness of their private and public acts. It is no longer possible for them to make a sharp distinction between the virtues most important only for politics, community, or private life. Everyday conduct of individual citizens is not just a matter for private life but increasingly important from the local to the global level for politics, community, and the character of the marketplace. The metaphor "footprints" captures the essence of this interconnectedness.[4] We leave *ecological, ethical, and public footprints* or consequences for others as we go about our seemingly daily private lives. Awareness of this, as in the examples above, implies an acknowledgment that everyday choices and acts by individuals play an important role for the future of political, social, and economic life. In short, every person is part of global responsibility-taking. Or in the postmodern language of scholars of global risk society "...individuals can feel themselves to be authors of global political acts..."[5]

The phenomenon of consumer behavior as political involvement and global responsibility-taking goes under many guises. It has been called consumer activism, ethical consumerism, and socially responsible investing. The term *political consumerism* is used in this book. It represents actions by people who make choices among producers and products with the goal of changing objectionable institutional or market practices. Their choices are based on attitudes and values regarding issues of justice, fairness, or noneconomic issues that concern personal and family well-being and ethical or political assessment of favorable and unfavorable business and government practice. Political consumers are the people who engage in such choice situations. They may act individually or collectively. Their market choices reflect an understanding of material products as embedded in a complex social and normative context.[6]

CONTROVERSIES OVER POLITICIZING CONSUMER CHOICE

Political consumerism is a controversial topic and an uncomfortable one for many scholars. It provokes social scientists because it signals that citizens are looking outside traditional politics and civil society for guidelines to help them formulate their more individualized philosophy of life and live as good citizens. It challenges our sense that money and morality cannot be mixed, as it is in green businesses, socially responsible investing, codes of conduct, and general trends toward corporate citizenship. Most importantly, it forces us to consider the role of the market in politics and the role of politics in the market.

Because the phenomenon is not well researched, it is easily misunderstood. Many scholars, particularly in the United States, consider empirical research on the phenomenon a political statement, and their comments at academic conferences reflect this view.[7] Some of them view political consumerism as representing a normative appeal for neoliberalism, economic globalization, and market capitalism and a call for the rolling back of the state. For them, politically smart shopping cannot rectify the wrongs committed by multinational corporations or make the world greener, better, and more just. This is the sole responsibility of government, and any talk of politically smart shopping diverts attention from the role that government must play and allows governments to engage in responsibility-floating. Other scholars are provoked by it because they see it as a left-wing statement and just another attempt by the political left to prohibit free trade and justify increased government regulation of business. They fear that politicizing consumer choice is the first step toward increased political control over the market. A third group takes a middle position by viewing it as an interesting political tool that may be able to play a role in civilizing global capitalism and creating regulatory mechanisms in areas where the state is unable to act effectively. They acknowledge the presence of economic globalization and concede that political globalization has been slower to develop. Political consumerism is seen as an (not the) attempt to fill in regulatory gaps. Others, like this author, see it as an interesting phenomenon well-worth studying because it challenges our traditional thinking about politics as centered in the political system of the nation-state and what we mean by political participation.

But can political consumerism deal effectively with political problems like child labor, environmental destruction, and depletion of the rain forests? The chapters in this book answer this overriding question by breaking it up into smaller ones about how political consumerism can be understood theoretically, why there is more concern about consumer choice today, how market-based regulatory tools are designed and work in practice, whether political consumerism can be explained by citizen dissatisfaction with government performance, if the marketplace is a new political arena, whether political consumerism is a reflection of profound changes in society, and who uses political consumerism as a form of political engagement and why they do so.

The task of this chapter is to address the theoretical understanding of political consumerism. The next section gives a bird's eye view of changes in the political landscape that are of relevance for explaining political consumerism and how these changes have been discussed theoretically by social scientists. The focus is then turned to the issue of consumerism as politics. The topic of the second section is what makes it political? Section four zooms in more closely on consumers as political actors. It discusses the political agency of consumers by directing our attention to the empowering force of political consumerism. Then I turn to the role of virtues in political consumerism and address the issues of why private consumer concerns can have public meaning by analyzing the relationship between the private and public virtue traditions of political consumerism and the role of self-interest in politics. The seventh section penetrates more closely why the everyday life of citizens is increasingly intertwined with politics. It introduces the concept of individualized collective action, which I believe helps us to understand consumers as political actors today. The chapter ends with a short discussion of whether political consumerism can renew democracy and the political community.

CHANGING POLITICAL LANDSCAPE

New thinking from different social science disciplines is needed to understand why changes in the political landscape can promote citizens to view consumer choice as a way of solving political problems and the market as an arena of politics. The nature of the phenomenon of political consumerism motivates this crossbreeding of academic disciplines. To understand how shopping impacts politics, scholars must follow political consumers who not only cross the border of the political and economic sphere in their actions but also the public/private divide that separates people as political individuals (citizens) from private actors (consumers and family members). Ideas discussed in this section are primarily taken from political science, sociology, and business studies, disciplines that in their own ways are studying how individuals and institutions use market action to create trust, control uncertainty, and solve common (public) problems. Governance and postmodernization are political science theories that set the stage to answer questions about the rise of political consumerism. Ecological modernization, reflexive modernization, and the risk society are the key theoretical elements from sociology. Theoretical work done on the audit society is the business studies' focus. These concepts and lines of thought point in one direction. They concern how globalization and individualization—two dominant shifts in the political landscape—are prompting citizens to take politics in their own hands and are creating new arenas for responsibility-taking.

As shown in this book, an important change in the political landscape over the years that encourages citizens to become political consumers is the difficulty that many states now have in ensuring citizen well-being. Problems such as environmental destruction, human rights violations, AIDS, smuggling, trafficking, and terrorism are examples of issue areas that states have difficulty controlling. Some states experience these problems more acutely than others. These challenges represent new kinds of governability problems. Solutions to these global problems require the cooperation of several states and new forms of politics that involve actors and institutions outside the political system. This entails the development of a new conception of politics. Politics can no longer be defined as the nation-state's authoritative distribution of values in society that is implemented either by force or by the legitimacy created by general popular agreement.[8] Neither is politics delimited to the proceedings of the different branches of government, that is, the political system. Today politics goes deeper than the public debate and public decisions. It concerns interactions among different spheres and levels of life or what political scientists earlier referred to as the environment of the political system.[9]

Governance is a theoretical perspective that recognizes this newer understanding of politics and the role of the political system in politics. A simple definition is the need for cooperation among the state, quasi-state, non-state (nongovernmental), and private institutions like corporations to solve collective-action problems and to take responsibility for citizen well-being.[10] This means that the political system and its environments are not only intertwined but also highly dependent upon each other. The governance perspective of politics acknowledges that the political landscape has changed dramatically. It is no longer the state that is necessarily the primary and dominant actor in politics. Rather, these tasks and responsibilities are often shared and coordinated in less conventional ways and through multilayered networks.[11]

What changes explain governance? Scholars have different ideas here. Some political scientists explain governance trends as a search for new policy tools—for instance soft laws and labeling schemes that involve consumers and business—because traditional government action has failed to reach its objectives. Others take their point of departure in the growing complexity of collective-action problems that is creating a need for new steering capabilities, which require the entrance of new actors in policymaking. Empirically it may not always be easy to distinguish between the two explanations in concrete settings because the two problems often are interrelated, but theoretically these distinctions are important. Scholars discuss government failure by highlighting a variety of state weaknesses including such legitimacy problems as public lack of faith in government solutions and problems with political competency and effectiveness. Examples of the latter are state inability to formulate successful and effective policy programs because of political deadlock or the need to compromise to create a majority, undue bureaucratic organization of problem-solving endeavors, group think, and lack of or improper use of resources.[12] Political scientists conclude that these problems lead to difficulty in formulating correct solutions and in implementing regulatory policies. They have implications for how people view politics. For example as discussed in chapter 4, Swedish environmental activists dissatisfied with how government was making policy regarding the environmental impact of business decided it best to "reroute" their environmental demands on business.[13] Rather than following their traditional path of calling repeatedly on government to regulate business, they decided to place their demands on business directly, as have other actors before and after them.[14]

Explanations that point to the need for new steering capabilities due to complexity consider even good government solutions and implementing potential as inadequate to solve today's difficult problems. The reason is that government policy alone cannot create the kind of compliance necessary to solve them. In these cases, "beyond compliance" efforts are required to solve common problems.[15] This means that the involved actors must be willing to go further than required by law. It may also be the case that problems defy national boundaries, which implies that transboundary coordination is necessary to solve them. This kind of coordination is often beyond the mandate of the state. Other cooperative frameworks, as those represented by political consumerist institutions, are necessary.[16] Without coordination over borders and levels, accountability is impossible and different actors and levels can pass off the problem to each other and engage in responsibility-floating. Thus, effective steering as a problem-solving tool in complex contexts requires active, positive involvement on the part of a variety of individual and institutional actors. These include governmental, nongovernmental, and corporate actors as well as individual consumers and citizens. In many cases it is crucial that the actors take the initiative to solve problems themselves. Policymaking need not, therefore, always start in the political sphere with legislation and executive branch regulatory or cabinet ministry documents. A measure of self-organization, self-reflexivity, and self-steering on the part of actors other than government may, therefore, be seen as necessary for successful policy ventures, as shown in the discussion on forest certification schemes in chapter 3.

Scholars of new regulatory tools and soft law argue that actors must view policymaking and regulation as a process in which problems are dealt with in appropriate and adaptable ways. This means that policymakers—be they government officials, civil society activists, individual consumers, or private corporations—must start by looking at the character of the problem and then decide which tools to use to manage or solve it. Tools other than government directives and civil servant involvement are possible. The messages sent to business by political consumers are an example of the kind of new policy tool referred to here. When governance in domestic or global settings works well it creates capable political actors who understand how political institutions work and who are able to deal effectively with them.[17] In many ways, this is a new way of doing politics.

Governance as an explanation for the rise of political consumerism ties in well with *postmodernization*, a theoretical perspective highlighting other general changes in the political landscape such as individualization, political conflicts over values (postmaterialism), and focus on consumption over production as a potentially powerful steering mechanism.[18] According to scholars of postmodernization, politics is not just a struggle among interest groups and political parties for state attention and action. Its sphere is larger than the political system and concerns issues packed with values and virtues, for example the struggle between consumers and private companies over how goods are produced. Postmodernization is also a debate over

how political problems are defined, which concerns ethical considerations about how individual citizens should be able to craft their own
circumstances to be able to live a good life. Individualization and
active citizenship stress the need for people to take more individual
responsibility for solving problems. This may require that they reflect
upon what ecological, ethical, and public footprints they are leaving
behind for others to cope with and how their daily routines affect
politics, for instance what signals family consumer choices send to
industry and the impact they have on the environment.

Concerns about green issues and environmental destruction are
changing our focus of what is important politically—locally, nationally, and globally. Recent theorizing on environmentalism and the
larger issue of sustainability emphasizes the role of individual citizens
and consumers in changing the business of consumption.[19] In many
ways, environmental and sustainability problems are forcing scholars
to develop ideas about governance of complex problems in complex
settings. Two important theoretical inputs here are ecological modernization and reflexive modernization. Sociologists theorizing on
ecological modernization and reflexive modernization consider ecological concerns a major change in the political landscape that affects
our problem-solving capacity and political strategies. *Ecological
modernization* views transboundary environmental pollution as
evidence that the modern state is in a governability crisis. This is the
case because it has severe steering problems in the field of environmental policy. Ecological modernizationists point to the need for a
paradigm shift in policymaking that takes its point of departure in
developing sustainable lifestyles and changing consumer behavior
rather than in legislation and policy tools that rely on state invention
and regulation. This blurs the distinction commonly made between
public and private life. Unlike earlier green thinking, ecological modernization also acknowledges that economic prosperity and environmental concerns are compatible. Morality and money can be mixed.
Its use of the footprint metaphor also implies a redefinition of the
relationship between the state, citizens, civil society, consumers, and
private corporations. New cooperative partners and arrangements are
to develop regulative processes that are "... characterized by the
principles of horizontal cooperation, consensual—and dialogical—
decisionmaking, less formal institutionalization and a growing importance of actors at the decentral level."[20] Green capitalism and green
political consumerism are examples of these new cooperative arrangements. Both imply a new brokerage role[21] for private corporations
and civil society associations, which are encouraged to build new

coalitions to develop new steering capacities. Coalitions of these kinds help create bridging social capital or trust among people who differ from each other on a number of characteristics.[22] Such political consumerist institutions as certification programs and eco-labeling schemes are examples of such capacities.

The *reflexive modernization* literature is similar to ecological modernization, but it has more serious implications for the way in which we understand how changes in the political landscape trigger political consumerism. For these sociologists, politics is no longer the prerogative of the state and civil society traditionally conceived. A new kind of politics—*subpolitics*—is emerging from below that encourages, empowers, and allows citizens to take more responsibility for their personal and collective well-being.[23] According to its theorists, subpolitics emerges more from the state's inadequacy in controlling the new uncertainties and risks created by industrial society than from its coordination problems and ineffective regulatory tools. Risk has less to do with the probabilities of problems occurring and more to do with the competency and trustworthiness of institutions that are created to assess and deal with them. Government's inadequacy in assessing and dealing with new problems is said to cause a crisis of state legitimacy, which according to risk-society theorists explains increasing high levels of political distrust and citizen flight from traditional politics.[24] The mad cow disease and other food risks caused by the industrialization of agriculture as well as the debate over genetically modified organisms are good examples of what risk-society sociologists consider the state's predicaments in dealing with problems caused by industrial society. Consumers in Europe and the United States who are concerned with these problems search for food that is problem- and risk-free, and their search is strengthening the need for organically labeled food products, which as discussed in chapter 3 are political consumerist institutions.

Business studies scholars answer the question about the rise of political consumerism by pointing to the establishment of new legitimate and trustworthy monitoring schemes that have been spurred on by such changes in the political landscape as government privatization, deregulation, and economic globalization. They view monitoring schemes as attempts to fill in regulatory vacuums and put some order into the regulatory chaos that has developed from changes in the political landscape. Examples of new attempts to solve problems are summarized in such new terms as *audit society*, audit explosion, and mobile networks for regulation, which describe different kinds of citizen, consumer, and particularly institutional activity. Many of these activities monitor and rank products and services.[25] They represent risk reduction practices based on the pragmatic idea of control and organizational transparency,[26] and as such are trends toward good governance and ecological modernization. Business studies scholars appraise monitoring activities as those political consumerist labeling schemes discussed in chapter 3 in terms of their institutional design. Their findings show that if these schemes are considered to have the necessary institutional characteristics they will be considered as legitimate and trustworthy by consumers, business, and government alike. The kind of conditions that business scholars consider necessary for legitimacy are: whether a trustful relationship between consumers, monitors, and business has been created; whether there is a good working relationship between auditing institutions and the companies they choose for evaluation; whether information has been collected and coordinated in such a way that satisfies all stakeholders, and finally whether the audit practice is based on institutional autonomy (that is, the evaluative tools cannot in any way be dependent on the companies whose products and services they evaluate for auditing purposes).[27] If these conditions of good institutional design are in place, auditors will be viewed as credible and trustworthy by consumers who will rely on them to make their purchasing choices.[28]

The theoretical literature discussed in this section explains the growth of political consumerism as a reaction to the de-rooting of politics from the context of the nation-state and the growth of risk-related problems like environmental destruction. These changes signify the need to conceptualize politics as increasingly independent of territory and a geographically defined place.[29] They imply that we need to view the political, economic, and even private sphere as interconnected and intertwined with each other as the actions of individuals and institutions penetrate all activities and spheres. Politics needs, thus, a new conceptualization. For political scientists the phenomenon of political consumerism is an example of governance or new steering alternatives and regulatory tools that are developing because of different problems experienced by the political system. It also reflects trends toward postmodernization, the increased importance of consumption in our lives today, and the role that values and virtues play for citizen involvement in politics broadly conceived. Sociologists emphasize even more the negative effects that industrial society has on the ecological system and how we conceive of politics and political problem-solving. They explain political consumerism as an effect of ecological modernization, reflexive modernization, and risk society, which considers cooperation of a variety of actors—from individual consumers and store owners to large transnational enterprises and state and supra-state actors and institutions—as necessary to develop sustainable politics in the world today. Political consumerism for them is, therefore, an example of creative and essential cooperation among actors and institutions from local to global arenas on issues of sustainable development. Business scholars also stress governability problems in risk society as the basis of political consumerism. However, the answer they give to the question about the rise of political consumerism is that good institutions are now available for consumers. This is the case because a greater number of legitimate auditing institutions are currently in place for consumers to use to make their daily shopping decisions.

Political consumerist actors also understand politics in this way. Hazel Henderson, economist at the Calvert Social Investment Fund, a political consumerist institution, writes: "The whole world has changed and we are now debating how we need to change the game, the rules and the scoring system..."[30] An activist in the Responsible Coffee Campaign joins in with the following words:

> "Globalization" is what's happening. At the simplest level, this means that more of what people consume comes from distant regions through complex transactions hidden from ordinary view....While most of us cannot escape participating in commodity chains, we can participate with greater or less insight and responsibility. That's a choice open to all consumers, obviously....On a range of issues, colleges and universities set standards for themselves higher than the law requires or the market delivers. Hate speech is one recent example. So why not campus consumption?[31]

CONSUMPTION AS POLITICS

Consumption has a rich meaning in today's globalized, postmodernized world. But this is not really a new development. A lesson from history is that many political struggles began when people—and particularly women—expressed problems about feeding their family. Consumer goods became politicized because of private, family woes. Considerations about family health also play a part in contemporary political consumerism. We see how people's outrage over food risks is creating a crisis in politics and problems for policymakers, be they civil servants, politicians, corporate actors, or consumer movements.[32] Today consumption involves broad concerns of global justice and solidarity as well as more specific private concerns about the ability to serve one's family a healthy, nutritious meal. As such, issues of consumption engage people who are both interested in furthering the public interest and those who want to protect and defend their private interests from detrimental outside forces. This combination of interests makes consumerism a potentially very powerful form of engagement. Its importance is stated forcefully by British political scientist Margaret Scammell: "Just as globalisation squeezes orthodox avenues for politics, through the state and organised labour, so new ones are being prized open, in consumer power." The importance of consumption challenges us to consider whether and how it is politics.[33]

Consumption can in certain instances be a *venue for political action*.[34] It offers people an inroad—venue—into policymaking that otherwise may be rather closed to grassroots citizen participation. It can create a venue because consumer behavior is difficult to regulate and therefore generally unregulated. This means that people excluded from such policymaking communities as corporate board rooms, diplomatic circles, and legislative arenas can use their market choices as a means for political expression and as political action. They can express their dissatisfaction with a product by organizing consumer protests in the hope of changing the image of the product as portrayed by business. In these protests, they can introduce issues that have not been part of the policymaking process. Studies show that ethical issues—for instance human rights and environmentalism—often enter policy discussions in this way.[35] A good example discussed in more detail in chapter 2, is the infant formula campaign, which changed the image of the product and created a negative public image of the Nestlé corporation whose products were the focus of the boycott, put the problem on the international political agenda, and led to an international agreement that restricted the selling of infant formula in developing countries. Another example is the Nike Email Exchange, which created a "culture jam" of one of Nike's most pronounced advertisement campaigns.[36] Thus, consumer choice and action can create direct input or participation in policy processes in both the political sphere and business community. Consumers' political input becomes more institutionalized once boycott networks and labeling schemes are established because, as discussed in chapter 3, such institutions create a institutional setting for public and private policymaking.

This view of consumption and consumer choice suggests that there is a *politics of product*,[37] which means that every product is embedded in a political context. The politics of products is an important issue in business ethics, a growing field in business studies concerning the community and public nature of private corporations (see e.g. *Journal of*

Business Ethics). The politics of a particular product is often latent, but as shown in history it can rapidly become a controversial issue for corporations, civil society, and government. Companies may find that their procurement policies and offshore labor policies make national and international news. Local, national, and global actors are often involved in politicizing product. Examples are easy to find. Most clothing and shoe manufacturers have experienced how their products can be politicized by grassroots' actors as illustrated in the Nike Email Exchange. Such embarrassing encounters explain their efforts in developing codes of conduct. Consumer involvement in product ethics is forcing business to concern itself with how and why it manufactures goods because these issues now affect its public image and goodwill. It may even be the case at times that company employees internally politicize company products because they want to fulfill their need for social acceptance and political involvement by demanding more ethical behavior on the part of their employer. They are frustrated with the ineffectiveness of established channels for citizen influence, which may also encourage citizens, employees, and even private firms to find new ways to participate politically.[38]

The politicization of products means that a greater number of actors from different spheres are seen as playing a public responsibility-taking role in the world today. A group of actors singled out is transnational enterprises. The economic importance and public prevalence of private corporations prompted an American political scientist to consider them *private governments* and public institutions because they are vested with state traits, among them power over people's lives.[39] Economic globalization recently led the United Nations, Amnesty International, and other international governmental and nongovernmental organizations to claim openly that they must rely on market actors to accomplish their goals. UN Secretary General Kofi Annan explains his decision to sign a global compact with business in this way: "let's choose to unite the powers of markets with the authority of universal ideals."[40] Amnesty International's Human Rights Principles for Companies urge businesses, citizens, and consumers to consider the direct responsibility that companies have for "the impact of their activities on their employees, on consumers of their products and on the communities within which they operate."[41]

The growing importance of private corporations in our world today helps explain why citizens are increasingly making demands on the market directly and requiring companies to follow the same ethics and modes of accountability as public government. There are even instances where consumer pressure has forced private corporations to behave more ethically in their practices than public government. A good case in point is by the large Swedish transnational clothing company H & M (Hennes & Mauritz) that for years now has worked on sustainable development and is acknowledged by the Clean Clothes Campaign for the progress it has made on these issues. Its code of conduct is superior to the one used in Swedish government procurement policy for clothing for the defense sector.[42]

Political consumerism is thus creating an arena for political action that expands the policymaking process by introducing new issues and participants. This book shows that political consumerism is politics when people knowingly target market actors to express their opinions on justice, fairness, or noneconomic issues that concern personal and family well-being. When they shop in this fashion they are using their consumer choice as an ethical or political assessment of favorable and unfavorable business and government practice. *Political consumers* are the people who engage in such choice situations. They may act individually or in groups. Findings reported in this volume emphasize that political consumerism often diverges from more traditional forms of political participation because its organizing principles and strategies tend either to be less collectivist or novel in orientation.

Political landscape changes explain this new political orientation on the part of people. The Nike Email Exchange can again be used to illustrate how these changes are creating new forms of citizen action. A classical political response on the part of the MIT student would have been to directly approach politicians and interest groups for better government regulation to improve the situation for garment industry workers, or to become a card-carrying member of a social movement or interest group mobilizing citizens in this field for a demonstration or other forms of political agitation. The focus would be on the national arena and actors, who would be able to deal with the problem satisfactorily because government policy could regulate shoe manufacturing. Economic globalization and concerns about global justice have, however, shifted the venue of politics to the market sphere and change the orientation of the action from pressure group politics and social movement agitation to targeting transnational corporations directly through purchasing choices and less-conventional political methods as culture jamming, hactivism, and guerilla media stunts. The purpose of these actions is to challenge the expensive corporate image-making process by making the politics of products visible for the global consumer.[43] Thus, whereas boycotts were embedded in social movement activities in the past,[44] efforts focusing directly on market actors are the main form of activity today.

The Nike E-mail and other examples reported in this book show how political consumer participation is playing a role in reinventing politics and democracy. Political consumerism carves out new arenas for political action by its involvements in the market and the politics of private corporations. It gives citizens a political voice by allowing them to participate in politics in new and different ways. It considers individual citizens as main actors in politics by emphasizing the responsibility of each and every citizen for our common well-being.

In sum, there are five basic reasons that theoretically justify conceiving of consumption as politics. First, consumption is at times an access point or venue for people to express themselves politically. It may be that they have tried unsuccessfully to enter more traditional political arenas or that they have been excluded from these arenas from the start. Consumption offers these people a space (an arena) to work on their political issues and helps them exercise influence to solve their problems. Second, people can use consumption to set the political agenda of other actors and institutions and to pressure them to the negotiating table, as in the case of the Nestlé's boycott. Third, consumption is politics because there is a politics of products that involves classical political issues about power relations and the allocation of values in society that are to large degree decided by private corporations. Thus private corporations are vested with political power and can be considered private governments. This means that it is justifiable for citizens to be concerned about corporate policy and practices and want to influence them politically. Fourth, consumption offers people market-based political tools like boycotts and buycotts that can be used to engage in political issues and struggles. They may use these tools to influence a variety of actors and institutions including private corporations, governments, and civil society. Fifth, consumption is becoming more political because of political landscape changes and the increasing global presence of transnational enterprises.

POLITICAL AGENCY OF CONSUMERS

That the ordinariness of daily life and everyday shopping choices has significance for societal, economic, and political development is an important theoretical position taken in this book. This means that actions by individuals and groups in common everyday circumstances like shopping daily for one's family or oneself can matter significantly. Action on everyday matters can take the forms of exit, voice, and loyalty decisions,[45] which for the phenomenon of political consumerism means boycotts, demands on producers, and smart shopping. These action alternatives signify a shift in the sites for citizen action[46] from politics traditionally conceived as involving the political system and public life to private life and the market sphere. Action involves both selection of issues and arenas for action. It is possible to analyze the phenomenon of political consumerism from the point of view of the importance of daily life for political and democratic development and to assess whether and in which ways consumers in actual situations function in this fashion.

The focus on choices in daily shopping situations as democratically important implies a new view of consumers as potentially important agents of political change. This means that the common view of consumers as manipulated, passive buyers of goods that capitalists produce to increase corporate profits needs to be questioned.[47] The phenomenon of political consumerism suggests that it is also necessary to consider "the productivity, creativity, autonomy, rebelliousness and even the 'authority' of the consumer."[48] Thus there is, as discussed by the cultural theorist Mica Nava, agency in consumerism.[49] This suggests that consumers at least theoretically can be understood as key actors in forming new and different democratic structures. When they shop smartly they combine their role as consumers and citizens and have the potential to act as exuberant *citizen-consumers*[50] with the power of agents to develop new content, forms, and coalitions to solve problems of risk society and global injustices. Their actions that combine the public role of citizens with the private role of consumers can be seen as having agency because they can help unfold new structures of operation and build new institutions to tackle global problems.[51] Some scholars even see consumers as playing the role of political entrepreneurs of our common future.[52]

This view of consumer behavior that equates it with political agency and embeds it with citizen qualities differs considerably from traditional views of consumer activism. It signifies that the modernist view of consumer activism, as a movement to improve the rights of buyers over sellers,[53] must be reconsidered in light of a postmodern or late modern view that takes its point of departure in the *active agency of consumers*. The theoretical argument is that this new consumer activism has the potential to transform society, economics, and politics. The starting point is the assumption that consumption is increasing in importance as a global structuring principle, which signifies that conflicts over what and where to consume are now central for understanding the functioning of affluent Western societies. This can even mean that consumers participating in boycotts can, for instance, be likened to resistance fighters. Yet unlike resistance or revolutionary conflicts of the past, citizen-consumers tend to direct their attention toward market rather than state actors.[54] Theoretically the importance of consumer choice can be seen as a new structuring agent that is encouraging citizens to "move into other spheres of life in order to secure a reasonable possibility of access to politics for all citizens."[55]

These ideas may seem theoretically far-fetched, but in many ways the explanation of consumerism as a site for political agency is the same as the theoretical and political attraction of civil society. Like civil society, consumers who use consumer choice politically is "a code name for people assuming responsibility for their own lives . . . "[56] Consumer responsibility-taking, the topic of this book, entails the practice of judgment, autonomy, and solidarity, which many scholars agree are three main aspects of citizenship.[57] Practicing judgment, autonomy, and solidarity requires that consumers be empowered with resources and civic skills. They must have both product knowledge and experience and the ability to assess both product quality and the values embedded in products.[58] Because arenas for consumer choice, as discussed in the next section and illustrated in the coming chapters, are less distanced from our daily lives than public decisionmaking ones, they at times represent more intense struggles over public values and virtues than those involving the government sphere and political system. The political richness and intensity of the market as an arena for politics and consumer choice as a political tool can be explained in one other way. Political consumerism can be characterized as a pluralist activity because it has looseness and an indeterminacy that appeals to citizens who tend to find themselves marginalized and alienated from formal political settings. It has, thus, been and continues to be an important instrument for reinventing citizenship.[59]

In particular, political consumerism has been shown to be connected to the citizen agency of young people and women. The attractiveness of political consumerism for young people is not well researched but it seems that an important explanation is the appeal of life style politics among the youth, trends toward individualization, and their tendency to find the formal political sphere alienating.[60] We know more about its attractiveness for women. There are three reasons that explain the role of women in political consumerism.[61] First, women are the gender that has assumed and still tends to assume responsibility for shopping for the family on a daily basis. Thus, women are more involved with consumer issues than men or children. Their responsibility for putting nourishing food on the family table and clothing their family gives them the opportunity to be more aware of the quality of goods that they bring into their home and give their family. Second, studies show that women have a lower risk perception threshold than men.[62] This means that women are generally more sensitive to risk society and react more negatively to the use of pesticides and other poisonous substances on goods needed for their family. Interview research reports a clear link between lower risk thresholds and green political consumer activism.[63] Third, because women have historically been excluded from institutions of the public sphere and their issues seen as nonpolitical, they have been forced to create other sites to express their political worries and work for their political interests. Consumer choice was, as shown in chapter 2, a site for women to participate in politics, a site for them to legitimate their interests, and a site for their struggle for public recognition. Active political consumerism empowered women as citizens. What is interesting is that consumer issues continue to do so today, as reported in the case study on green political consumerism in chapter 4.

The political agency that develops from consumerism is, therefore, rooted in the integration of citizen concerns with consumer choices. Consumers view their choice of products in a political fashion, and citizens find that they can work on political causes in the marketplace. The political consumer or citizen-consumer is a responsibility-taking actor who sees market transactions as having interesting political potential. Daily trips to the market can, therefore, in certain situations and under certain circumstances be empowering acts. They can open up an arena for political involvement for people who otherwise may not have easy access to politics. They can also help people develop a public space for political action on issues of importance for them. Finally, work on consumer issues allows people to develop their general civic skills in situations that are comfortable for them and in which they feel confident about the appropriateness of their actions and involvements.

PRIVATE AND PUBLIC VIRTUE TRADITIONS OF POLITICAL CONSUMERISM

To equate consumer choice with citizen engagement is controversial. It is controversial because, as discussed earlier, it questions our distinctions between politics and economics, causing some scholars to lament trends toward neoliberalism and others to fear a new left-wing argument for political regulation of the market. Scholars also argue that smart shopping in the form of politically informed consumer choice cannot be considered political involvement because traditional political actors and institutions—interest organizations, political parties, and government—need not be present. They motive their standpoint by maintaining that consumption and consumer choice is part of the private economic sphere of oneself and one's family. For them, the site of politics must be tied to the public sphere and government and choices that concern these arenas. This is where citizens participate in politics. These scholars thus confine the role of citizens to voting in elections, joining political parties and civic associations, and a few channels for direct contact with traditional political actors. On this basis they argue that consumer choice does not play a role in politics and democracy. Their opposition to smart shopping as political action rests on a conventional, common, and narrow view of politics.

Political consumerism is a fascinating and challenging phenomenon for social scientists because it shows how our different spheres are interrelated and how our private lives and actions impact public concerns locally and globally. It illustrates how citizens are seeking new sites for political activism. What is particularly interesting is the way it ties together self-interest and public interest in uncommon interpretations of political life in real life practice. This is done in two ways, which in political philosophy is called the public virtue tradition and private virtue tradition of politics.[64]

Let us first examine how the phenomenon of political consumerism applies the *public virtue tradition of politics*. This occurs when public-oriented citizen-consumers practice their public principles in everyday settings and actions that are not conventionally conceived as political in orientation. They buy products for political, ethical, and social reasons. This means that on their daily trips to the market they boycott some products, question the politics of others in their contacts with store managers and owners, and when available follow labeling schemes to purchase certain goods over others. They use exit, voice, and loyalty consumer choice alternatives to express themselves politically at the marketplace. They choose or refrain from choosing products for other-oriented or public virtue motivations. In some cases their choices require restraint on their part because their political conscience tells them not to buy the product they want for other reasons like price, looks, and taste. They exercise self-sacrifice and self-restraint, a virtue closely associated with the public virtue tradition of politics, when deciding in this fashion even when they really want it for personal reasons. In other cases, they may want to express solidarity with others (another public virtue) when they choose a more "ethically produced" good that is more expensive, inferior in quality, or perhaps more time-consuming to purchase because it is not readily available in neighborhood markets. In these instances, their shopping choices express public-oriented values and interests and are part of a larger political commitment. Smart shopping may be just another way or possibly the only way for these people to express and practice their political commitment in concrete settings. Their actions reflect a common line of reasoning in political philosophy that good citizens must be emotionally engaged with the polity and its principles. This first case of political consumers represents a well-accepted view of good citizens as enthusiastic, self-sacrificing, solidaristic, public-spirited and who willingly subordinate their personal interests and private desires for the good of the public. Its roots are civic republicanism and communitarian democratic theories.[65]

A second view of political engagement, *the private virtue tradition of politics*, can also be found in the phenomenon of political consumerism. Its point of departure is the realization of self-interest. Smart shopping is initially a good way to express private concerns. Here self-oriented consumers buy certain products over others to solve what we may call private problems. These problems are the starting point that ties the individual consumer's self-interest to public-oriented interests. The goals of consumers are to promote their family's interests, for instance to find soap to buy that does not cause their child who is prone to allergies to scratch wildly after a bath, and this may mean that parents buy the same soap as the political consumer activist concerned about water pollution or sustainable trade who represents the public virtue tradition of politics. The reasons for the parents' consumer choice are different but their choice of product is the same. In fact, they may be more dedicated to promoting the product than the political activist because its use directly solves a problem that involves their loved ones. They may be more willing to exert effort in boycotting harmful products, contacting producers in attempts to influence them to change their ingredients and manufacturing practices, and more adamant in consistently buying certain products over others no matter the time required to find a store that carries them or the costs incurred in purchasing them. Their intense private concerns may cause them to exercise the exit, voice, and loyalty choice alternatives more intensely and fully than consumers of the public virtue orientation.

Their actions may also give them the opportunity to realize that their private worries are shared by others. For example, in their search for good soap for their child they may meet other families in stores who have the same or similar problems. The families may decide to pool their private worries and engage in collective action in very concrete, problem-oriented local networks. We see this clearly in some of the historical instances of political consumerism discussed in chapter 2. The family's search for good choices for their family may even force them to assume political responsibility in a broader context than the local problem-oriented network. The parents in our example become political leaders. They exert energy to mobilize people to join their cause for boycotts and organize mass contacts with producers. A goal of their cause is to encourage and mobilize others to consistently purchase certain product brands to assure their availability in neighborhood markets. Their point of departure is still self-interest, and their concern is still satisfying their private consumer worries. But by now the parents are political consumer activists, which is a spillover effect of their private concerns. They may even, as discussed later, find this kind of political engagement or individualized collective action comfortable because it allows them to stay within their competence, experience, and desperate need for involvement in solving problems of a private nature.

Many social scientists are uncomfortable with accepting this private virtue tradition of politics. They argue that it legitimizes the role of self-interest in politics, a development that they believe has negative consequences for democracy.[66] There are, however, good normative theoretical reasons for accepting it and the empirical findings reported in this book show that self-interest can play a constructive role in democratic political development. The American political activist Saul Alinsky once said, "the only time you stand up in righteous moral indignation is when it serves your purpose."[67] For him, morality began at home, and outrage over personal problems was the starting point for collective action. Studies of green political consumerism show the same thing. Many people who buy green products do so to solve personal problems. They feel what scholars call a "closeness" to environmental problems,[68] which as discussed later in this section makes people more willing to engage in collective action.

In a convincing way, the American political philosopher Shelly Burtt has theoretically shown how private self-interest and the private virtue tradition contribute to civic virtues and how they can benefit the common good. For her, it is theoretically unsound to equate virtuous citizenship only with people who renounce their purely private concerns for the greater good of the political community, as in the case of the public virtue–oriented political consumerist activist discussed earlier. She sees this as an illusory ideal because such publicly dedicated people are far too few in number, and as individuals they run the risk of overexertion if their only source of commitment is the interests of others and the public good. The demands on an individual's time and emotional resources are, in short, way too high for this to be a realistic scenario to encourage in real life. The ideal has, therefore, low normative appeal. She contrasts these public-oriented or self-sacrificing virtues with private-oriented, self-serving civic virtues and asks if "...it is at least conceivable that individuals would be able to serve a civic regime without possessing the passionate attachment to the polity and its needs that grounds the more familiar sort of publicly oriented civic virtue...."[69] For her, a politics of virtue must include private self-interest. Her theoretical point is that this is one of the few ways to develop more participatory self-rule. Otherwise, politics will be reserved to an elite few with the proclivity and time for purely other-oriented engagements, while other citizens who must or choose to focus their attention on private woes are normatively chastised for avoiding political responsibility.[70] She grounds her philosophical argument in the writing of Tocqueville, Rousseau, and others who included issues that concern the everyday lives of citizens in their discussions on the politics of virtue. It is from these seemingly private issues that individual citizens see how their own lives are affected by the lives of others and vice versa. Her way of viewing the role of self-interest in political life differs considerably from scholars like James Buchanan and Anthony Downs who focused on the importance of worries about private economic life for the development of private-oriented political preference orders to determine voting behavior and the expression of self-interest in representative democratic structures.[71] Burtt's position concerns direct citizen involvement in politics and what is needed as an impetus to spur citizens into active political involvement and responsibility-taking.

From this section it can be theoretically concluded that self-interest is an important motivational source of an individual's positive contributions to politics. More problems can be brought to the public fore once politics is opened to self-interest and private concerns. Energy and resources packed in private worries need to be released in public channels for involvement. Opening up politics for private concerns thus renews the political community because citizens find that their everyday interests, problems, and concerns are part of the struggle and debate over the public good. They become engaged in their own issues and seek political forums and alliances to promote them. If traditional political channels and actors are closed to them, they seek new arenas and the cooperation of other actors.

This is exactly what has happened in many cases of political consumerism, several of which are discussed in the coming chapters.

Citizens concerned about how consumer choice affects them personally join together. They find each other in very local, everyday arenas like the butcher store, workplace, church group, even in their own family, or now via the Internet. Historically speaking, geographical closeness has been important for initial contacts, but today it may be argued that geographical closeness can be accompanied or replaced by Internet closeness. In the past physical geographical closeness gave and today cyber geographical closeness gives people a practical way to discuss their common personal problems, share their common worries, and create common knowledge. Perhaps they, as in the parents who slipped into political activism above, learn that their problems are not unique. There is, thus, a bonding function in these kinds of political consumerist activities, which creates trust and social capital among likeminded people.[72] The fact that they are near each other physically or via the Internet creates solidarity and strong ties, and these ties, as we learn from theories on collective action as well as historical cases of political consumerism, became important structures for participation.[73] Group pressure may even develop from feelings of physical or Internet closeness, thereby forcing family and friendship networks to participate in the cause as a friendly gesture or out of a sensed need for family peace. These people decide that support is the best thing to do. Or put in more formal collective-action language, they believe that support is the optimum long-term strategy for them to follow.

Moreover, the need to find a solution for personal problems is so strong that the people initially involved disregard all costs of collective action. They are not worried that uninvolved and disinterested people—free riders—also will be rewarded once the problems are solved.[74] Neither do they care initially whether their cause is on the agenda of mass organizations. Their decision to become involved is not dependent on high support rates from other people.[75] All that matters to them is that they can depend on and trust each other and can find a way to solve their own common problems. Sociologists who study social capital, trust, and collective action call these individuals "low threshold people" because it is easy for them to "slip" into active involvement together with others. Political scientists may refer to them as everyday political entrepreneurs or perhaps we can call them political venture capitalists, because they are willing to use resources—time, money, and civic skills—and take private and perhaps public risks to solve political problems of a private nature. Their enthusiasm may encourage other people not personally affected by the problem to join the cause. Perhaps they heard about the cause from people in the immediate environment of the initial supporters. A mass movement may, therefore, emerge, and established political institutions may decide to take notice. In this way, everyday settings and people working on concrete problems in a hands-on way are important links for new collective action and a hothouse for the growth of new forms of citizen involvement in politics.

Both the virtue traditions discussed in this section acknowledge that consumer choice can be political choice and the market can in certain circumstances be an arena for politics. Yet they do so in different ways. According to the public virtue tradition, citizens take their public concerns with them when they engage in contacts with market actors through shopping and non-shopping choices. Thus, they bring politics to the marketplace. The private virtue tradition begins with private individuals in their role as family providers and family shoppers. These people first bring their private problems to the marketplace and then understand that their worries are political. The private virtue tradition shows how absorption in solving private concerns that involve marketplace transaction can release an abundance of resources—physical energy, time, creativity, and so on—which can serve a public purpose. The urgency for action and problem solution that is embedded in this kind of involvement withstands many of the pitfalls of traditional collective action based on self-sacrificing public virtues. Typical pitfalls found in numerous studies include free riding and activists feeling burnt out and in need of a shift in involvements from self-sacrificing political activism to a quiet family-oriented private life.[76]

POLITICAL CONSUMERISM AS INDIVIDUALIZED COLLECTIVE ACTION

Political consumerism can be said to fit a general pattern in contemporary politics that is reflected both in the discussions in this chapter and social science research. Studies on civil society, political involvement, and social capital show that citizens are tending to view politics and political participation in a different light than in the past. Citizens in the Western world are moving away from many traditional forms of political participation focusing on the political system per se. Traditional forms of political participation are frequently viewed as time-consuming, limiting in terms of individual expression, and lacking a sense of urgency.[77] Instead people are increasingly attracted to less bureaucratic, hierarchical kinds of involvement characterized by looser, egalitarian, and informal structures that allows them to express themselves more individually and experience the thrills of participation.[78] They are now seeking issues and arenas for involvement that are more flexible, network-oriented, hands-on and that allows them to combine their daily lives with political causes. This kind of involvement may actually take more time and effort than traditional forms of political participation, but many citizens are willing to invest their resources as long as it fulfills them personally. Self-assertive responsibility-taking characterizes this kind of involvement, which refers both to taking care of one's own self and the well-being of others, and therefore reflects a new mix of the role of public virtues and private virtues that was discussed in the previous section. An example of this new mix is political consumerism.

I am developing the concept of *individualized collective action* to capture the essence of this form of citizen engagement that combines self-interest and the general good. The three words are carefully chosen. I do not mean "individualized political participation" or "individualized political action." With these three words I want to make a clear theoretical distinction between citizen-prompted, citizen-created action involving people taking charge of matters that they themselves deem important in a variety of arenas (individualized collective action) and conventional definitions of political engagement, involving taking part in structured behavior already in existence and oriented toward the political system per se (collectivist collective action, political participation). While individualized collective action occurs in a variety of settings and more spontaneously, political participation is involvement that takes place in a given arena and in accordance with a given mode of activity and given agenda. New citizen engagement can take place all over the place in a variety of settings, which motivates my decision to choose the term collective rather than political action so as not to confuse readers who view political action as focusing specifically on the political system per se.

The concept of individualized collective action reflects the political landscape changes of postmodernization, risk society, and globalization that were discussed earlier in this chapter. These landscape changes imply that citizens must juggle their lives in situations of unintended consequences, incomplete knowledge, multiple choices, and risk-taking. Political engagement and citizenship is, thus, a task that people must deal with on an increasingly individual basis. It is not laid out as in the first modernity (industrial society and nation-state dominance) in which citizens define themselves more directly in terms of established institutions and social positions.[79]

My *working definition of individualized collective action* acknowledges the impact of these political landscape changes on our view of politics and political involvement. It is the practice of responsibility-taking for common well-being through the creation of concrete, everyday arenas on the part of citizens alone or together with others to deal with problems that they believe are affecting what they identify as the good life. Individualized collective action involves a variety of different methods for practicing responsibility-taking including traditional and unconventional political tools.

This section develops the concept by contrasting the theoretical construct of individualized collective action with the conventional view of political participation, here called collectivist collection action, and embedding the concept of individualized collective action theoretically in social science literature discussed earlier and further developed in this section. It should be noted that scholars have not generally given the concept of political participation an articulated theoretical grounding. Rather, political scientists have generally concentrated most effort in developing an operational theory of political participation useful for survey research. This situation explains the infrequent use of reference to theoretical works on political participation in this section. The concept of collectivist collective action developed here is based on a general summary of empirical works of quantitative and qualitative nature on political participation concerning civil society and citizen contact with the political system per se. The theoretical constructs of collectivist and individualized collective action are formulated as ideal types, which following Weber are abstract descriptions, constructs, or models of social actors, social situations, or social processes that cannot in their entirety be found in real life.[80] They are presented in figure 1.1. The key theoretical aspects of the concepts are given in italics in the figure and are focused on explicitly in this section.

As shown in figure 1.1, the prerequisites for collectivist collective action are established structures and procedures that individual citizens can enter to find a home to channel and mold their political voice or identify their societal interests. Involvement in *membership-based* interest groups, civic associations, and political parties are examples of such established political homes. The theoretical basis of this kind of collective action can be said to be liberal, representative democracy.[81] Membership in the interest articulating and aggregating structures implies that individual citizens find an institutional home through which their political voice and identity is filtered, adapted, and molded to the political preferences and priorities of these representative structures. Thus their political voice and responsibility is *delegated* to organizational leaders. Individual citizens are, therefore, encouraged and perhaps even pressured to craft and construct their

Collectivist collective action	Individualized collective action
First modernity collective action: identity with structures and social positions, *unitary identity* that follows life paths, role models	*Late modern* collective action: identity and social position not taken for granted, map out your own life path, be your own role model, *serial identity*
Participation in *established political homes* such as membership-based interest groups and political parties	*Use of established political homes as base and point of departure* to decide own preferences and priorities and create and develop individualized political homes, e.g., home pages
Participation in *territorial-based* physical structures focusing on the *political system*	Involvement in networks of a variety of kinds that are not based in any single physical territorial level or structure, *subpolitics*
Participation that is channeled through *grand or semi-grand ideological narratives* (traditional political ideology)	Involvement based on self-authored individualized narratives (*self-reflexivity*)
Participation in *representative democratic* structures	*Self-assertive* and direct involvement in concrete actions and settings
Delegation of responsibility to leaders and officials	Responsibility is not delegated to leaders and officials, it is taken personally and jointly, *self-actualization*
Member interests and identity filtered, adapted, and molded to political preferences of these *interest articulating and aggregating* institutions, *socialization*	Dedication and commitment to *urgent causes* rather than loyalty to organizational norms, values, standard operating procedures, and so on
Loyalty to established structures, acceptance of organizational norms, values, standard operating procedures, and so on	*Responsibility-taking* for urgent causes, *active subpolitics*
High thresholds for active participation in established organizations; *high costs* for active involvement in terms of time, seniority, socialization, and other resources	*Everyday activism* in variety of settings; *low thresholds* for involvement; urgent involvement may be *high cost* in terms of being time-consuming and requiring considerable effort on the part of individuals

Figure 1.1 The ideal types of collectivist and individualized collective action.

political preferences to these structures. They become *socialized* in
these organized settings. Studies show that it is not uncommon that
citizens are forced to compromise their preferences and interests to fit
the issue frames that characterize *interest articulating and aggregating structures.* At times, new members burning with enthusiasm to
work together on current problems find that they must conform to
organizational time frames, put their priority issues on hold, and
instead work on matters that they do not consider the most important for the organizational cause. They must do so because their
urgent issues are not given organizational priority.[82] Political involvement of this kind tends to be hierarchically organized and based in
the *representative democratic structures* that characterized traditional
civil society associations. It signifies that citizens who become members accept the norms, values, and rules that structure collective
action. Collectivist collective action thus requires that citizens join
associations and support the association's politics. While, this kind of
collective action seems to have worked well for a considerable part of
the twentieth century, labeled the *first modernity* in figure 1.1, studies in social science of the past few decades show that it easily leads to
a passive membership, responsibility-avoiding behavior, free riders,
and difficulty for the association to renew itself due to problems with
inflexibility and organization maintenance.[83]

The concept of *individualized collective action* is grounded in a different theoretical point of departure. Individual citizens do not seek a
prefabricated political home for expression of their interests to be represented by organizational leaders. They do not need someone else or
an outside structure to take care of their interests for them. Rather,
they *create their own political home* by framing their own aims and
channels for political action. This can be done by using established
political housing as a base to work with their own preferences and priorities, as is discussed in the case of green political consumerism in
chapter 4, or through the creation of their own political homes as a
self-assertive responsibility-taking response, for example as Jonah
Peretti did with his Nike Email Exchange and its relevant home
pages.[84] An important difference between this logic and the traditional
one is that individual citizens do not need to join and show loyalty
toward interest articulating structures to become involved in what
they deem are urgent issues of politics and society. They can become
involved outside these structures by showing commitment to causes
and assuming responsibility in a more hands-on way. *The physical and
territorially based structures* of the earlier part of the twentieth century
with their *grand or semi-grand ideological narratives* (first modernity

and collectivist collective action) are not necessary for citizens to achieve strength in numbers in the twenty-first century or what is labeled *late modernity* in figure 1.1. Sufficient knowledge about problems can be achieved outside traditional political channels and on a more individualized basis. These citizens may use established government, private, civil society, and Internet institutions as information sources as well as engage in chat sites to gain perspective on the information produced by these sources. They may achieve political strength or influence by joining consumer networks, using checklists developed by home pages for on-the-spot street-level monitoring, and act politically in very specific and time-delimited settings.[85] These activities are characterized by *everyday activism* involving contact with store managers about their assortment and contact with other everyday activists via home pages. They represent responsibility-taking in loose networks in geographically close settings. In short, people do not need collectivism for collective action, which explains my choice of the word individualized for the new conception of political involvement here called individualized collective action.

The social science concepts of subpolitics, everyday-makers, new citizenship, and serial identity help us with an initial understanding of the role of daily activism and local and even global responsibility-taking in individualized collective action. These concepts inform us theoretically about how politics and democracy is brought down to the level of individual citizens in their daily, more personal concerns about public and private life. This theoretical approach implies a reconcretization of politics and democracy, and a revision of the roles of citizen and politician, that is, of follower and leader and political representation.[86] Each will now be discussed in some detail.

The concept of *subpolitics* has developed from work on risk society.[87] Risks are defined broadly in this literature and include such concerns as environmental pollution, food risks, personal problems with the welfare state, and worries about multiculturalism. Subpolitics signifies politics emerging in places other than formal politics: the site of the conventional political science definition of politics and political participation. It is politics emerging from below. This is occurring for different reasons, among them are such political landscape changes as the government's inability to understand and control the new uncertainties and risks created by public and corporate policy. This is causing a responsibility vacuum that is being filled by *active subpolitics*,[88] which involves responsibility-taking by citizens in their everyday, individual-oriented life arena that cuts across the public and private spheres. The point that needs emphasizing for the discussion in this chapter is that this development should not solely be analyzed as flight from politics, cocooning, retreat from public concerns, or defense for a purely self-oriented and self-interested private life. Rather, it is quite possible that the self-orientation or individualization apparent in sub-politics is responsibility-taking for the well-being of oneself and others by means that differ considerably from those of conventional political participation. The differences concern the role that private-oriented virtues (duty to oneself) play publicly and the importance of a feeling of self-fulfillment from energy exerted in hands-on involvement for public issues (duty to others).

The theoretical argument is that individual citizens increasingly act politically in their daily private lives. The reason is the interconnect-edness of private and public acts, as exemplified by the impact of private consumption on the global environment and for workers' rights in Third World factories. We leave ecological, ethical, and public foot-prints as we go about our seemingly daily private lives. Awareness and self-reflection of this impact imply an acknowledgment that everyday acts by citizens have the power to potentially restructure society. This is the meaning of *self-reflexivity*. In the postmodern language of scholars of individualization, "...individuals can feel themselves to be authors of global political acts..."[89] and "[w]hat appeared to be a 'loss of consensus,' an 'unpolitical retreat to private life,' 'a new inwardness' or 'caring for emotional wounds' in the old understand-ing of politics can, when seen from the other side, represent the struggle for a new dimension of politics."[90] Their point is that poli-tics, when seen as the need for collective action to provide for our common well-being, is moving into the sphere of everyday life.

The theoretical implication of subpolitics is that everyday acts by citizens have the power to potentially restructure society. Citizens are seen as the key actors in forming new democratic structures. In particular, "exuberant citizens" based in civil society networks have the power to develop new content, forms, and coalitions to solve problems of the risk society. For postmodern scholars like Ulrich Beck "(t)he 'political entrepreneur' of the future is not an elected repre-sentative..."[91] This implies that what we do as individual citizens can have global political significance. This view of politics gives citizens a central role in the *responsibility-taking* for our common future and couples together the public and private sphere in a way that is unfamiliar in traditional politics.

The concept of everyday-making (hverdagsmager) developed by Danish political scientists to understand local citizen initiative fits this understanding of politics as hands-on, local action well.[92]

Everyday-makers are citizens characterized by governance and the values of postmodernization.[93] They become involved with issues in a very local and specific way. Everyday-makers may work alone or in ad hoc networks organized outside the formal system of politics and across traditional, political ideological boundaries. They organize sub-politically. Danish research shows that everyday-maker issues include local health care, park improvements, or locations and relocations of government services. In line with this, we can view everyday-makers as street-level political entrepreneurs who seek solutions for very concrete or local problems concerning the welfare state. However, it seems clear that issues of consumption and even concrete consumer goods as coffee, jeans, toilet paper, and tropical wood should be considered as everyday-maker concerns. These concerned consumers also function as street-level auditors of government and corporate performance who either want to keep service up to standard or make service conform to a level of standard that goes beyond compliance to regulatory rules and practices. Like subpoliticians, everyday-makers are contributing to a newer understanding of democracy that takes its point of departure in individualization, that is, self-interest, self-organization, and self-responsibility.[94] They put democratic values to practice daily and in so doing make democracy tangible.[95]

To understand the role of self-interest, self-organization, and self-responsibility as a mobilizing force we need to consider political identity formation.[96] Identity is an important aspect in active subpolitics and everyday-making and an essential part of the concept of collective action. However, political identity in collectivist and individualized collective action differs considerably from one another. Traditionally we have understood *political identity as a unitary notion* created by belonging to well-established institutions oriented to the *political system*—political parties and unions to name just two examples. This means that you, for example, identify yourself as a democrat, social democrat, republican, or member of the working class. Political identity is, thus, not so much a matter of active, individual choice as it is defined by one's position in society. The implication is that people in the same position in society have the same political identity because they have common experiences and share the same social, political, and economic interests. Scholarship on class identity illustrates how we have lumped together people in one social class because they are born into it and are associated with it through their position in the means of production. Research over the past decades finds that changes in the political landscape as those discussed earlier force us to reconsider our view of political identity formation. A good starting point for understanding this development is theoretical work on seriality, which implies that our political identities are not fixed but flexible and embedded in concrete situations rather than social structures. Seriality means that we move among and in and out of various identities.[97]

Iris Marion Young reintroduced the concept of seriality and serial identity to research on political participation to understand why women do not identify themselves with organizations representing women's interests by becoming members. Her main point is that it is wrong to consider political identity as based on "a collection of persons who recognize themselves and one another as in a unified relation with one another." This is what in figure 1.1 characterizes *first modernity* collective action. Her theoretical alternative is to understand identity as fragmented rather than homogenous and contextual rather than structural, that is, not a given but social constructions, and characteristic of late modernity collective action. She calls this *serial identity*, which develops from feelings of commonness with others in the same context or situation as ourselves: "To be said to be part of the same series it is not necessary to identify a set of common attributes that every member has, because their membership is defined not by something they are but rather by the fact that in their diverse existences and actions they are oriented around the same objects...."[98] Thus, depending on the situation and mind-set of people on a particular day, they can, for example, identify themselves as taxpayers, bike riders, political consumers, dog owners, political scientists, or local citizens irritated with the municipal service. Each of these identities can lead to solidarity with others in the same situation and spark individuals into collective action. Citizens can craft or self-author their own personalized, individualized political narratives and adapt their political involvement thereafter. This is the meaning of *self-reflexivity*. We can decide for ourselves on a more individual basis which events, issues, and phenomena will politicize us. People with opposing views, experiences, and interests may even find that they, in certain contexts, have common ground for collective action because they strive to solve concrete problems rather than allowing established political institutions and ideologies to position them politically. We can also change political identity rapidly over time. Identities may, therefore, be temporary and highly contextual. We craft our personalized, individualized political identity and adapt our political involvement thereafter. We can even hold seemingly conflicting political identities. This is possible because our identities, as expressed by another theorist, are an articulation of an ensemble of subject position that are "constructed within specific discourses and always precariously and temporarily sutured at the intersection of those subject positions."[99]

The concept of serialized political identity, subpolitics, and self-assertiveness is implicit in new citizenship theories, which argue that the idea of citizenship should not be restricted to the relationship between people and the state. Rather, citizenship is a relationship to institutions regardless of sphere. It is commitment to working with institutions—to defend, improve, and reform them.[100] *Self-assertiveness* on the part of citizens is active involvement and entails civic or political competence—that is, attitudes and skills—necessary to create an institutional context for responsibility-taking through collective action. These ideas reflect an understanding of the impact of changes in the political landscape, which show how contemporary citizens are demanding more arenas for self-expression and *self-actualization* as well as more opportunities for involvement that allow them to take both individual and collective responsibility for their own needs and interests.[101]

Ideas about responsibility and *responsibility-taking* are central for the theoretical discussion used to develop my concept of individualized collective action. They are also central for political consumerism. Responsibility-taking goes beyond citizen obligations and rights and the civic republican demand that citizens participate in their territorially based community and political systems. It is part of the normative theory of cosmopolitan citizenship that considers citizens as embedded in wider issues of responsibility for nature, unborn generations, and in a variety of settings representing a diversity of private and public spheres.[102]

New citizenship and serial identity theories help explain what triggers citizens to act individually and collectively as, for instance, political consumers. Scholarship on subpolitics and everyday-making explain the arenas for this kind of citizen activism and establish the market as a venue for politics. Together the concepts help craft the concept of individualized collective action. They stress how individual citizens adapt their involvement so that it is appropriate for the problem and responsibility-taking at hand. A multitude of identities and contact with sites for involvement help citizens develop the necessary competence to assess which venues and kinds of action are best for solving complex contemporary problems. Gone are the ideas of solving political problems solely in the political system and mobilizing for action on the basis of established political identities, ideologies, and organizational settings. Flexible thinking and flexible involvement is part of individualized collective action.

An important implication of the concept of individualized collective action is that political problems need not solely be dealt with in the political system, by established political actors and channels, and through mobilizing for action on the basis of established political identities, ideologies, and organizational settings. Rather, the market, the home, and other seemingly private or nonpolitical arenas are also appropriate venues for general responsibility-taking. A second implication is that citizen activism crosses the public and private divide that has determined our conception of political participation and politics. Finally, this new form of citizen activism implies that responsibility for problem-solving cannot be delegated to other actors and spheres and the actors and institutions of representative democracy. It must be taken by each individual who leaves footprints after their actions and choices.

Subpolitics, everyday-making, serial identity, and new citizenship are concepts that help us recognize how structural changes in the political landscape can be understood at the level of individual actors. The structural and actor-oriented political landscape changes discussed in this chapter imply a need for renewal of the political community to fit our contemporary needs. A political community that functions well not only includes procedures for solving collective-action problems. It also educates its members in the values of involvement and encourages them to renew their involvement and institutions through deliberative feedback. Today citizens are creating new ways to understand, channel, and safeguard their interests. They are inventing new forms of political involvement. Some of these forms are establishment-challenging because they circumvent routine or conventional politics, which has traditionally been based on production-oriented Left–Right politics. Newer channels allow citizens to attempt to use their serial identities to build bridges between actors who normally do not work together.

Renewing Democracy and the Political Community through Political Consumerism

When political consumerism works well it brings issues of justice, human rights, and the environment down to the level of choices made by individuals and groups of individuals in their daily routines. This kind of responsibility-taking on the part of individual citizens can play an important role in reconstituting the political community because it connects public-oriented politics and our private lives. It signifies that citizens should not theoretically be construed as just passive recipients of rights that are protected by law. They have also the opportunity to act as grassroots rights–enforcing agents and promoters of justice in a variety of settings, among them the market. Thus, political consumers can in this way be said to be participating in the reconstruction of the political community. They can, to borrow a phrase from Ulrich Beck, be conceived as the moral material of new ways of private and public life.[103]

As shown in this book, political consumerism reflects new trends in political involvement that concern the individualization of political conflicts triggered by the political landscape changes discussed earlier in this chapter. These changes imply the need to reassess the division of responsibility among spheres, actors, and institutions. A way of summarizing the impact of these changes is that we are currently in the process of striking a new balance for *the responsibility for the responsibility*.[104]

As argued in this book, theoretically political consumers can individually and collectively, in certain circumstances, play a central role in the discussions on the responsibility for the responsibility. Consider the following theoretical scenario reflected in empirical examples in the coming chapters. Individuals begin by worrying about a private matter—wanting to provide a healthy meal for the family, work a shorter day for personal health and family solitude, or buy new furniture for a barbecue planned on the patio—and soon find that their private issues and interests have a public side to them as well. This is what earlier was called the politics of products. Healthy food for one's family may mean finding where one can buy it, leading to a demand for organic foods and a movement for eco-labeled produce that takes a stance against genetically modified organisms, and finally in institutions that audit and label food products to ensure their environmental quality. A shorter workday may require collective action in the form of calling for codes of conduct, the right to become members of trade unions, and an end to sweatshops. A desire to have a barbeque on a newly furnished patio may force the individual to consider the impact of purchasing tropical wood furniture on the rain forests, how farming tiger shrimp affects the working conditions of fishermen and waterways in Thailand, and what effects coffee plantations have on the ecosystem in Latin America. Thus political consumerism has the potential to renew democracy by wanting full citizen rights to apply to all people alive today and for future generations.

Consumption can also be a site of political action for citizens with a public-interest orientation. These publicly virtuous individuals may grieve over the exploitation of children as laborers in developing countries or the cutting down of rain forests in Indonesia and

South America. They may decide that they want to engage themselves politically to help solve the problem. However, they may find that they lack an institutionalized means (an established political home) of voicing their grief politically or feel frustrated with the way that governmental and nongovernmental institutions work with these issues. They may decide that the best way for them to quell their political hunger for urgent action and change is by working with the issue directly and target business through their consumer choices. Political consumerism thus renews the political community through new ideas, action arenas, methods, and new groups of participants.

Political consumerism has also the potential of uniting private-oriented and public-oriented people in common action repertoires. It is quite possible that the most rational (i.e., resource conserving and preference maximizing) form of engagement for both groups of individuals discussed above is to follow the shopping advise provided by the labeling schemes discussed in chapter 3. In this way, political consumerism gives people a way to practice virtuous civic activity in their everyday lives. It can encourage self-interested individuals to engage in serialized collective action on matters of particular private concern to them. Here self-interest is the most important impetus for an individual's positive contributions to the public good. Political consumerism can also give public-oriented citizens a channel for political action. Because of its more hands-on character, it offers them a sense of political efficacy that they may find lacking in other participatory channels and it gives them concrete, everyday political tasks that satisfy their hunger for urgent direct involvement. The methods used in political consumerism make each person a global stakeholder with responsibilities for their conduct and choices (their footprints). For both groups of people, political consumerism can give them the energy and willpower to continue participating even during campaign setbacks or bad personal times. This is because involvement has been integrated into their daily routines. It is an everyday practice that can renew democracy by sensitizing people to democratic deficits in the marketplace and also revitalize the political community by introducing it to new ways of conceiving and doing politics.

2

HISTORY OF POLITICAL CONSUMERISM

GOING BACK IN TIME

Political consumerism is not a new phenomenon. Scholars of history know intuitively that issues of consumption—particularly food supply and prices—lie behind all revolutions. Yet the role of consumption in politics has not traditionally been an important focus for the social sciences. Recently more scholars have begun to study it historically. Some of them even consider consumption as the vanguard of history.[1] Their research shows how women, ethnic groups, civil society associations, and states have used consumption as a tool for change. With the help of previous research, this chapter sketches the political contours and historical impact of consumerism. The research cited is mainly American. Information on political consumerism in other countries and particularly Sweden has been collected to complement the American findings. Nevertheless, much more research is needed for a complete history of political consumerism. The chapter is an initial attempt to compile, juxtapose, and draw conclusions about the virtues, values, and action involved in political consumerist events, the relevance of consumerist activities for people in their private and public lives, and the role that consumer choice plays in politics.

BOYCOTTING BOYCOTT: HISTORY OF THE TERM

It would seem that political consumerism finds its origin in boycotts. At least this is the impression one gets from historical studies. Boycotts have been used for hundreds of years by citizens to protest injustice and unfairness. *Negative political consumerism* or the choice not to buy products or services is called boycotts after Captain Charles Cunningham Boycott, the Earl of Erne of County Mayo in Ireland. Boycott owned a considerable amount of agricultural land, which was worked by the Irish peasantry who were his tenant farmers and farm laborers. Their situation was not good, due to the famine of 1878 and actions of the landlord class. The peasants were displeased with how Boycott treated them. They began to mobilize themselves for some kind of action to protest against his treatment and policies.

The Land League, a prototype farm workers' union, was formed to represent their interests. It encouraged the peasants not to use violence and to avoid any communication with those who refused their demands for lower tenant rents and higher wages. The Land League encouraged the farm workers who worked for Captain Boycott to take action against him. They decided not to harvest his oats because he paid them a lower wage than their regular one. After a few other incidents, they agreed to break all contact with Captain Boycott and his family. Boycott was forced to request military assistance and the help of hired men to gather his crop.

An American journalist and an Irish priest who sympathized with the peasant cause took note of the event. While the journalist wrote about the event for a newspaper, the two men discussed what to call it. They were the first to use the family name "boycott" as a noun and a verb for the action of the peasants. A scholar who has written on morality and the market summarized the boycott of Boycott in the following words: "No one would work for Boycott, speak to him, or supply him with goods or services; ultimately he was driven out of his home, and out of Ireland. More importantly, the boycott action made many people in England and Ireland aware of grave injustices."[2]

The boycott of Boycott showed how common people could exercise influence by using their meager economic power in a collective fashion. The peasants' actions would today be called a strike. In the early 1900s the word strike would be used to describe the refusal by groups of people to purchase goods because they believed them to be too expensive. Both strikes and boycotts are actions that involve collective action to influence transactions in the marketplace. The main difference between them is that strikes are the refusal of people to work for their employer for various reasons. Strikes are a production-oriented tool while boycotts are consumption-oriented. Boycotts are now commonly defined as attempts "by one or more parties to achieve certain objectives by urging individual consumers to refrain from making selected purchases in the marketplace."[3]

BOYCOTTS IN REVOLUTIONS: THE CONSTITUTIONAL SIGNIFICANCE OF EVERYDAY GOODS

It can well be that the American journalist who covered the peasant revolt in Ireland became interested in the action because he knew the history of his country well. Of all countries in the world, the United States is most noted for using boycotts as a political tool. The reason, as stated by a historian of American consumer society, is the importance of consumption for the material and ideological components of American identity.[4] Boycotts were used frequently in the War of Independence. Sympathizers of the revolutionary cause refused to buy English goods as a protest against the passage of the Stamp Act in 1756 and the tax on tea. The deterioration of the relationship between the colonies and the British government made many colonists worry about their own private economic dependence on Britain, which was a consequence of their purchasing of British goods and their reliance on the credit that British retailers generously extended to them. Tea, clothing, and other goods imported from Britain became embedded with political meaning and identity. A scholar of this "consumer revolution" states:

> Americans who had never dealt with one another, who lived thousands of miles apart, found that they could communicate their political grievances through goods or, more precisely, through the denial of goods that had held the empire together. Private consumer experiences were transformed into public rituals. Indeed many colonists learned about rights and liberties through these common consumer items, articles which in themselves were politically neutral, but which in the explosive atmosphere of the 1760s and 1770s became the medium through which ideological abstractions acquired concrete meaning.[5]

Local colonial merchants were the first groups to organize boycotts. They had, of course, a vested economic self-interest in the struggle for independence. However, the most important group behind the boycotts was the general consuming public. What motivated their action were their private concerns and the desire for economic and political independence from England. Both the public and private virtue tradition of political consumerism thus drove people to activism. They used what was called subscription lists to mobilize support for their cause. The lists provided information on the purpose of the boycott and requested a written pledge of support. The names on the lists were tabulated and announced in the local newspapers. The goal was high numbers. Anyone and everyone—not just white males with property—were encouraged to sign up. This mobilization strategy makes them particularly interesting as it shows their rather egalitarian character. Another important aspect is the presence of women. In some cases, women organized their own subscription movement when men refused to let them play an active role in general list campaigns.[6] Thus, we see how the politics embedded in British goods sold in the American colonies opened up an arena for citizen participation for all groups of people. Just providing consumer goods for the family became, therefore, interlocked with the high politics of diplomacy and the constitutional status of the colonies.[7] A historian of American consumerism concludes:

> The American Revolution was in part a consumer revolution. The identity of the colonies as a nation, an "imagined community" to borrow Benedict R. O'G. Anderson's phrase, grew out of the practices of wearing homespun clothing and boycotting British goods, most notoriously during the Boston Tea Party. The revolutionaries became the first in a long line of Americans to link consumption—or its withdrawal—and politics.[8]

An American political tradition of fighting for justice by "putting one's money where one's mouth is" was, thereby, established. Boycotts continued to play a central role in other constitutional disputes later in history. One poignant instance is their place in the events leading up to the Civil War. Northern abolitionists called on all shoppers to boycott goods produced by southern slave plantations. The issue was the injustices of slavery and the need to convince citizens and government that it must be prohibited constitutionally. Boycotts of slave-produced goods were one of the means used by the international antislavery movement in its struggle.[9]

Boycotts have been important in other revolutionary settings as well. India is a good example. The issues were much the same as in the United States: economic dependence and political injustices caused by colonialism and the colony's need to create an independent political or national identity. Britain was also the target of the Indian boycott. Mahatma Gandhi's nonviolent struggle for independence from Britain demanded that Indians practice the public virtue tradition—self-denial and self-sacrifice—in their struggle for justice and equality that was seen as part of their political and economic independence. Many Indians supported the boycott of British goods, and it is of interest for this book that women were key actors in the Gandhian movement for independence.[10]

Swadeshi, meaning use of things belonging to one's own country (i.e., indigenous goods) was central to Gandhi's strategy for independence. He integrated the Swadeshi Movement from the early 1900s in his struggle. Swadeshi became a central ideological tool for him. It can be seen as a primitive kind of political consumerist labeling scheme. Swadeshi helped build national unity and identity, and it promoted domestic industry. Like American colonists before them, Indians were encouraged to "buy Indian" cloth and other domestically produced goods.

Another aspect of special interest about the Swadeshi political movement for this book is that a number of key groups found that the campaign fell in line with their own private interests. The private virtue tradition is, therefore, evident in the Swadeshi movement. Many Indian capitalists supported Swadeshi because it promoted their private interests as domestic textile manufacturers. They also believed that Swadeshi would help better their own economic standing by improving the economic standing of Indian industry generally. This in turn was seen as benefiting the interests of domestic workers. Swadeshi even met with the approval of the Indian educated class because they were not dependent on selling British goods for their livelihood. Thus, Swadeshi gave manual labor dignity, helped alleviate rural poverty and underemployment, and the private virtue character motivated people to act together. As a consequence, it united educated and uneducated Indians in a shared experience.[11] The movement was also helped by a fall in the exchange rate, which raised the price of imported cloth. Higher prices meant that people could no longer afford imported cloth. This was an economic incentive for people to change their consumption patterns and indirectly helped to strengthen the campaign.

The author of a 1931 report on the use of Swadeshi and the anti-British boycott stresses its ethical quality and characterizes the public virtue tradition of political consumerism present in it in his description of the practice of virtues by the Indian people:

> The present movement is not entirely political; it has a higher and an ethical aspect, although it may at times be lost slight of by officials and their apologists.... There are many Indians, who feel that they cannot make the supra-sacrifice for their country. There are some again who believe that resistance even against "lawless laws" is unconstitutional. It is subversive of orderly Government. There are others again, who feel that antipathy against the imports from a particular country engenders hatred which must be eschewed as evil in itself. But they all agree in the belief that they should make some common sacrifice for the cause of their country and that could best be done by religiously encouraging *Swadeshi*. When one buys an indigenous product, probably of worse

quality or at a higher price than the imported product, he does this, for the good of the nation as a whole. It is these little conscious acts of self sacrifice which have contributed to weld Indians into a nation, in spite of their superficial differences. It is for this reason that many Indian nationalists prefer *Swadeshi* to protection, which, they agree, cannot give the same impetus to efficiency and economy or the same inspiration to national endeavour as "*Swadeshi*" can. According to them, there must be free and unrestricted competition with imported goods in order that on the one hand Indian manufactures may not slacken their efforts at constant improvement and on the other, Indian consumers may know and feel what sacrifice they are making in the interests of the nation. As against this, there is the view that when an industry is in its infancy, it has to be helped in its upward growth by artificial aid in the shape of protective tariff.

In either case, it will be clear that if and when boycott is called off, *Swadeshi* will stay and will be adhered to religiously by most people.... [12]

BOYCOTTING FOOD FOR SOCIAL JUSTICE: CONTRASTING AMERICAN AND EUROPEAN EXPERIENCES

Products used by families on a daily basis have been and continue to be the focus of political consumerist activities. Once politicized these products create an arena that juxtaposes the household and the community.[13] Sometimes, as in the cases discussed in the previous section, goods were boycotted because they were embedded in struggles for national independence. They symbolized the needs and wants of emerging nations-states, and they helped mold national identity. In other cases as those discussed here, constitutional principles were not at stake, but politics is clearly present. The political issue of the food boycotts of the 1900s, social justice, shows this quite clearly. Consumers in Europe, the United States, and elsewhere expressed their dissatisfaction with the supply, quality, and price of agricultural produce in meat and milk strikes. A particularly active group was working-class housewives. Scholars are now beginning to write their history, with work on the United States being the most comprehensive. This section uses a political consumerist theoretical lens to interpret historical instances of food strikes and boycotts. It begins with the American experience, then offers examples from Europe, and ends with an articulation and analysis of the contrasts between American and European experiences.

Between the 1920s and 1940s, American urban and rural housewives across the nation voiced public dissatisfaction about the price of food. The revolts by housewives were, in the words of one historian, "far more widespread and sustained, encompassing a far wider range of ethnic and racial groups than any tenant or consumer uprising before it."[14] The revolts have not gone unnoticed in the social sciences. Political philosopher Iris Marion Young uses the housewives' revolt to explain seriality and serial identity, a theoretical concern in chapter 1. She discusses how focus on a particular, every-day problem like chicken prices in the lower East Side of Manhattan led angry women to organize and express their dissatisfaction with the situation publicly and how this, in turn, helped them to understand better their role as wives, mothers, and women in society.[15]

In these revolts, women mobilized into ad hoc networks to boycott food products and, thus, organized themselves as class-conscious mothers and consumers. Their tactics did not always reflect peaceful collective action, as shown by a group of angry Polish house-wives from Chicago who poured kerosene over thousands of pounds of meat to state their case that meat shortage was not the reason for high prices or other women who threw meat and poured milk and flour into the streets.[16] But in many instances they learned the strategies and tactics of nonviolent collective action as well. Women labor unionists used their know-how to help organize housewives as consumers and to forge consumer alliances between working women and housewives. Some organizers for the Communist Party used mother-hood as a parole to unite women because they realized that "when appealed to as mothers, apolitical women lost their fears about being associated with radicalism in general and the CP in particular."[17] The appeal to women as mothers and wives thus lowered the threshold for collective action, a feature of the private virtue tradition of political consumerism discussed in chapter 1. It sanctioned the role of private concerns for the family as legitimate public worries, and this gave women the incentive and push they needed to become involved in a political struggle. The focus on family concerns gave them courage to voice their complaints publicly, and it allowed them to do it in geographically close areas that were comfortable and familiar.

Historians view the housewives' neighborhood councils and networks created in the 1930s as sophisticated collective-action groups. They are also examples of more individualized collective action, an important theoretical concept for political consumer research introduced in chapter 1. They were relatively stable structures, and the women who belonged to them were successful in using the radio and print media—the information communication technology of the time—to put pressure on producers, retailers, and government.

These networks can be characterized as political consumerist pressure groups, and their demands on both government and private industry "reflected a complex understanding of the marketplace and the potential uses of the growing government bureaucracy."[18] They show how women consumers were able to politicize agricultural products and hold their own against producers who were men. Here we see clearly the political agency of consumers, that is the interactive relationship between empowered consumers and the marketplace[19] discussed in chapter 1.

The housewives' revolts in the United States are important events in the history of political consumerism. They illustrate how private concerns have a public face, which requires organized action that is put together in new ways and places—as serial identity and individualized collective action aimed at the marketplace. The revolts also put the concerns of the everyday woman consumer on the public agenda. Women began to speak with one another about the injustices of high food prices. In their casual talk, they found that many housewives had the same experience, and they began to see their worries as a problem that needed to be dealt with as a group and politically. The housewives were forced by concern for family nutrition and health to find a solution to the problem, and this drove them to public action. This is a clear example of the private virtue tradition of political consumerism. Participation in councils and networks empowered them and gave them self-confidence. They also used a rather new information communication technological invention—the telephone—to mobilize women nationwide.

The actions on the part of these women are interesting because they illustrate how civic skills gained from contact with such established political homes as trade unions could be applied in new and innovative ways when housewives organized to solve family problems. Serial identity is evident among the housewives because they stepped out of their established political identities created by social class, region, religion, and ethnicity to identity themselves as mothers and wives in order to work together in concrete everyday problems and in close-to-home settings. Immigrant urban women created networks with rural women to target the actors who profited from high food prices. Local neighborhood women's councils created to fight food prices often cut across ethnic and religious lines. Women taught other women in the networks to read, write, deliver speeches, and lobby government. They took pride in their empowerment as political actors. Many women remained members because the networks enhanced their self-esteem and gave them a sense of camaraderie. The situation was different in most other civil society associations, where women as a rule were marginalized as members. Not surprisingly, these political consumerist networks threatened men. They politicized motherhood, the family, and the home. They also built bonds between women. This led to conflict with the worker's movement of the time, which felt threatened by the politicization of the housewife and the attention on consumption over production in the class struggle.

The conflict over production and consumption as organizing principles in politics and the role of labor and consumerism for the class struggle in particular is also evident in European experience with food boycotts. A good example of a European way of dealing with the tension is the 1909 margarine boycott in Sweden. The boycott is not well-researched, but we know that a rather new civil society association at the time, the Swedish Cooperative Union (*Kooperativa för-bundet*, KF), which established cooperative grocery stores catering to working-class family needs, called a boycott of two of the largest producers in a margarine cartel. It called this boycott because the cartel had decided to discontinue giving the KF a rebate on margarine that they gave to private wholesalers. Private wholesales had complained about the KF's use of the rebate to lower margarine prices in its stores. All cartel members decided to stop selling their margarine to the Cooperative Union. What makes this example more European than American is the way the KF dealt with the situation. At the same time that it called on consumers to boycott margarine, it bought a margarine factory and began selling its own margarine brand in its stores. It had managed to raise money for the loan to buy the factory through contributions from its local units, individual citizens, and other sources. This move and also changes in Swedish trade policy forced the margarine cartel to reform its policy. Once it began to sell margarine to the cooperative again, the KF sold its factory and called off the boycott.[20] The "margarine struggle" (*margarinstriden*), as this incident is called in history books, is interesting because it shows that a European umbrella consumer cooperative opted to solve its problem by choosing a production over a consumption solution. Rather than concentrating on mobilizing consumers in a national boycott and using the market as an arena for the struggle for lower margarine prices and a fight against food cartels, the consumer organization purchased a factory and became a producer.

The limited and scattered information available on food boycotts in European history shows both differences and similarities between American and European use of political consumerist tools in the struggle for change. One important difference involves the organization of political struggles. Europeans have tended to view the boycott weapon as a political tool that is more difficult to control and therefore less appealing than other more organized forms of struggle.[21] A second difference is that government has played a more important role in the political consumerist struggles in Europe. An interesting similarity is that food boycotts in Europe also mobilized individual citizens and involved women. Networks were also created but they were organized differently than the ones discussed above.

For instance, a network of well-to-do Swedish women was founded in 1914 to offer consumer education to less fortunate citizens. To accomplish this, it applied for and received government funding for some of its activities.[22] At about the same time that this network was in operation a spontaneous and disorderly working-class food protest movement emerged in Stockholm. This food boycott movement worried the KF, which had become part of the political establishment. It disliked the protest group and its tactics. The KF also saw it as a competitor. Even the social democratic party in Stockholm was skeptical about this renegade group but decided to tolerate it given the mood of the country. The social democrats were pleased that citizens took matters in their own hands by using the market as an arena for politics, and they even stole some of the group's ideas. But the party also believed that the best strategy for promoting the interests of consumers was for them to organize in one, united political home, the KF. Food prices and food supply were an agenda item in politics during these years. But this did not stop all spontaneous protests of women wanting to feed their families a nourishing meal. Many working-class women took to the streets when potatoes, a staple of the Swedish people, were in low supply. The police were called in when their desperate search from store to store for potatoes turned violent. These "hunger uprisings" by women in the early years of the 1900s politicized food products. Women used the market as an arena for politics and their activism is considered part of the working-class struggle for social justice and equality.[23]

Another example that shows the difference between the European and American approach to the politics of products is the "ideological experiment" (*det ideologiska försöket*).[24] It was an organized attempt by parts of the Swedish social democratic movement to give consumption as high an ideological priority as production. The target group was women as homemakers. The social democrats behind the attempt believed that "[i]t is, of course, housewives that decide which goods in the country should be sold and which should not be utilized. In this way, housewives become consumer leaders—and in some ways even production leaders."[25] The idea was for women consumers with their everyday knowledge about homemaking to adapt production to the needs of their families. Together with their working husbands, they would gain control over the means of production. An old KF slogan, "power of the food basket" (*korgens makt*), was used here. The movement taught women about good taste as consumers and sound home economics. They learned that good taste was based on functional choice and bourgeois (middle class, nonsocialist) taste was bad taste.[26] The experiment was not long lasting, and it failed because it put emphasis on consumption and women rather than on production and men.

Established political actors in Europe have been skeptical about the use of the market by women as an arena for politics. An example from 1972 is telling. This account given here is based on newspaper reports of that period as scholarly research is nonexistent. This spectacular event produced about 100 articles in the daily newspapers. What happened was that women from the Stockholm suburb of Skärholmen organized a food revolt, which the media labeled "Skärholmen Housewives" (*Skärholmsfruarna*). They called a weeklong boycott against what they considered the unjust price of milk and meat. The boycott mobilized many supporters and spread all over Sweden. It ended in a protest demonstration that attracted 6,000 participants in Stockholm. Newspapers reported that retailers and dairies noted a dramatic decrease in milk sales during the boycott. This was the first widespread food demonstration in Sweden since World War I. That women—or protesting ladies (*protestdamerna*) as one journalist called them—politicized food prices in this fashion was duly noted by the media and politicians. "Housewives' Milk War Becomes a Political Threat" was one telling newspaper headline.[27] Parliament addressed the group's concerns; Prime Minister Olof Palme called them to a meeting to discuss high food prices, and a popular political issues program on national television (Kvällsöppet) invited the women to debate food prices with Kjell-Olof Feldt (Minister of Trade) and supermarket chain representatives. Not all participants in the television show considered the points raised by the women as well-informed and relevant. The Minister of Trade was criticized later for telling the women that they were ridiculous and not worth listening to.[28] Yet their demands fell well in line with popular discontent over high food prices. Shortly thereafter Parliament passed a bill to subsidize milk to lower its price. Some public reactions to the events showed a rather negative view of women as political activists and ridiculed the tactics that they chose to use in their struggle. Yet the group fits in well with the wave of extra-parliamentary protest activity by loose networks and new social movement outside established political homes that characterized Sweden in these years. The political establishment's reaction is also typical of its time. It viewed all new women's and youth's groups with skepticism and considered their interpretation of justice and fairness as out of line with conventional Swedish thinking on these matters.[29]

European responses have five general characteristics: production-orientation; organized or group collective action; established civil society associations' attempts to capture and monopolize the consumer interest; strong role of the state; and dominance of male values. These characteristics seem to apply to other forms of European political consumerism as well.[30] More systematic research is needed to establish the political and cultural differences between the United States and Europe but it seems quite probable on the basis of the discussion in this chapter that emphasis on production is the most important explanation for the different historical developments in Europe and the United States. The general impression is that European skepticism of political consumerist boycotts is explained by the historically stronger European socialist workers' movement that could successfully use production as the focus for the political struggle. The situation was quite different in the United States. Political consumerism, and particularly boycotts, which have formed part of American political identity, have been seen as "a principal means of political communication since the birth of the Republic"[31] and have offered the labor movement a way of working with their issues in situations where employers and government have opposed them. Because the socialist workers' movement was never strong in the United States, labor unions were forced to use consumption as an effective method for their political struggle.

For Europeans, consumption has generally been viewed as secondary to production as a focus for political change and the promotion of political and civil virtues. Consumption has traditionally been conceived as the simple satisfaction of basic human needs. Focusing on it has not until quite recently been seen as a way to solve societal problems. Nor did most European states considered it as an organizing tool. In earlier decades of the 1900s, many socialist leaders even believed that more focus on consumer issues would give workers bourgeois values and thereby weaken class-consciousness and class identity. Prominent social democrats in Sweden for instance initially opposed the cooperative movement for just this reason. Like their American counterparts, these men also feared that consumerism would politicize the home and empower women in the wrong way—that is, it would help them develop into independent citizens. Significant parts of the consumers' cooperative movement in Sweden and other European countries also held this view. Some leading Swedish social democrats had, however, a different opinion. They agreed with their American counterparts that consumer power could play an important role in the movement and could ease the class tensions in society.[32] However, they differed from their American counterparts who saw production as necessary for consumption and consumption as the goal of all economic activity. The labor movement in Europe was far stronger and could use labor strikes, collective bargaining, and corporatist collaboration with the state to pressure for more labor rights. For American trade unionists, the union movement needed consumerism to reach its goals.[33] It could not rely on strong socialist parties or on government for help.

Two other explanations for the different historical experiences give an indication of the methodical, organized nature of European political culture. The case of Sweden is illustrative. Collective action that was not channeled through established civil society associations, as in the case of the spontaneous uprisings in Stockholm and its suburb Skärholmen in the 1970s, have been viewed with suspicion because, like boycotts, it was potentially uncontrollable. Thus, for organized action to be viewed as legitimate, at least in the past, it needed to be conducted in a highly structured, organization-oriented way, and channeled through such established political homes as interest organizations and long-term social movements. Members became socialized and disciplined followers of these political homes. Until quite recently, more individualized collective action has been viewed with skepticism and even considered as unwanted and unnecessary extra-parliamentary activity. It was unwanted because it disrupts representative democratic structures and routines and unnecessary because encompassing associations as the trade unions and the consumers' cooperative have generally believed that it is their responsibility to represent the interests of consumers. Their handling of the issue has, however, been influenced by the interests of production, suppliers, and male workers. Over the years Europe has become a consumer-oriented society. This transformation is influencing all spheres of life, and it is a change that is leading to a reevaluation of the role of consumption in economic, societal, and political development. A question worth pondering is why Europe is now more open to the use of labeling schemes than the United States. Perhaps the impact of globalization on Europe is the key to the answer.

EARLY "NO SWEAT" LABELING SCHEME

Political consumerism as a form of citizen engagement in politics involves more than boycotts. Although boycotts have dominated in the past, there are a few examples in the history of institutions that have been created for *positive political consumerism* (so-called buycotts) that encourage people to purchase goods following an established set of criteria. A particularly interesting early example is a labeling scheme called the White Label Campaign (1898–1919). It was organized by the National Consumers' League in the United States.[34] The campaign shows a number of interesting similarities with later-day successful labeling schemes and will, therefore, be discussed in some detail.

Florence Kelley, general secretary of the National Consumers' League, was an innovative political entrepreneur. She wanted to renew the organization by giving it a new mission. To accomplish this, she developed the White Label scheme. Today we would call it a fair trade (no sweat, non-sweatshop) label. Its success depended on mobilizing smart shoppers, targeting a mass product for labeling, establishing viable labeling criteria, and identifying manufacturers willing to allow themselves to be evaluated by the criteria. The tar-geted group of smart shoppers was middle-class women, a choice motivated by their economic means to pick and choose among product brands. Kelley decided it best to focus on a few manufactured products nationwide. (The other option was a narrow geographic scope and a large number of target goods.) The chosen product was women's and children's machine-made white, cotton underwear, a product purchased in great numbers particularly by middle-class women. The market was competitive, and there were few manufacturers worthy of the label so it was possible for women to make a smart choice from the start. Qualifying for the label demanded transparency and what we may call certification of manufacturers. They were required to obey state factory laws, make all their goods at the factory location (no home work), regulate working hours so that no one had to work overtime, and refuse to employ children under the age of sixteen.[35] With the criteria in place and the target groups of consumers and producers identified, Kelley began to mobilize support nationwide for the campaign and to establish local League chapters to participate in the labeling movement. She kept in touch with the different chapters and the headquarters through the information communication technology of the time: she sent letters.

The White Label Campaign is an example of a positive political consumerist, market-based activity with roots in an established civil society organization. It is a positive political consumerist activity because it encouraged people to purchase certain products: a buycott. It is market-based because rather than lobbying government to regulate the manufacturing sector more or enforce its present policy more stringently, the campaign asked the consumer to choose White Label goods to promote certain manufacturers and to encourage others to improve their labor policies or go out of business. It also illustrates governance and, as such, represents an early example of new regulatory policy or soft laws as discussed in chapter 1. Government's role was restricted to the factory legislation it had passed, which formed some of the criteria for labeling. Other criteria used by the campaign represented the concerns prevalent in the early years of industrial society. Manufacturers were not only encouraged to follow state ordinances but to adopt more progressive labor policies than demanded by law, that is, "beyond compliance" policies. The label was effective. It changed factory workplace conditions and improved the situation of workers. Over time, the label outlived its usefulness. One problem for its creators was that certified manufacturers used it as an argument against unionization, which illustrates how political consumerism can conflict with other struggles for citizen rights, in this case the right to join unions.

 Like boycott actions, the labeling campaign also showed that women could be involved politically through their consumer choices. It informed them about the politics of products. Kelley was well aware of the potential for citizen influence inherent in consumerism. She said: "No one except the direct employer is so responsible for the fate of these children as the purchasers who buy the product of their toil."[36] The campaign also gave women access to the political community. It gave them an arena for political action, and their purchasing choices became a tool to exercise moral and political power in a time when men dominated formal civil society and government settings.[37]

USE OF POLITICAL CONSUMERISM BY LABOR UNIONS

Trade unions in different countries have used political consumerist tools in labor struggles. Some unions, as those in the United States, used boycotts to unionize the workplace. Others called boycotts as part of the larger workers' movement struggle. Union participation in international boycotts is an example here. Unions have also employed positive consumerist tools. They have encouraged their members and others to buy goods manufactured by unions ("buy the union label"[38]) and to shop at union or workers' movement stores. In more recent years, unions have focused on how and where they invest their capital and have, therefore, become involved with socially responsible investing, a topic of chapter 3. Capital may be in the form of money accumulated by the unions and invested in the stock market or may concern how money for pensions is invested in funds. This section illustrates the role that political consumerism has played in the history of the union movement in the United States. The focus is the American case because it is richer in examples than Europe. European unions have also been involved in boycotts but most of them seem to have an international orientation, as discussed later in this chapter.

Union activists in American history perceived boycotts to be as important as striking and picketing. Both had the same goal—just treatment of workers. In cases where labor laws made it impossible to strike, boycotts were called instead. Government and industry could not prohibit individual citizens from choosing what to purchase at the marketplace, though they could and did at times prohibit organized labor's use of "we don't patronize" and "unfair to labor" consumer guides.[39] Boycotts also gave women a public space in trade union activities. It was important that they, as homemakers and union member wives, understood union goals and applied them in their everyday shopping activities.

An interesting example of this that has been studied in some detail comes from Seattle, Washington. In the 1920s, the unions encouraged men and women of the working class to come together as consumers. Unions created their own businesses and asked their members and members' wives to patronize them. In doing so they began to erase the clear boundary between the public spheres of politics and work on the one hand and the private sphere of family and home life and private economic considerations on the other hand. A historian who has studied unionism in Seattle draws the conclusion that once the unions "chose to politicize consumption, they also sought to change the way housewives performed their unwaged labors of consumption."[40] The class struggle was, therefore, fought on two fronts—production and consumption.

At times, boycotting was the preferred tool of the American labor movement. The reason was weak support for the unions in the community and among workers. Frequently workers lacked the skills, knowledge, discipline, and experience needed for successful strikes, and their unions lacked the necessary economic resources and organizational tools to make strikes successful. Lack of resources meant that it was very easy for employers to replace striking workers with others desperately in need of work. The history of the farm workers' movement in the United States is illustrative.

Several unsuccessful attempts had been made to unionize American farm laborers. Not only were the political establishment and laws working against them, it was difficult to use the strike weapon because it was almost impossible to create a sense of workers' identity and solidarity among migrant farm laborers. The unions also lacked the necessary economic resources to provide for a proper strike fund for their members. Boycotting was, thus, one of the few available options. We see the influence of Mahatma Gandhi and nonviolent political action in the attempts in the 1960s to improve the working conditions of farm laborers. César Chavez, leader of the United Farm Workers' Movement and boycott organizer, conducted a number of political fasts when the boycott was called to create a public spectacle to underscore what he and his movement considered the unjust treatment of farm laborers. His fast and nonviolent political movement received considerable mass media attention and the support of such influential political leaders as Martin Luther King and Robert Kennedy. At first other trade unionists viewed the boycott with skepticism, but they soon changed their minds when they saw that it became the most important tool for the farm workers' movement.[41] The boycott spread to other parts of the world. Networks were set up in many different countries to protest the treatment of Hispanic farm laborers in California. The boycott symbolized more than unionization. It became a struggle for human rights, workers' rights, social justice, and ethnic pride.

At first the boycott organizers pleaded with the American public to follow their boycott call by appealing to citizens' public virtues. They asked consumers not to buy certain brands of grapes to show solidarity with the farm labor cause. This strategy was not all that successful. What is worth noting is that the boycott really began to have an impact in the United States when the union decided to give its struggle an everyday consumer focus. The union informed consumers that the pesticides used on grapes were hazardous to their own and their families' personal health.[42] Their outrage over how growers viewed consumers and about the risks involved with eating grapes spilled over into a public concern about how growers treated farm laborers. Thus, once the union changed its strategy and began using the private virtue tradition of political consumerism, it found that more consumers were willing to boycott grapes. This is an example of how private concerns can create virtues that are more public in orientation. Politicization of table grapes proved successful. It showed the world that farm labor concerned everyone—not just individual pickers and their families but all people who enjoyed eating grapes. The text of a boycott poster used at the time illustrates the politics of grapes well: "Every California grape you buy helps keep this child hungry."[43]

BOYCOTTING FOR CIVIL RIGHTS

Civil rights imply equality regardless of people's religious beliefs, group associations, ethnicity, gender, sexual persuasion, and political views. Frequently a list of civil rights is included in national constitutions. The problem for many groups is that these constitutionally protected rights may not apply to all spheres in society and may not be fully realized in the political system. Consumer boycotts have been used in different countries to focus attention on the violation of civil rights in different spheres and particularly to put pressure on private corporations to treat all groups equally and with respect. Boycotts called by unions to force companies to allow their employees to use their civil right of freedom of organization—unionization—as well as those called by humanitarian associations to improve the human rights of particular groups have been rather frequent and are still in use. Today it is common for marginalized groups to use boycotts to improve their political, economic, and social standing. Boycotts have been and continue to be an important part of many transnational advocacy groups that work to improve the labor, human, and citizen rights of people in distanced countries.[44] Boycotts put pressure on institutions and call public attention to their cause.

In this section, I draw on a few examples of the use of consumer boycotts in the African American civil rights struggle to illustrate the importance of political consumerism in this field. The choice of the American civil rights struggle does not imply that other countries and groups have not used political consumerist action. Women, gay people, Native Americans, Mexican Americans, and other ethnic groups in the United States have used the boycott tactic to improve their standing in society.[45] My choice of the American civil rights movement is based on the fact that American researchers have focused more on it than on other cases. There is, thus, more scholarship available for interpretation through my political consumerist lens.

Consumer boycotts for civil rights are often part of nonviolent action. They have been combined with political fasts and civil disobedience. Boycotting for civil rights by African Americans was highly influenced by the Indian struggle for independence. Many influential civil rights leaders, among them Martin Luther King, were inspired by the Gandhian movement discussed earlier in this chapter. These civil rights leaders found a number of similarities in the Indian and African American struggle. Economic dependence and economic enslavement are two of them. African Americans began to teach themselves how to use nonviolent tools in their struggle for desegregation and integration in American society.

Many bus boycotts occurred in the 1950s, but the one in Montgomery in 1955 is most famous. Rosa Parks, a politically aware woman, started it by refusing to accept that the money she paid for a bus ticket did not entitle her to sit anywhere she wanted on the city bus. She was arrested because she refused the bus driver's request to give her seat to a white person. A leader in the Montgomery African American community found her arrest to be a good test case to challenge segregation in court, as litigation had for years been the preferred political tactic of the community. But even before her arrest and its politicization, a women's political group in Montgomery had begun to discuss the possibilities of using a boycott as a means of resistance, and they considered the city's bus system a good target. Buses were a good target for two reasons. Many African American people took the bus but were not really dependent on them as their destinations were within walking distances. Their frequent use of buses (reason one) and their ability to get around without them (reason two) were two critical prerequisites for making the boycott successful. People could follow the boycott and express their dissatisfaction with segregation without having to sacrifice themselves to a great extent for the cause. Thus, boycott involvement was individualized collective action with a rather low threshold.

With these prerequisites in mind, church leaders in the African American community decided to support the Montgomery bus boycott. Churches were used as meeting areas where the boycott could safely be publicized. Boycott organizers printed about 37,000 flyers for distribution; the women's political group used the telephone to mobilize supporters, and information on the boycott was leaked to the main local newspaper. Here we also see cleverness in boycott organizational strategy, another reason for its success. Before the boycott was officially called, its organizers had already sounded out potential supporters. They found that the response from the African American community was overwhelmingly in favor of the boycott and, therefore, worth calling. Martin Luther King was appointed its leader.

The boycott gave the antidiscrimination movement a new focus. Churches became an important force in the struggle. They were resourceful institutions in the African American community, an important arena for social contacts, source of social capital, and less harassed by white supremacists than the community's political organizations. Also, the boycott legitimized direct action as a political tool and the market as an arena for political action. The traditional tool that had been used by the civil rights movement was legal action, which explained the National Association for the Advancement of Colored People's (NAACP) reliance on lawyers and court proceedings. The bus boycott showed that direct action and market-based actions could be just as or more effective than court challenges for desegregating America and improving the standing of African Americans. Moreover, boycotts involved citizens at the grassroots level. Boycott organizers demanded that individual citizens assume responsibility for their own and their group's well-being. This responsibility-taking required courage, a degree of self-sacrifice, group solidarity, and even patience on their part; virtues discussed again in chapter 5. The year-long boycott tested and empowered African Americans. It gave them racial pride. As King put it, they were more willing to walk in dignity than ride in humiliation. The boycott ended when the U.S. Supreme Court declared local laws requiring segregation on buses to be unconstitutional. The bus boycott was effective. It changed municipal policymaking and set an example for both African Americans over the entire United States as well as for marginalized peoples globally. King declared that the decision was a victory for justice and democracy.[46] The boycott proved that market-based action could play a crucial role in breaking the cycle of history.

What is particularly interesting for this book is the role that women played in the boycott. A woman instigated the Montgomery bus boycott, and many other women mobilized support for it. White women also helped the boycott because they began to drive their African American housekeepers to and from work. In doing so they went against a proclamation issued by the city major to fire all African American domestic workers. Boycotting as a tactic was well-suited for African American women, and research shows that women have played an influential role in African American political consumerist actions and, therefore, for the civil rights struggle. For instance, African American women initiated many of the early efforts later categorized as part of the "Don't Buy Where You Can't Work" campaigns. These women were often politically active, well-known in their community, and economically resourceful. They formed the African American middle class. An example of their use of political consumerism comes from Harlem. In the 1930s a group of "serious and determined women" from the Harlem Housewives League decided that chain stores in their neighborhood should use a racial quota for hiring employees. The idea was for African Americans to be hired in proportion to the amount of money they spent in the stores. The group mobilized women to boycott the local branches when they refused to implement the quota policy.[47]

African Americans have used the boycott tool frequently. They have boycotted to change segregation policy, as in the bus boycotts and their precursors the streetcar boycotts of the early 1900s, and to open up employment opportunities. Some boycotts started by the African American community even show similarities with the Indian and American revolutionary struggle. Their basic goal was to create a separate and independent economy for black America. The groups supporting them were black nationalists and they, at times, found themselves in disagreement with the "Don't Buy Where You Can't Work" boycotts. These latter boycotts did not necessarily support African American businesspersons or an independent black economy. Their goal was African American employment in the community and integration into the workforce. Frequently the groups targeted chain stores owned and managed by white people and, when effective as they often were, the group encouraged African Americans to spend their money in them. At times this meant that the chain stores owned by whites were patronized more than those owned by African American.[48] People going in and out of these stores were carefully monitored and African Americans violating the boycotts were harshly criticized. Vandalism was also present in these early boycotts, which show that boycotting is not necessarily and always a nonviolent act. Obstructionist tactics like blocking telephone lines were also frequently employed.[49]

Boycotts continue to play a role in the African American struggle for civil rights and equality. Some of them such as boycotts of stores run by Koreans in African American ghettos can still become violent.[50] Other boycotts call on people across the American nation. Two examples are the NAACP tourist boycott of the state of South Carolina for flying the confederate flag over public buildings and the joint NAACP and AFL-CIO boycott of Crown Oil for its gender and race policies.[51]

International Boycotts and Economic Sanctions

For many years, political consumerism has been used to condemn the behavior of institutional actors in other countries, to gain publicity for the plight of foreign peoples, and to reinforce global perceptions of morality. Consumer boycotts and economic sanctions are a way for citizens to show moral outrage beyond state borders. They have for centuries been part of the strategy of international activism, as shown in the anti-slavery movement mentioned earlier and in the examples that follow. The League of Nations was overly optimistic when it hoped that boycotts and international economic sanctions would be an effective alternative to war; or perhaps it was exercising foresight in suggesting this idea by foreseeing such developments as economic globalization, postmodernization, governance, information communication technology, and the establishment of labeling schemes as new regulatory tools.

It is often difficult to discern the effect of international boycotts and economic sanctions on the political affairs of other countries. And like their domestic counterparts discussed earlier in this chapter, international boycotts and economic sanctions only work when a number of situational characteristics are in place, among them is the ability of boycott organizers to frame causes as influenced by consumer choices, mobilize consumers to participate, and if possible isolate a target that can be influenced to change its policies because of a boycott threat or action.[52]

Yet regardless of the potential effectiveness or ineffectiveness of international boycotts, they seem to be growing in number. A scholar of the American situation estimates that international boycotts are the category of boycotts with the most growth in recent years in the United States.[53] Boycotts allow concerned citizens to express their sense of urgent outrage about international affairs. Citizens turn to boycotts when they consider other options as hopeless. This is currently illustrated in arguments for an academic boycott of Israel that has begun in many countries and the divestment in Israel stocks movement on American university campuses.[54] Thus, we see a similarity between international and domestic boycotts. They are often used by groups of citizens who believe that they must use other forms to influence politics and therefore feel frustrated, marginalized, and/or shut out of participation in conventional means of exercising influencing in politics.

International boycotts focus on foreign governments and transboundary corporate actors. Globally they call for people, particularly consumers in the more affluent Western world, to resist purchasing certain targeted goods as a way of either influencing transnational corporate enterprises or government policy. When they ask consumers to boycott goods produced by private corporations within

a particular country as a means of influencing governmen
they are participating in what we may call international mark
pressure group politics. Boycott organizers and citizens who boycott
goods in this fashion view their consumer choice as a way of voicing
their political concerns to foreign governments via the marketplace.
This means that they view businesses as representative channels that
have the capability of carrying citizen messages to their political
system. They function similar to political parties and interest groups.
International boycotts target governments and may involve one or
more countries that agree to cease all cooperation with a particular
country. At times international government or supranational organizations, such as the United Nations and European Union, are
involved in them. It may also be the case that a "boycott war" is
declared, which means that the boycott is directed at two or more
countries.

As the main theme of this book is political consumerism as citizen
engagement in politics and responsibility-taking for their own well-
being and that of others, this section will now highlight the role that
citizens play in a few well-known international political consumerist
activities. We begin with the well-known international consumer boycott of a private corporation involving the food manufacturer Nestlé.
The boycott is an excellent example of how problematic the politics
of a product can become for a multinational company. It also shows
the limitations of boycotting as a new regulatory tool. The boycott of
Nestlé is discussed in some detail. Then I examine one aspect of the
South African boycott to discuss the problems involved with a boycott that is long lasting and requires self-sacrifice on the part of business and consumers alike. The section also mentions the role of
citizens and civil society associations in other international boycotts.

The general boycott of Nestlé (1974–84) was called because the
corporation manufactured baby milk substitutes or infant formula, a
substitute for breast milk used commonly in the Western world and
which Nestlé as well as other companies marketed in Africa and Asia.
It was well-known in medical circles that giving small babies this
product was the reason for increased levels in infant mortality in
Africa and Asia. Since the 1930s medical doctors had warned against
the use of infant formula in developing countries. Infant formula
powder needs to be mixed with water, and since clean water is scarce
proper preparation is difficult in certain countries. Various groups had
brought the issue to the United Nation. Infant formula companies,
including Nestlé, were aware of these medical results but continued
to sponsor maternity units and encourage women to use infant

formula rather than breastfeed their children. They even went out into the communities to market their products in what today would be considered rather unethical ways.[55]

Nestlé was a particularly good target for the boycott because it was the largest multinational company that manufactured infant formula. It was a well-known company that promoted itself as oriented toward family values and quality goods and had even been very successful with its trademark and logotype. It had high visibility in the market and was vulnerable to consumer pressure and a boycott because it was easy for consumers to identify Nestlé products in their supermarkets and decided not to buy them. Like the Nike case discussed in chapter 1, Nestlé's success in advertising itself made it sensitive to criticism. Its critics could successfully latch onto the company's crafted image and skillfully declared it to be hypocritical. Nestlé also inadvertently helped promote the boycott because of its decision to sue the German Arbeitsgruppe Dritte Welt (Third World Action Group) for libel for its translation of a report called *The Baby Killer* into German with the title *Nestlé totet Babys* (Nestlé kills babies), which was given considerable media publicity. The judge who heard the case ruled in Nestlé's favor but cautioned the company about the marketing tactics it used in developing countries.

The public attention given to the court case together with the moral credibility of the cause due to the involvement of many church groups encouraged other groups to participate. There was sufficient support to call a boycott. A group that monitors church investments in the United States decided to found the Infant Formula Action Coalition (INFACT), which called a boycott of all Nestlé products in 1974. Many churches, nuns, and missionaries working in developing countries were mobilized for the cause. Activists came from all over the world, and then the International Baby Food Action Network (IBFAN) was established. Together they—and many of them were women—developed new forms of international cooperation as part of their boycott efforts. They demanded that Nestlé stop marketing infant formula, hiring milk nurses, passing out free samples, and using direct advertisement in developing countries. It even called an Infant Food Day in Minnesota (the INFACT headquarters) on April 13, 1978 that was endorsed by the Governor of Minnesota. The publicity it received put the issue on the American congressional agenda. These events and others pushed the issue higher up on the United Nation's agenda. WHO and UNICEF hosted an international meeting to discuss the issue in 1979. Two years later the International Code of Marketing of Breastmilk Substitutes was adopted.[56]

According to all accounts, the boycott was *successful*. It had the right issue, actors, and setting for success. Organizers found a good boycott target and a good way to frame it so that a sufficient number of consumers worldwide could support it. Also, it was easy for consumers to participate in the boycott; all they needed to do was buy another brand name. It was difficult for Nestlé and other infant formula manufacturers to argue against the medical evidence (the consensual knowledge) that had accumulated over the years. The civil society associations forming the boycott campaign were able to work together successfully, and they had scientific knowledge, hands-on experience, and testimonials on the effects of the use of infant formula in developing countries as well as testimonials to convince others to support them. Facts and everyday examples were on their side.

Two international governmental organizations, the WHO and UNICEF, became the setting for negotiations between industry and the transnational boycott network. A code of conduct was negotiated among the concerned actors and finally ratified by the participating actors. It prohibited direct advertising and promotion of infant formula to mothers. The boycott was not entirely *effective* in terms of changing company policy or ethics about the use of infant formula in developing countries. Here we see the limits of boycotts as a policy tool and the difference between successful and effective boycotts (see chapter 3 for a discussion of the distinction between successful and effective boycotts). Infant formula companies found loopholes in the code and legal ways to get around it; only a few countries incorporated the code into national legislation, and no provision was made for monitoring its implementation.[57] As a consequence, the IBFAN reinstated its boycott of Nestlé in 1988.[58] The boycott has been in place for over three decades and has fallen out of the public limelight.

The Nestlé case shows that a successful boycott can open up a window of opportunity for a policy process that includes all concerned grassroots, governmental, corporate, and global actors. But it is only the beginning of a long process to change the behavior and mentality of a number of different and diverse policy actors and to solve problems. Yet it can, as research on international activism on human rights is showing, and did in the infant formulate case "break the cycles of history" by opening up agendas and arenas for alternative visions and information.[59]

The boycott of South Africa is another well-known case of international political consumerism. Citizens in many countries showed their moral outrage over the government policy of Apartheid by joining campaign groups and by refusing to engage in any cooperative dealings with South Africa. Many universities participated in this effort by ending all contact with South African academic institutions and colleagues. Groups now called "transnational principled issue networks" developed and internationalized the struggle against Apartheid. A scholar in this field declares, "the campaign against apartheid was ultimately able to mobilize a broader base of supporters than virtually any other human rights campaign to date."[60] The account that follows considers one aspect of the movement as a way of illustrating the role that citizens and businesses played in the boycott and the kind of commitment that is possible in boycotts that lasts for decades. There are different reasons for focusing on Sweden's role. First, other countries and many transnational networks have viewed Sweden as a moral role model for others to follow, quite probably because of such statesmen as Dag Hammarskjöld, Raul Wallenberg, and Olof Palme all of whom are well-known for their efforts for international humanitarianism.[61] Second, Swedes show high levels of mobilization for international humanitarian causes.[62] Third, Sweden has a dense civil society populated by a diversity of organizations and movements with high levels of membership and good mobilization potential.[63] Fourth, the consumer boycott was sanctioned by the Swedish state, civil society, and received wide public support. Many of the criteria for a successful boycott were in place in Sweden. Why did it fail?

Swedish citizens became involved in the South African struggle in the late 1950s. The boycott of South Africa mobilized many Swedes, was a highly politicized activity, and involved different political and civil society actors. The International Confederation of Free Trade Unions decided in 1959 to encourage North American and West European trade unions to show solidarity with the plight of South African nonwhites by boycotting South African goods. The Swedish Trade Union Council (*Landsorganisationen i Sverige*, LO) actively supported this decision and called a boycott of South African goods for a few months in 1960. This was the first phase of the Swedish South African boycott. Swedish criticism of Apartheid grew stronger in the early 1960s after a number of highly violent incidents between black political activists, the white police, and the South African government. The South African situation was an important issue in the Swedish public debate in these years. Politicians, journalists, and civil society leaders agreed that Apartheid was unjust and that Sweden should take action to end it. Apartheid was also an item on the agenda for the United Nations and many international nongovernmental organizations.[64]

Swedish civil society mobilized people to protest against the treatment of nonwhites in South Africa. The Committee for South Africa (*Svenska Sydafrikakommittén*) was established in 1960 and successfully set up local units in many cities and mobilized supporters from different political parties and civil society associations. It was the Swedish domestic branch of the transnational advocacy network against South African Apartheid. What is interesting about the Committee for South Africa is that it broke through the traditional ideological pillars in Sweden. People with different political leanings from the Right to the Left came together in this joint effort to rid the world of Apartheid. The Committee for South Africa also began a cooperative endeavor with the umbrella organization, Sweden's Youth Associations' Council (*Sveriges Ungdomsorganisationers Landsråd*, SUL). The SUL presented a motion at the World Assembly of Youth in 1962 that called for a worldwide protest action again racial oppression in South Africa, which was passed unanimously. The Swedish protest action, which involved other civil society associations, took the form of information politics, financial contributions, and boycotts.[65]

The civil society associations that were involved sought to prohibit all trade with South Africa to pressure the South African government to end Apartheid. Their goal was to convince the Swedish government to use economic sanctions in the form of an official boycott or trade embargo. Rather interestingly, they saw their call for a consumer boycott as the first step in opening up a policy window to start the legislative process for an official government response. Consumer support of the boycott can, therefore, be likened to an opinion poll or referendum that would show the government that Swedes were ready for action and dedicated to the cause. The second phase of the consumer boycott began in 1963. Its supporters held demonstrations, passed out flyers, and used their voice in local party organizations. The limited scholarly accounts on the boycott show that it engaged many people and received considerable publicity. The publicity and citizen-consumer support convinced institutional consumers—in this case several large supermarket retailers—to stop buying South African fruit and other South African goods to sell in their stores. The state alcohol retailer monopoly (*Vin- och Spritcentralen*) decided in 1965 that it would not sign new order contracts with South Africa. This meant that no spirits from South Africa would be imported and sold in Sweden. Also, Swedish food wholesalers decided to decrease their import of fruit from South Africa, which meant a drop of about

10 percent between 1963 and 1967.[66] The boycott was a short-run success. However, it was not effective because it failed to fulfil the goal of convincing the Swedish government to pass a law imposing a trade embargo of South Africa.

The boycott continued on a less successful note. Its long duration was taxing commitment and shows some of the difficulties in prolonged boycott activity. The Committee for South Africa and SUL were experiencing organizational problems and were unable to continue mobilizing consumers to boycott.[67] The Swedish Cooperative Union, the KF, discussed earlier in this chapter for its early involvement in boycott activity, found that its decision not to import South African fruit was having a negative effect on its cooperative store chain, *Konsum*. Customers had stopped their boycott and began to shop at other supermarkets to purchase the less expensive South African fruit as well as other family food supplies. Thus, the KF's commitment to the boycott when other supermarket chains had decided to discontinue their support had a negative effect both economically and organizationally. The KF was in a moral dilemma and had to choose between wanting to support a losing cause it believed in politically and seeing its customers go elsewhere to shop. They were forced to choose between money and morality.

The failure of the South African boycott in Sweden reveals many of the traits of other unsuccessful and ineffective boycotts.[68] Part of the problem was that it did not reach its goal as mass market-based consumer pressure for an official Swedish trade embargo. Over time consumers began to believe that their shopping choices and the self-sacrifice that the boycott entailed in the form of extra costs for fresh fruit were not urgent and crucial efforts in the long-term campaign against Apartheid. They chose money over morality and let the public virtue tradition of political consumerism fall by the wayside. They also wondered whether a small state like Sweden could have an impact by instigating a trade embargo. Finally, they knew that their boycott could not embarrass the South African political regime, which did not care if its reputation was tarnished with accusations of racism and unfair treatment of its nonwhite population, an important motivation for the boycott in the first place.

Other examples also show that international boycotts alone do not always solve political problems. In fact, their contentious nature can lead to the escalation of hostilities and end in boycott wars. The Arab boycott of Jewish goods that began the year World War II ended is a case in point. This boycott has impacted citizens and corporations greatly, increased hostilities between Arabs and Jews in the

Middle East, and led to a Jewish boycott of Arab goods. The Arab boycott has been called the economic war against the Jews.[69] It began in 1945 when the League of Arab States asked everyone to stop buying goods produced by Palestinian Jews because they promoted Zionist political aims.[70] Technically speaking, the boycott was against Zionists not Israel or Jewish people. But it was not easy to uphold this distinction in the heated political environment of the postwar period. In 1952 the boycott was extended to foreign companies doing business in Israel. The number of blacklisted companies grew over the years and by 1970 around 1,500 American companies were on the list. Many companies fearing retaliation from the oil-producing Arab countries decided to play it safe, and disassociated themselves with Israeli and Israeli-connected companies. One of the side effects of the boycott was the general discrimination of Jews as workers and businesspeople. Companies feared that a Jewish presence would jeopardize their dealings with Arab countries and decided to keep a low profile in the political dispute over human rights and Palestine.[71]

Citizen reaction to the boycott was louder and stronger. Citizen groups and many civil society associations in different countries fought for anti-boycott legislation and proclaimed that the companies blacklisted by the League of Arab States should be put on their white list, a list of companies to patronize for their support of Zionism and Israel. Citizen groups also called counter-boycotts in which they shunned companies that followed the Arab boycott. The boycott war was fought on two levels and involved different sets of actors. On one level, a regional governmental organization, the League of Arab states, called for a boycott of what they called Zionist goods. On the everyday level of individual consumers, Jewish sympathizers called for a boycott of goods from companies that stopped their transactions with Zionist actors and even encouraged boycotts of companies reluctant to invest in Israel.[72]

There are many other examples of international consumer boycotts organized globally by citizens to express their moral outrage. The international workers' movement has participated in them on many occasions. Radical organizations in Sweden and other European countries became members of a transnational advocacy network in the 1920s that criticized the court ruling on the socialists N. Sacco and B. Vanzetti. They called a boycott of American goods and particularly American films in the late 1920s as a response to the court ruling of guilty for charges of robbery and murder. Sacco and Venzetti were given the death penalty. Although many European socialists considered the verdict unjust, they had difficult in mobilizing support for the boycott. In Sweden a demonstration in Stockholm gathered

50,000 people and one in Gothenburg 10,000 protestors, but mobilizing socialists to participate in a demonstration was different from convincing the general public to boycott the American movies they were so fond of seeing on a Friday or Saturday night.[73] The boycott was neither successful nor effective. Sacco and Venzetti were executed.

Another boycott that involved the international workers' movement was the international boycott against German goods in the early 1930s. Its purpose was to express moral outrage against German treatment of its Jewish population. The AFL-CIO, the Swedish Trade Union Council (LO), as well as other labor movements supported it. The boycott created considerable public debate and many labor unions felt the need to defend their involvement. Other civil society associations also supported the boycott and in the mid-1930s an umbrella organization, the World Non-Sectarian anti-Nazi Council to Champion Human Rights, was formed to coordinate the activities of the various anti-Nazi boycott groups. Many large department stores in different countries decided to boycott German goods.[74] But this action did not stop the German government's anti-Semitic policy.

PROBLEMATIC POLITICAL CONSUMERISM: DILEMMAS OF MARKET-BASED COLLECTIVE ACTION

This chapter has shown how citizens have used the market to express moral outrage and fight for social justice, labor rights, human rights, and constitutional freedoms. At times boycotts have been organized by existing institutions like social movements and civic associations. On other occasions citizens have used existing political homes as a platform to create local, national, and international boycott network. It would, however, be wrong to conclude that political consumerism always promotes good public virtues, democracy, equal treatment, and morality. There are numerous instances where political consumerism has been used in an undemocratic fashion to oppress groups of people. This section looks at a few such examples. It illustrates how political consumerist actions may attract people who agree on the action, promote the main goal of the action, but differ considerably on the basic root of the problem. The exact same acts of political consumerism may both promote the rights and interests of one group while at the same time oppressing those of another group, thus resulting in conflicting messages to the targeted company, government, or the general public at large.

Probably the best example of problematic, undemocratic, and discriminatory political consumerism is the boycotts against Jewish merchants in the 1930s to promote anti-Semitism and ruin Jewish economic society. Little has been written about these boycott movements, but they started at the end of the nineteenth century. The boycotts reinforced anti-Semitic laws that were in place in many countries at that time and even encouraged "beyond compliance" behavior on the part of market actors (suppliers, retailers, and individual consumers). Groups actively declared that citizens should not buy Jewish goods and that they should not buy from Jewish merchants. Boycott activities were particularly intense in Germany in the 1930s. They were also violent. Even though "Don't Buy Jewish" campaign movements most likely started in Germany, they existed in many countries, including the United States, Sweden, and other European countries. Scholars call them the cold pogrom of the interwar years that "undermined the livelihood of hundreds of thousands of Jews."[75] The boycott was publicly supported by national socialist parties in various countries and by individual consumers privately sympathetic to the cause. The parties put up advertisements on stores owned or operated by Jews and in daily newspapers in their attempt to mobilize consumers to boycott Jewish merchandise. Local Swedish newspapers carried such advertisements. One declared: "Swedish goods should be bought by Swedes from Swedish businessmen. Do not participate in the international Jewish big business exploitation of Swedish workers and businesses."[76]

Political consumerist efforts can involve a wide range of participants. Some supporters may be moderate in their views on the issues involved in the boycotts. Others may have a more fundamentalist or fringe perspective. What brings them together is the need for a political consumerist campaign to root out problems. The "Don't Buy Where You Can't Work" campaign discussed earlier in this chapter is a good case in point. It began as a moderate effort on the part of primarily women's and church groups to encourage stores through dialogue to invest more in African American neighborhoods. The campaign then changed its tactics to picketing and boycotting, which engaged other more radical groups in the effort. As the campaign evolved, it developed two contradictory branches: a Black Nationalist group running a "Buy Black" campaign that used occasional anti-white and anti-Semetic racist rhetoric and an integration-minded group advocating white-collar job opportunities for African American residents. The groups could unite on methods (boycotting) and even on the general problem (low employment rates) but ideologically they differed considerably from each other. The ideological differences—integration versus black separation and economic independence—created internal divisions. This internal disruption led to disunity and weakened the campaign. Not only did the internal disputes scare off and alienate potential supporters but also storekeepers and owners were displeased by the boycott protests and pickets that had become more confrontational and disorderly. In the end, the campaign failed to reach its goal of higher employment because the merchants decided to back out of agreements that they had made with the campaign on hiring African Americans.[77]

Like all forms of collective action, boycotts and labeling schemes, which are the two main political consumerist actions, can attract a variety of supporters for different reasons of virtuous and less virtuous nature. Politics, as the saying goes, makes strange bedfellows. The long and on-going boycott of the Walt Disney Company is an excellent example of the dilemmas and contradictions of market-based political consumerist collective action. For decades the Disney Company has been a target of criticism. In the 1960s, student, hippy, and left-wing groups focused on its conservative and discriminatory nature. Some of the criticism of discrimination can still be heard today, but other issues have come into play in the boycott of Disney. Many different groups—church groups, racial groups, and supporters of fair trade—support this boycott. As activists before them, they agree that Disney is an offensive company and call on citizens globally to protest it. They also agree on the means, a boycott, and have put together an impressive home page "Disney Boycott. Your Official Disney Boycott Site!"[78] The problem is that the groups have different and contradictory reasons for considering Disney offensive and engaging in the boycott.

Numerous religious groups in the United States—including the Southern Baptists, the Catholic League, Oklahoma State Church, and General Council of the Assemblies of God—support the Disney boycott because it offends Christian and family values.[79] A Christian protest poster from 1999 declared "Disney funds abortion, sodomy, violent films."[80] Disney is criticized for providing health care benefit policies to "live-in partners of their HOMOSEXUAL EMPLOYEES" and is therefore betraying its commitment as "a FAMILY oriented company..."[81] The Ethics and Religious Liberty Commission lists "twenty-three reasons (and counting) to be aware of the 'Magic Kingdom'" including Disney's support for paganism; criticism of Christianity; release of dubious movies from a Christian moral standpoint, and smears on the reputation of the American founding fathers.[82]

Other groups supporting the same boycott have different grievances. The African American community argues that Disney is racist
in how it portrays African Americans in its productions and treats
them as employees. "Disney Pictures has yet to create animated films
featuring African-American characters other than having them portray animals."[83] Criticism of Disney's ethnic stereotyping is also heard
from Italians, who staged a protest demonstration against the film
"Mafia" in 1998, the National Hispanic Media Coalition,[84] as well as
Arab groups who state:

> A Disney Muslim is often an ugly, sinister, violent character of color,
> something yelling "Allah" and "Death to America," while abusing,
> shooting, or taking a beating from either a Caucasian or, recently (a
> more sinister twist), an Asian hero, as in Operation Condor. Enough is
> Enough! Is this innocent entertainment or a high-tech defamation of
> Muslims and Arabs on a global proportion...When was the last time
> you saw a movie where the hero was an African Muslim?[85]

The Disney boycott is also part of the general Boycott Israel
Campaign supported by many Arab groups. What has provoked Arab
groups is a costly Disney investment entitled Walt Disney's
Millennium Exhibition. According to Friends of Al-Aqsa, this exhibit
promotes Israeli occupation of Jerusalem and signifies that it "has
stepped into [the] political arena to promote Jewish claims over
Jerusalem."[86] A final listing on the official boycott site involves
groups concerned about fair trade and "Disney Sweatshop, Child
Labor and Union Bashing." It claims, "...the Southern Baptists are
right in boycotting Disney. But they are doing it for all THE
WRONG REASONS. If they want to boycott Disney, it should be for
Disney's blatant exploitation of women and children who work under
sweatshop conditions through the world..."[87]
    Collective action will always have the kind of problems discussed
in this section. Its dilemma is that there is no guarantee that all
citizen involvement always promotes democracy, public and private
virtues, equality, and justice. Political consumerism like collective
action generally can serve the purpose of expression of hostility to
outsiders.[88] Yet it may be the case that market-based efforts, as represented by political consumerist boycotts discussed here, are more
problematic as forms of collection action than those directed at the
political system per se. The problem is well-phrased by a scholar of the
history of political consumerism: "Political consumerism provides an
important vehicle for community expression when blocked from
operating within traditional political frameworks. It gives voice to the

voiceless. But precisely because it operates outside traditional politics, it can be dangerous in that it lacks the buffers against bias, ill-considered action, and vigilantism that such frameworks provide."[89]

POLITICAL CONSUMERISM AND DEMOCRACY

This chapter's interpretation of history through a political consumerist lens shows that the market has been used as an arena for politics for centuries. Political consumerism is not a new phenomenon. The discussed examples illustrate the linkage between shopping, morality, ethics, and politics. Most of the time the linkage—the politics of products—is not readily apparent. It is latent or concealed. Citizen concern and action is needed to bring the politics of products to the fore. In the cases from the past, we see how citizens who lacked political empowerment turned to the market as an arena for the expression of their opinions and used boycotts as their means of political expression and as a political tool. At times boycotts were the only available way for people without money, connections, suffrage, social status, and education to show others where they stood on issues of importance to them. Consumer boycotts helped them articulate their demands for greater justice. They have allowed these marginalized citizens to publicize their grievances, put pressure on institutions to change their policies, and develop their own sense of self-worth. In this sense, political consumerist actions form a fundament of struggles for democracy around the world. A view of consumer choice as false consciousness thus misses the potential impact of consumption for the development of the "agency of the consumer." Consumption not only pacifies people, it can also empower them.

We see this clearly in the revolutionary settings and civil rights struggles discussed in this chapter. The struggles also show how political consumerist activism can lead to ethnic, racial, and gender pride. These actions also function as a policy tool for civil society associations, be they trade unions or churches. Humanitarian organizations find boycotts to be a useful first step toward improving regulatory standards in situations where legislative authority is lacking or dispersed among different institutional actors or on many governmental levels. Thus, boycotts play a role in the development of democratic accountability. The consumer-citizen campaign against Nestlé illustrates how boycotts can encourage institutional actors who are involved in two- or even three-level governmental games to assume joint responsibility for regulatory norms and structures. Citizens have also engaged in international boycotts that target particular states to express their dissatisfaction with the domestic situation in that country even when their own governments have been reluctant to do so. In this sense as shown in the South African boycott, they have found a way to formulate a grassroots foreign policy.

Political consumer activism in the past was, most assuredly, much more extensive and richer than it has been possible to portray in this chapter. Indications of this are events from history, such as government debates on the legality of boycotts in Europe, the establishment of a boycott court in Norway, U.S. Supreme Court decisions restricting unions' use of boycotts, and the antiboycott organizations created by private industry.[90]

Political consumerism has always been a controversial phenomenon. Market-based political action is problematic and is characterized by many of the dilemmas of collective action. The fear that shopping has the potential to replace more established forms of political participation and turn citizens into consumers should not be taken lightly. Recent studies show that some of the new patterns of consumerism that developed in the American industrial society of the 1920s in fact replaced traditional community involvement and activism in trade unions. Older research explained this development by the pacification thesis that views consumption as surrogate satisfaction of needs and interests.[91] Today scholars analyzing the 1920s developments are more inclined to look elsewhere to explain this declining activity in the political system. They find explanations in the difficulty of established institutions in the past to adapt to newer circumstances. Scholars of the American situation in the 1920s argue that citizens left traditional forms of civic engagement because they felt that they catered less to their needs and desires. Economic prosperity of the early 1920s had changed the position of workers, and this meant that the workers' movement also needed to change. In Seattle, Washington, for instance, unions became more focused on issues of the politics of consumption than on issues of the politics of production. Their goal was to transform the structures of the American society by organizing how and where people purchased goods. This meant that they made visible both the workplace concerns of housewives and paid wage earners. Union-run cooperative stores were essential for this trade union strategy. Unions also used boycotts and labeling schemes as policy tools to shape shopping and saving habits. The general idea was to organize the purchasing power of workers rather than their labor power. The working class was, thus, transformed into the consuming class and gender issues became part of the class conflict.[92] An important condition for this effort was economic prosperity, and changes in the economic setting toward the end of the 1920s made it a short-lived effort. The effort was also before its time. But its failure raises an important question about the stability of political consumerism as a political tool and a political solution. Is it only successful when people have money to spare and can without much self-sacrifice follow the public virtue tradition of political consumerism?

The American experience of the first two decades of the twentieth century did not go unnoticed in later years. Political actors understood well that consumption could, if nurtured properly, play an important role in politics. During the New Deal, consumerism was an arena for struggles over democracy and political power. The struggle involved the creation of a political culture of consumerism that could renew trade unionism and develop an American version of social democracy.[93] The sociologist and New Deal policymaker Robert Lynd wrote articles for scholarly journals with eye-catching titles like "Democracy's Third Estate: The Consumer," "The People as Consumers," and "The Consumer Becomes a 'Problem.' "[94] His basic point was that government, business, and trade unions must consider seriously the interests of consumers. Consumers were not objects of manipulation. Rather the public interest should be redefined as a consumer's interest. Established private and public institutions needed to promote the agency of consumers or what they called at the time "the ultimate consumer." Individual citizens were not envisioned as accomplishing this alone.[95]

Other New Dealers agreed that institutional backing was necessary. They wrote about the politics of products or, in their own words, ". . . 'a complete check upon industrial processes from the raw material to the finished good and its distribution to the ultimate consumer.' "[96] Setting up standards for positive consumerism was on the New Deal agenda. The Director of the National Bureau of Standards at the time considered certification plans and labeling plans as essential for the consuming society.[97] Today we would consider his ideas as weak on accountability, transparency, and legitimacy. But they were rather progressive for his time. Other participants in the public debate on how to end the "economic illiteracy" of consumers were wary of self-labeling schemes.[98] As discussed in chapter 3, we are showing interest again in developing institutions to give consumers a new deal and to help them sign a social contract with global business.[99]

3

CONTEMPORARY FORMS AND
INSTITUTIONS

POLITICS IN THE GLOBAL MARKETPLACE

Today the global marketplace is an arena for political struggle. The Battle in Seattle, as the third ministerial conference of the World Trade Organization in 1999 has come to be called, is only one example of its contentious nature. Humanitarian organizations are increasingly focusing their attention on the global marketplace as an important arena for the promotion of their causes. Governments are no longer the sole targets for Amnesty International and the United Nations. Citizens of different countries are also participating in growing numbers in marketplace activities to promote global sustainable development. Not all contemporary political consumerist involvement is anti-globalist in nature, and most of it occurs in a much less public and vocal fashion than witnessed in Seattle in 1999 or at the time of the G-8 meeting in Genoa. The only sound may be the clicking of a computer mouse for cyberspace access, the hum of a fax machine, or a wallet opening to purchase goods at the neighborhood grocery store. Contemporary political consumerism also takes on a variety of forms. The global marketplace is the focus of demonstrations, boycotts, buycotts, involvement in transnational networks, and particularly Internet information campaigns and contacts with companies. The general issues of contention are ecology, fair trade, and human rights broadly conceived. They are reflected in political struggles on a single product like coffee or for a global norm as the rights of children.

Political consumerism is not a well-researched phenomenon but available studies from different countries show that citizens are increasingly becoming more concerned about the politics of products and their involvement in political consumerist activities is growing.[1]

Why is this happening? An important basic shift that explains this increase is our growing reliance on the global marketplace for the provision of goods. There is no other viable option for most consumers. We must shop to survive. These days few of us produce our own food and clothing. In order to live we must purchase commercially produced goods. It is important that we trust the producers and their goods because we are dependent on them. Our vulnerability is underscored when scandals force us to question the quality of goods. Food scares, concern about genetically manipulated organisms, and reports on sweatshop conditions and ecological disasters caused by manufacturing practice make it clear to us that we lack control over production processes upon which we depend for our daily existence. Consumption occupies a larger part of our lives and is taking on greater economic, political, and social significance. Citizens are demanding a voice in the marketplace.[2]

Another shift is globalization, which is interweaving the lives of citizens in different parts of the world in new ways. We have a greater number of products in common thanks to more cosmopolitan tastes, multinational companies, transboundary access, and free trade. At the same time we find it difficult to trace the commodity chain of the products offered to us on the global consumer market. We may not be able to discern where the raw materials come from and where the product is manufactured. Frequently we do not know the land or lands of origin of the product. Globalization has, thus, made the commodity chain longer and less transparent.

A third important development is our desire to express our individuality through consumer goods. We pick and choose among products of the same category in a way that was unimaginable in the past. For some people, lifestyle politics means the desire to harmonize politics and private life, with consumer choices playing an important role here. For others, the need to express individuality in for instance dressing in certain ways has opened up a new global market for mass customized goods, which is leading to labor problems and problems of sustainability in the global garment industry.[3] Thus, another important shift that explains the increase of political consumerism is individualization. Consumer choice is now part of the individual life style.

More consumer choice is leading to new forms of responsibility-taking. For a growing number of people, particularly in the Western world, increased wealth implies the economic means to consider aspects other than the relationship between material quality and price in their marketplace transactions. Thus, their involvement with products concerns more than price and quality. These people politicize products by asking questions about their origins and impacts. This politicization of products represents the fourth important shift. It is a shift in understanding of the origin of problems and the responsibility of individual consumers and citizens in problem-solving efforts.

In its most basic expressions, political consumerism is citizen desire to influence business. Through consumer choice, citizens express their opinions about and attempt to exercise influence over the politics of products. In certain circumstances, political consumerism can raise the consciousness of consumers and force producers to change their production methods. The phenomenon of political consumerism encourages us to think about business influences on world trade, global politics, business ethics, and its consequences for government and citizen involvement in public affairs.

This chapter discusses these issues by focusing on the forms and institutions of contemporary political consumerism. I discuss their scope, variety, and common characteristics. The first section compares political consumerism with other methods of exercising influence over the marketplace and regulating industry. The chapter then continues with a series of sections on different categories of political consumerism: boycotts; labeling schemes; stewardship certification; and socially responsible investment. Toward the end of the chapter, I offer more general reflections on the phenomenon of political consumerism. I compare older forms with new forms and consider whether political consumerism can be understood as a new global framework or a great transformation for the relationship between politics and economics.

REGULATING INDUSTRY AND THE ROLE OF POLITICAL CONSUMERISM

There are three broad and general ways to classify the regulation of industry: whether it is (1) production- or consumption-oriented; (2) compulsory or voluntary; and (3) older or newer in form. Production-oriented regulatory tools focus directly on changing production methods. This regulation may come in the form of legislation or is incorporated in collective bargaining rounds between employers and labor. Citizens and consumers play an indirect role. As citizens we can vote for a political party or candidate that promises to regulate business in a way we find satisfactory or takes action for better consumer protection. Consumption-oriented tools focus on changing production methods through consumer choice. These tools give people information on production methods and alternative products for them to make informed consumer choices, which may even include refraining from purchasing a particular good or category of good. Consumers and citizens are more directly involved in the use of this kind of tool. The driving force behind consumption-oriented tools is the role that consumer choice can play in affecting business' monetary profit and goodwill in society and the marketplace. Ideally consumers voice their views on companies by choosing a particular product over another one. They act in this fashion to encourage industry to change its production methods before its profits are cut and public image is damaged. At times, as shown in chapter 2, businesses may have difficulty in understanding the message sent by consumers. Perhaps as in the Disney case, it finds the messages confusing, contradictory, and therefore easy to sidestep. On other occasions, a media scandal is necessary for private corporations to get the point and act on the issue.

Compulsory ways to regulate industry, the second general category, legally sanction violators. The so-called government "*command and control*" policies and litigation are examples of a compulsory regulatory tool. Company violation of legislative enactments may lead to legal sanctions in the form of fines, prohibition on continued production, or imprisonment. Litigation on a company's policies and practices may be brought to court by employees, their representatives, consumers, other companies, interest groups and social movements, as well as the general public. When effective, the sued companies must compensate the injured parties economically and possibly discontinue their production practices. In contrast, schemes that are voluntary encourage compliance through membership in them or involvement in certification or labeling programs. These schemes frequently encourage industry to apply standards that are not required by law. They are so-called "*beyond-compliance*" schemes. The final category is the age or maturity of the regulatory tool. Older forms of regulation are those that have been in regular use and institutionalized for decades. Newer forms have a more recent origin, which generally implies a rather immature institutional structure and more need to create legitimacy publicly.

An old production-oriented regulatory form is politics. Legislation is passed that creates *public policy*, which regulates how products are manufactured and produced. This legislation may pertain to working conditions, wages, ingredients used in products, environmental pollution, and other matters involving the production of goods. It is often national in focus and thus only applies to goods produced domestically. Governments allocate funds to public agencies to monitor how well industry follows the legislated rules and regulations. Compliance is compulsory. As discussed in chapter 1, public policy is not always well-suited to the problems that it is mandated to solve. Public policy may be the product of a political compromise, public agencies may be ill-equipped to monitor industry effectively, or may be only a partial response to a problem that is transboundary in character. Many political consumerist, standardization, and management system institutions discussed later have been established as a reaction to government failure to solve problems caused by more international industrial trade and manufacturing practices. Their founders believe that government acts too slowly, and its policy goals are too lenient. They may even consider government to be the wrong institution to solve certain problems caused by industry. Transboundary problems are difficult for separate national public bodies to target successfully. Problem-solving may also require that citizens alter their opinions and behavior, and it may prove difficult for government to provide the necessary framework for this to occur.[4]

Another old and production-oriented tool for regulating industry is *standardization*. Standards are "documented agreements containing technical specifications or other precise criteria to be used consistently as rules, guidelines, or definitions of characteristics, to ensure that materials, products, processes and services are fit for their purpose."[5] They differ from public policy measures because they are voluntary in nature and are often run by standardization organizations. These nongovernmental organizations are the children of industrial society. In their infancy they set quality standards for industrial products. The first standardization organization, the International Electrotechnical Commission, was created in 1906. National standardization organizations were established shortly thereafter. Their establishment created a need to harmonize national standardization criteria and apply them globally and industry-wide. The International Organization of Standardization (ISO) was created in 1947 for this purpose. It is a nongovernmental organization. Membership is voluntary. Members are national standardization organizations. Free trade, globalization, as well as lack of national and supra-governmental action to regulate industry have increased the importance of international standards. Export-oriented industries have pushed for international standards to break down national technical barriers to trade. Contemporary standardization organizations have a much more ambitious agenda than in the past. International standards are set up to enhance product quality and reliability, to improve health, safety and environmental protection, to increase compatibility and interoperability of goods and services, and to facilitate distribution efficiency and ease of maintenance. Examples of internationally standardized products are telephone and banking cards, measurements, paper sizes, and symbols for automobile controls. The ISO has even developed environmental labeling and marketing guidelines that are quite similar to the eco-labels discussed later. What is interesting about these new standardization guidelines is that they are more consumption- than production-oriented. They have developed more as a response to green political consumerism than industry's need for standardization for trade purposes.[6]

Management systems are a rather new way to regulate industry. They offer internal management standards that respond to industry's need for risk management. Risks can vary greatly in kind. Management systems are similar to standardization and political consumerism because they are voluntary. Many of them follow the standards set up by the ISO. Consultants sell these systems to companies and help in their implementation. These management systems are production-oriented in the sense that they are implemented inside businesses, but they differ from traditional standardization because they do not standardize material goods. Rather they standardize work conduct and conditions. Unlike some of the other regulatory tools discussed in this section, they do not set substantive goals or specify final outcomes. Instead they are process-oriented. As such, they represent a move toward self-reflexivity within industry. The basic idea is to change production methods by changing industry's mentality or its shared beliefs, assumptions, and values of the managers.[7] Management systems can be seen as a form of corporate social responsibility and corporate citizenship.

Three kinds of management systems are in operation now. The most well-known and widely used are those that concern environmental management systems (EMS). Two dominant schemes are ISO 14001 created by the ISO and the EU's Environmental Management and Audit Scheme (EMAS). The standards are not completely similar but the EU allows its member states to adopt either one.[8] The ISO system is considered by environmentalists to be less stringent and it poses a potential threat to more rigid national environmental standards and EMAS.[9] The second kind of management system is for global working conditions. Social Accountability International, founded in 1997 as the American Council on Economic Priorities Accreditation Agency (CEPAA), developed a social accountability management system modeled after the ISO quality control auditing system and based on the principles of international human rights norms as delineated in International Labor Organization (ILO) Conventions, the UN Convention on the Rights of the Child, and the Universal Declaration of Human Rights. It has nine core areas: child labor; forced labor; health and safety; compensation; working hours; discrimination; discipline; free association and collective bargaining; and management systems. The process includes certification of compliance and accreditation, which makes it similar to labeling schemes. Companies that are certified can display the SA 8000 certification mark and use it as a selling point for consumers and shareholders. Principles of transparency and external auditing are applied.[10] The aim of the final and newest, gender management systems, is to promote mainstream gender equality at the workplace. It is similar to the SA 8000 and also uses the ISO as a model. EQ 2000 targets the way that company managers plan, implement, revise, and evaluate their work with gender equality issues.[11] At present it does not certify companies.

An older form of corporate regulation is *codes of conduct*. Codes of conduct are voluntary agreements that state formally the values and practices that should govern in the marketplace. They may be short mission statements on the part of a corporation or a sophisticated document requiring compliance with criteria or benchmarks with the power of enforcement. Codes of conduct can be production-oriented when companies draw them up and apply them internally. They can also be consumption-oriented if they are drawn up and enforced by nongovernmental organizations. Codes of conduct received renewed attention in the 1970s in connection with the controversy that arose over the role of multinational enterprises and the negative social and environmental implications of large-scale foreign investment. International organizations developed voluntary codes of conduct to deal with these issues. For instance, the United Nations developed the International Code of Marketing of Breastmilk Substitutes and the International Code of Conduct on the Distribution and Use of Pesticides. Consumer and nongovernmental organization pressure, as discussed earlier in the Nestlé boycott, has not led corporations to fully abide by the standards included in these documents.

Codes of conduct are once again a primary focus. The concern today is economic globalization and the relocation of production to developing countries with lower social and economic standards. Numerous codes of conduct that are global in orientation have been drawn up by international governmental and nongovernmental organizations, trade unions, corporations, governments, universities, and business associations.[12] Different reasons explain the growing interest in codes of conduct. Some codes have come about because industry decided that self-regulation was better than anticipated government regulation or as a way of appeasing consumer mobilization for independent codes of conduct. Others have been created because of citizen-consumer pressure or competition from other companies. Still others can find their origin in a company's desire to improve its public image and goodwill. At times the impetus for code creation is a combination of all reasons.

Voluntary codes are seen as having interesting potential given the problems presently experienced with furthering political globalization. They can be formulated to apply across national boundaries and government jurisdictions and, thus, avoid some of the problems involved with the restrictions that states usually apply to regional and international trade agreements.[13] Codes of conduct are often seen as an important complement to government regulation. However, their use is difficult to monitor, and there are problems with how transparent, fair, and open the code is when implemented.[14] In particular, environmental and humanitarian groups have been very active in what may be called the code of conduct movement in the 1990s. Research on codes of conduct that regulate child labor shows that the ones which have been developed by nongovernmental organizations tend to be more specific and those developed by business associations the least specific.[15]

Political consumerism is the final general way to regulate industry. It is similar to standardization and management systems in that it is voluntary. A difference is political consumerism's involvement of many more people than most of the other mechanisms. Also, the role of citizens and consumers is more pronounced. Political consumerism is not a new tool, though it is used more frequently now and in ways that are different from the past. There are several different kinds of political consumerism. *Negative political consumerism* is represented by people refusing to buy specific products and brand names. Boycott is the common name we use for this purchasing behavior, and as discussed in chapter 2 they can be rather difficult tools to wield effectively. *Positive political consumerism* is also called buycotts and involves conscious attempts to encourage consumers to purchase specific brand names. Consumers learn about boycotts and buycotts through information provided by civil society associations, cyber networks, media actors, informal contacts, policy institutes, and various government bodies. Information may be published in report and book form (e.g., the book *Shopping for a Better World* published by the Council on Economic Priorities or the Swedish book entitled in translation *Buy and Act Environmentally* discussed in chapter 4), or can be downloaded via the Internet. It can also come in the form of organized campaigns outside local places of business (e.g., supermarkets) and through media reports. Other important sources of information are labeling schemes, certification, and special institutions with websites catering to consumer interests. All illustrate the more institutional nature of the phenomenon of political consumerism. Political consumerism is *successful* if citizen-consumers participate in it and is *effective* as a regulatory tool when it leads to changes, which can, as discussed in chapter 5 and in the appendix, be defined in at least five ways and concern words, deeds, and outcomes.[16]

The main difference among the regulatory devices reviewed in this section involves the role of consumers and citizens or "citizens-consumer," to use an interesting term introduced earlier to understand how our roles as citizens and consumers are becoming more intertwined. Otherwise, they have quite a lot in common. Many regulatory schemes model themselves after other regulatory arrangements. An important model for imitation is environmental labeling schemes, which are used as a prototype for constructing social accountability and gender management systems. Some regulatory schemes even overlap as is the case of eco-labels, organic labels, and fair trade labels. Labeling schemes can be embedded in standardization organizations, and management systems can easily develop into labeling schemes.

Regulatory schemes covering the same area often compete with each other. Competition is beneficial when it encourages the different institutions to monitor each other and develop their criteria and mission further. Pluralism can also give business and consumers the opportunity to choose among alternative systems. A negative aspect of competition occurs when powerful actors decide to use a particular system to force other ones to close down or to establish their own system with less transparency and more modest goals, as discussed in the section on forest stewardship certification. High information costs for individual consumers are a consequence of the existence of several alternative systems. The presence of a variety of schemes monitoring the same products may also confuse consumers who have difficulty understanding the differences among them. It will be interesting to follow the development of political consumerist labeling schemes in the near future to see how they deal with these problems. One trend discussed later in this chapter is the creation of umbrella organizations that assist in coordinating the several schemes through a joint mission statement and harmonization of goals under the rubric of sustainable development.

Information is crucial for all regulating tools. The sources of information must be viewed as reliable and trustworthy regardless of whether the information comes from politicians, civil servants, nongovernmental organizations, citizen networks, business, or consultants. Otherwise the regulatory arrangements will lack the necessary legitimacy for cooperation among industry, government, civil society, and consumers.[17] Thus, essential characteristics of all regulatory tools are cooperation and trust among regulatory actors, transparency, and accountability. Business must open up its company doors for external review and reveal the ingredients that go into its products. The auditing institutions—public agencies, standardization organizations, management systems, and labeling schemes—must assure business, government, and the consuming public that the standards and criteria they use for evaluation are reasonable and honest. This requires a good measure of openness on their part as well. They must convince all involved actors that their criteria are objective, that is, that they are not biased in favor of a particular company and are not based on vested interests. The same requirement applies for boycott organizers. A boycott called on the basis of incorrect assertions, as arguably was the case in Greenpeace's Brent Spar boycott in 1995,[18] can seriously damage the reputation of its organizers. The issue of accountability is also important here.

CONSUMER BOYCOTTS TODAY

Probably the oldest kind of political consumerist activity is boycotts. Generally their success depends on extensive grassroots support and/or media attention given to the boycott threat and cause.[19] At times boycott campaigners try to influence the purchasing behavior of institutional consumers. Government procurement offices and the purchasing practices of large nongovernmental and private organizations are attractive targets for what we may here call boycott lobbying.[20] An example of boycott lobbying is presented in chapter 4. All available evidence shows dramatic changes in the use of boycotts and a marked increase in their number.[21] Scholars also state that boycotts are changing in character. When compared to the past, they now focus on different kinds of issues and involve new strategies and tactics. In particular, media-oriented boycotts are becoming more prevalent. Boycotting has also become institutionalized and more globalized. Newer issues revolve around sustainable development and a growing number of people who boycott do so for other-oriented reasons.

As illustrated in figure 3.1 today boycotts are called to protest industry's involvement in human rights violations, discrimination of minority groups, homosexuals, women, and indigenous peoples, environmental destruction, animal rights, and unfair trading practices with developing countries. In some of the examples in figure 3.1, individual citizens participating in boycott actions are affected by the injustices they seek to set right through adjustments in their purchasing behavior but in a different way than in the past. They are affected by what they consider to be the risks taken by the companies for sustainable development. In other examples, consumers are not affected directly by the injustices they are boycotting against. Rather, they are protesting for other people, as in the case of the Nike or woodchipping boycott. This is a change from the past and shows the dominant role of the public virtue tradition of political consumerism. Scholars call this kind of consumer civil action "lent consumer power," that is, "usually international, collective action involving, through consumption, both poorer producers and workers, and those wealthier communities which have influence over production and trade by virtue of their vast purchasing power."[22]

Although many of the boycott actions included in figure 3.1 call on consumers and citizens to play an active role, an important difference with the past is that boycotts can be effective even if they do not induce economic problems for the company, that is, lead to lower profits because fewer people buy their products. Boycotts can reach their goals through the media attention focused on them and on the companies they target for action. Harm to corporate reputation, the corporate logotype, expensive corporate advertising, as well as corporate goodwill can be just as threatening. The reason for this is the more vulnerable public position of companies in the transparent media and globalized society of today.[23] Finally, the examples in figure 3.1 show that boycotting is frequently embedded in civil society associations or nonmembership campaign networks for specific boycott actions. Many civil society and nonprofit organizations in the United States and Europe advertise boycotts and offer links to other boycotts on their websites, as illustrated by the American union AFL-CIO's national boycott list, the network Consumers Against Food Engineering, and CorpWatch.[24] Special publications and boycott websites also illustrate how boycotting is becoming more institutionalized. Examples include a website dedicated entirely to boycotts, www.boycott.org, the American publication *The National*

Boycott name	Boycott target	Boycott caller/duration	Stated reason for boycott
Boycott South Carolina	South Carolina's tourist industry	National Association for the Advancement of Colored People (1999–)	Flying of Confederate Flag on state property, which is seen as a racist expression
Say No To Monopolies	Microsoft products	Moral High Grounds (1996–)	Microsoft's anticompetitive practices
Boycott French Products	France via French products (wine, cheese)	International Peace Bureau, supported by many nongovernmental organizations (1995)	France's decision to resume nuclear weapons' testing
Change Your Brands! Blood on Your Hands! P&G Kills	Procter & Gamble products	Uncaged, In Defense of Animals (1996)	Procter & Gamble's animal testing policies are considered cruel and lethal
Just Do It!	Nike products	Variety of networks, social movements, interest organizations (1997–) with specific and diffuse boycott calls	Labor abuses in Nike factories
Divest Now from Israel	University-owned stocks in companies with significant operations in Israel	University networks of students, staff, faculty, alumni from Harvard, MIT, Princeton, University of California (2000s)	Human rights abuses against Palestinians by Israeli government, continued military occupation and colonization of Palestinian territory by Israeli armed forces and settlers

Figure 3.1 Examples of contemporary boycott action and network.
Sources: Information directly from the campaigns and campaign organizers. See bibliography.

Campaign	Target	Organization	Demand
Boycott Woodchipping	Boycott wood products by Amcor, North, Boral and Bunning, and other Australian woodchip exporters	Environmental groups in Australia started Boycott Woodchipping Campaign (1996)	Logging last remaining Australian native forest is an environmental and social disaster
Stop Bottle Baby Deaths—Boycott Nestlé	All Nestlé products	International Baby Food Action Network (1988-)	Nestlé is violating the International Code of Marketing of Breastmilk Substitutes
Starbucks/Frankenbucks$ Global Days of Action	All Starbucks products	U.S. Organic Consumers Association (Feb 23-March 2, 2002)	Starbuck's allowance of recombinant Bovine Growth Hormone and other GMO ingredients in its products
Global Days of Action	Monsanto Roundup Ready Soybeans, Ciba-Geigy Maximizer BT Corn	Foundation on Economic Trends, Pure Food Campaign, Council of Canadians, Friends of the Earth, Pesticide Action Network, Forum sur la Globalisation, Women's Environmental Network, and others (April 21–26, 1997)	Monsanto and Ciba-Geigy engage in forced commercialization of unlabeled, untested gene-altered food products
World Bank Bonds Boycott	World Bank Bonds	Center for Economic Justice (2000–)	Debt cancellation, end structural adjustment programs, other environmentally and socially destructive World Bank policies

Boycott name	Boycott target	Boycott caller/duration	Stated reason for boycott
Give Swordfish A Break	Swordfish	Seaweb, National Resources Defense Council (1998-)	Swordfish is targeted because it is a popular fish emblematic of the problems facing marine fish. An adequate recovery measure for it will be a model to replicate for other depleted fish
Don't Buy E$$O	Esso/ExxonMobil Corporation	Greenpeace, Friends of the Earth, People & Planet	Esso/Exxon deny reality of global warming, do not invest in alternatives to fossil fuels, sabotaging global environmental action

Figure 3.1—cont'd.

Boycott Newsletter, and the electronic newsletter *Boycott Action News* (BAN) at the website of Co-op America, a nonprofit association founded in 1982, which among other things offers a chart of current boycotts as well as updates on the progress and success of others.[25] The embeddedness of boycotts in these institutions may be an expression of their increased legitimacy as a means of changing politics and the market. They are an example of more individualized collective action used by established political homes discussed in chapter 1.

What is boycotted? Boycotts are either commodity- or institution-oriented. They can target products and services that consumers use on a daily basis, as illustrated by swordfish in figure 3.1. Other examples taken up in this book are batteries, entertainment, and paper. Institution-oriented boycotts involve campaigns against specific companies and governments with objectionable practices or policies.[26] Well-known boycotts of companies illustrated in the figure involve Nestlé, Microsoft, Esso/Exxon, Nike, and Starbuck. A repeated target for boycotts for a variety of reasons is Shell Oil.[27]

A boycott that deserves more scholarly attention is the 1995 grassroots global boycott targeting sensitive French economies, particularly wine and cheese. It is an interesting boycott for two reasons. First, although France's nuclear testing in the South Pacific Ocean was criticized and condemned by several national governments, many European political parties and the United Nations did not officially endorse the boycott. Second, the boycott is an example of how private companies can be used as a liaison to government. The boycott targeted farmers with the hope that this highly organized, vocal, and politically influential group in France would pressure their government to end its nuclear weapons tests. All French goods were part of the boycott, but the decision to focus particularly on wine and cheese was a strategic one. A number of European politicians sanctioned it unofficially by participating in it and demonstrating publicly against France. The International Peace Bureau mobilized its 158 member organizations in 46 countries in its call for the boycott, which was supported by a long list of social movements.[28]

Other countries or government units have also been the subjects of boycotts. In some instances, boycotts are part of an international economic sanction package that has been ratified by supra-national political bodies and individual states. In other instances, organizers have called tourist boycotts of particular countries and American states. Turkey was boycotted in the 1970s for its insufficient human rights policy. American states, which did not ratify the Equal Rights Amendment, have been boycotted by women's and professional organizations. Today Israel is the target of many boycotts; the one illustrated in figure 3.1 concerns boycotting shares in companies with investment in Israel and is an example of what can be called negative socially responsible investing. Boycotts of countries and particular American states target all institutions and actors within the geographic area no matter what position they take on the boycott issues. In this sense, they are insensitive to the plight of third parties that are affected by boycott action.[29]

Why boycott? Figure 3.1 shows that concerns about sustainability are behind most contemporary consumer boycotts. People boycott goods to express their political convictions. Boycotting is, therefore, part of ethical purchasing behavior. Fairness and justice are its foremost values. Examples in this category are boycotts for human, women's, children's, ethnic, racial, workers', and gay rights. When boycotts are a part of ethical purchasing behavior, they are often the first step in endeavors to institutionalize political consumerist action. As such, they are trial balloons or pilot projects to test the market for other political consumerist actions. The origin of many labeling schemes is in boycott actions.

Do they work as a form of political protest? Boycotts, as with all forms of political participation, do not always reach their goals. They may, as discussed in chapter 2, also have different and even conflicting goals. Three distinct goals that need to be coordinated in successful and effective boycott actions are (1) publicity for the boycott cause; (2) naming, shaming, and punishing the producer; and (3) producer compliance with the boycott demands. The examples in figure 3.1 involve all three goals, but it should not be concluded that they are successful and effective boycotts. Such an assertion requires empirical study. Other boycotts may be called primarily to gain the attention of the media, raise the consciousness of citizens and consumers about the politics of products, or put the issue on the political agenda. Still others may seek to satisfy consumer displeasure with a company and its products and an urgent need to react in some way.

It is common to make a distinction between successful and effective boycotts. When boycotts mobilize large numbers of consumers to participate, they are successful. A boycott is effective when it reaches its goals. A well-organized boycott may be effective even if large numbers of consumers do not participate in it. Good boycott organization, strategy, and careful choice of the good to be targeted are the keys to effectiveness. In these cases companies may decide that it is better to acquiesce to boycott demands than allow a boycott action to catch the eye of the media, change consumer purchasing behavior, and harm the company's public image. Most boycotts are not fully successful or effective. Many are complete failures because they are ill-conceived and are more similar to spontaneous, short-lived, grassroots urgent expressions of protest than serious commitment to a political cause. There is a political, social, psychological, and an economic side to all phrases of boycott actions—from their preparation, organization, targeting, launching, and calling off or folding.[30] Institutions supporting boycotts like Co-op America offer guidelines on how they should be organized. Part of a successful and effective boycott strategy is the availability of suitable alternative products to replace the boycotted commodity and company brands. Boycott organizers must convince their supporters and potential supporters that this is the case. Otherwise, a boycott may mean personal sacrifice on the part of the consumer, which as discussed in chapter 1 in the section on the public virtue tradition of political consumerism, may be asking too much of individual citizens. Organizers must also convince their supporters that boycotting can make a difference. Websites offer information on the expected impact of boycotts and give examples of successful and effective ones. Boycotts vary also in duration, as shown in figure 3.1, and it may be difficult to determine who calls them and when they are called off.

SEALS OF APPROVAL LABELING SCHEMES

Product labeling politicizes products by calling on producers and consumers to look behind product brands. Many governments require industry to label the contents of its products and in certain cases list their land of origin. The demand is transparency from producers so that consumers receive information to decide among alternative products. This is not a new phenomenon, but it seems that product labels are increasingly important today given long commodity chains due to globalized free trade and the health risks associated with agricultural products. Use of labeling at times leads to heated political debate because they concern power relations and control over industry. The controversy surrounding genetically modified organisms (GMO) in food is a current example.[31] The labeling schemes discussed in this section differ from government-decreed labels in that they introduce voluntary and new criteria to help consumers to judge industrial production. They are "beyond compliance" regulation, and most are fairly recent in origin. Their market-based character means that the actors necessary to put them in operation differ from those present in "command and control" public policy regulatory control.[32] Contemporary labeling schemes cover five general and related areas: ecology; fair trade; organic foods; forestry; and marine life. They are run by government, quasi-governmental bodies, national civil society associations, and global nongovernmental organizations.

Voluntary labeling schemes differ in how they politicize products. *Type III* is the simplest one and only includes information on product content on packages. *Type II* is developed by manufacturers themselves. These self-certification or self-declaration schemes allow companies to highlight certain values in their products for marketing purposes. They promote commercial transaction. There are self-certification schemes for environmental products, healthy foods, and forest and marine stewardship. At times industry decides to establish a self-certification scheme to avoid pressure to voluntarily comply with type I schemes, as in the case of forest certification discussed in a later section. Both types II and III schemes offer citizens some information for product choice, but they lack the kind of transparency, quality control, and accountability that is involved in type I schemes, which require independent third party monitoring of products on the basis of agreed-upon criteria.[33]

Type I are the most advanced labeling schemes in existence today. They reflect newer trends in how risks should be managed in society. Their way of managing risks is through transparent market-based instruments that stimulate the supply and demand of alternative and less hazardous products. They are an example of reflexive monitoring of society, which means that both producers and consumers have responsibility for creating sustainable lifestyles. Their purpose is to provide consumers with shopping guidance. This is a new and different approach to policy and represents trends toward governance, ecological modernization, as well as active, responsible citizenship.

The labeling schemes discussed here have a number of characteristics in common. Stakeholder is a key characteristic of all type I labeling schemes. Its use underscores the responsibility of industry, civil society, and consumers to work together in the development of sustainable consumption. The implication is that citizens can no longer point their finger at industry as the perpetrator of badness and request the government to take the proper disciplinary measures. Consumers must also understand that their consumption patterns leave footprints and are part of the problem. An important characteristic of successful schemes is consumer and public awareness of the role that consumption plays in problems of sustainability. Therefore, the schemes exert considerable effort in informing consumers and producers about the negative impact of certain kinds of production and consumption and about the advantages of labeled goods for sustainable development. A feature increasingly common on labeling schemes' websites is discussion of the importance of good consumer choice and its impact on the politics behind products. Testimonials from producers in the South and information on market shares are used to discuss the effectiveness of political consumerism as a tool of change. Market research shows that people who do not believe that their choices are effective are less likely to choose political consumerist products.[34]

Another characteristic is the role of government or nongovernmental organizations in sponsoring, initiating, or establishing labeling schemes. Some schemes are run by government; others by civil society associations or institutions created by them. They are, therefore, embedded in established institutions that may sponsor them financially or through moral support. The schemes also have the goal to become self-financing through money collected from companies seeking certification. Therefore, they must be attractive to business. Companies seeking certification do so because of strong incentives. Consumers, employees, and institutional actors may pressure companies to certify themselves. Such information may be communicated in boycotts or in opinion polls. Businesses may also seek certification because of characteristics of the market. Influential incentives are certification of competitors and involvement in export-sensitive markets. Two other reasons for certification are the profit motive (money can be made from selling certified goods) and the image motive (certification will payoff in goodwill).[35]

Certification costs money. Companies pay both for product evaluation and for use of the labeling scheme's logotype on approved products. It is also time bound, and companies must periodically seek recertification. Once certified, the labeling schemes indirectly market the company's products in their publications and on their home pages. Their shopping guides frequently contain lists of certified products and the names of the companies that manufacture them.

Supply and demand concerns are important to the labeling schemes discussed here, legitimacy being the key word.[36] Not only must businesses assess them as fair and trustworthy. Consumers must consider them as providing attractive and trustworthy shopping guidelines. All the schemes are dependent on good consumer contact and want to increase the consumer demand of their certified products. Like other market actors, they commission market researchers to investigate consumer recognition of their labels.[37] Many schemes also publish newsletters or magazines, and all have well-developed websites. Labeling institutions market their services in different ways. They take great efforts to make information transparent regarding which actors are involved in the formulation, the adopted evaluative criteria, and how the evaluations are done in practice. This is their way of assuring consumers and businesses that their evaluations can be trusted and are characterized by transparency and accountability. They also take great care in displaying their logotypes in information materials and in carefully monitoring attempts to misuse and falsify them.

The term *eco-labeling* describes product labels that provide consumers with information about the environmental quality of products. Environmental quality concerns the use of poisons, pollutants, and chemicals in products. The most developed eco-labels are type I external life-cycle evaluations of products. Eco-labeling institutions that establish independent life cycle criteria assess the environmental impact of the production, use, and disposal of goods. These eco-labeling schemes include a selected area of products that are in high consumer demand such as household chemicals, paper, and paints. Some of the schemes as the EU-Flower have a broad array of products while others, the Swedish Good Environmental Choice discussed in chapter 4, have concentrated on a more limited area of products.

About 30 type I eco-labels are in operation on four continents today. Examples of countries with type I eco-labels are the United States (Green Seal), Canada (TerraChoice), Germany (Blue Angel), Japan (Ecomark), United Kingdom (which uses the EU-flower scheme), Australia (Environmental Choice), and Sweden (see chapter 4).[38] Two regional schemes exist: the EU-Flower and the Nordic Swan. There is also a nonprofit association, Global Ecolabelling Network (GEN), established in 1994, to coordinate, improve, and promote national eco-labeling globally.[39] In 1978, the first type I eco-label, Blue Angel (Blau Angel), was established in Germany. It is government-run by Germany's Federal Environmental Agency, important domestically, and a model for other countries.[40] The symbol of the German eco-label is made up of the United Nations environmental logo and for this reason was nicknamed the "Blue Angel" by the public. Evaluation of the scheme's effectiveness ranges from claiming that it is a success story about product policy and consumer behavior to a more modest view claiming that it has impacted business and government procurement practices and the setting of environmental standards for certain product groups.[41] The different opinions are interesting because they reflect general views about the significance of labeling schemes. One view considered eco-labels and all market-based regulation as a viable alternative to public policy; a second view more cautiously considers them to be a supplement or complement to control and command regulatory policy; and finally there is an oppositional view supported by major multinational consumer product manufactures based in the United States that considers them misleading, ineffective, and a hindrance to free trade.[42]

The Nordic Swan was started by the Nordic Council of Ministers in 1990 and is a public-supported eco-label. It was the world's first multinational, independent scheme, which is in use in Denmark, Finland, Island, Norway, and Sweden. The EU-Flower eco-label established in 1992 is not as well-known as the Nordic Swan label and has been less successful in receiving support, mainly because EU member states have been hesitant to agree on common criteria and to give the labeling scheme complete European status,[43] as such it is an example of the debate in Europe over whether the EU should remain a body of member-states or develop into a federation. Both regional schemes are quite expansive in their product categories. The Nordic Swan includes office furniture and equipment, washing machines, paper, household chemicals, detergents, shampoo, batteries, soap, paint, textiles, DVD players, and truck tires in its certifiable categories. It has even begun to label hotels. Since it began in 1992, the EU-Flower has grown to include washing machines, refrigerators, tissue paper, dishwashers, soil improvers, bed mattresses, footwear, textile products, laundry and dishwashing detergents, indoor paints and varnishes, light bulbs, and portable and personal computers.[44]

Sweden has two unique environmental labeling schemes, which are also members of Global Ecolabeling Network. Both were started by civil society associations. Good Environmental Choice is the eco-labeling scheme established by the Swedish Society for the Conservation of Nature. It is a special scheme because of its consumer citizen-input and is the focus of chapter 4. TCO Development is an eco-label and also a certification system for "excellent workplaces," that is, working environment products like computers and mobile phones. It started as a project within the umbrella union Swedish Confederation of Professional Employees (*Tjänstemännens Centralorganisation*, TCO), which became increasingly concerned about the health effects of the new computerized working environment for its white-collar members. Although embedded in a member-strong union movement of over 1 million, it lacks a grassroots profile. TCO Development is highly respected by producers and consumers and sets the global work environmental standards for computer equipment. Its vision is the " 'sustainable office' where all employees can contribute to a good work environment through participation and skills, is based on sustainable consumption and production patterns grounded in ecological, financial, and social values."[45] Today it is a stock market company with information centers in Chicago and Munich. Its website offers consumers easy on-line access to work environmental information on the computer equipment they are considering purchasing. Most people—and even many Swedes—do not know that the "TCO" in the label of approval is the acronym for a large central trade union organization.

A second kind of type I labeling scheme concerns fair trade. *Fair trade* or alternative trading organizations (ATO) recognize the important role consumers play in improving the situation for producers in developing countries. Fair trade labels encourage consumers to support workers in developing countries by buying labeled goods that ensure them a fair price for their labor and sustainable living. This is the lent consumer power referred to earlier. It focuses on trade with marginalized producers and promotes trade relations with farmers' cooperatives and farmer-owned companies. As such it is considered to represent "a reasonable blend of market-based economy, and social justice and environmental interests."[46] Goods consumed on an everyday basis are the subjects for fair trade: cocoa, coffee, tea, honey, bananas, and textiles are the most well-known. Its supporters consider fair trade a crucial global issue. While the consumer prices of these goods have not risen in real terms, their production costs have increased substantially. There are also problems with price stability. The problem that fair trade focuses on is the wages and working conditions of the people who grow these crops. Fair trade is the only systematic attempt to develop an alternative international trade market in existence today. As such, it implies criticism of the World Trade Organization for its inability or unwillingness to create a viable framework for social and environmental regulation of international trade.[47]

Fair trade is a very interesting form of political consumerism. It has evolved and grown over the years as well as professionalized its activities. Now its network is immense. The movement is well-connected with policy institutes, foreign aid public agencies, nongovernmental organizations, and university institutes in industrialized nations and is embedded in a number of international-oriented humanitarian social movements. Fair trade can be seen as a movement in its own right. It is reliant on voluntary citizen and consumer activity, which is mobilized by campaign networks that reflect more individualized collective action as well as traditional membership organizations. Fair trade also gives old membership-based social movements like the Red Cross,

Oxfam, and trade unions a new mission, and it is recreating the traditional consumers' movement. Some scholars and activists even view fair trade as a better way to help developing countries to solve their economic and democratic problems than development aid provided by government. They call it a new paradigm representing a change in mentality because it rejects the view of poor people in the Third World as victims and emphasizes the role that consumption plays for their economic empowerment and well-being. Many scholars argue that the fair trade movement has a real capacity to influence mainstream business.[48]

The roots of the fair trade movement are from the 1950s and 1960s and the stores (now called world shops) that sold goods from developing countries. People initially bought goods from them even though the quality at times was inferior. They shopped to show solidarity with people in developing countries and, thereby, exercised the public virtue tradition of political consumerism. In the 1960s, different groups concentrated on making consumers aware of the relationship between the price they pay for products and the money paid to producers. Two decades later, fair trade represents an important alternative trading market.[49] It has become serious business thanks to the Dutch Max Havelaar Foundation.

The history of the Max Havelaar fair trade label is worth describing because it clearly shows the politics of products and a new way of regulating industry. The name comes from the title of a book, *Max Havelaar or the Coffee Auctions of the Dutch Trading Company*, written in the 1800s by a resident of the Dutch East Indies who criticized how Dutch coffee plantations treated their workers.[50] The Max Havelaar Label was created in the Netherlands in 1988 as a response to a plea from Mexican coffee farmers for help. It formulated a set of criteria for companies purchasing coffee. If they adopted the criteria they received an independent mark or seal of approval from the Foundation. The label gained in importance when coffee prices plummeted after the International Coffee Organization's coffee agreement was suspended and no attempt was made to fill the contractual vacuum.[51] Unlike earlier alternative trade organizations, its goal was to mainstream fair trade coffee by inviting the traditional coffee industry into cooperative endeavors. This guaranteed the Max Havelaar label a place in neighborhood supermarkets, which meant access to more consumers. Its efforts with coffee were repeated with other products. In 1993 the first labeled chocolate bar appeared. Five years later fair trade labeled tea was introduced. Criteria for other products have also been formulated, and more are on the way. The Dutch experience shows that fair trade labeling is a viable market concept, and this is encouraging citizen-consumers in other countries to establish their own associations.[52]

Today there are many different groups, networks, and institutions working for and with fair trade. Some of them are labeling schemes; others are involved with consumer awareness and mobilization. The EU has become interested in fair trade and conducts opinion polls on it.[53] Fair trade has received the support of the European Parliament.[54] The global Fairtrade Labelling Organizations International (FLO-I) was founded in 1997 to coordinate the various national associations. Its members, not all of which are labeling schemes, represent 17 countries; among them are the United States, France, Germany, United Kingdom, Canada, and Japan.[55] The FLO Certification Programme is involved with inspection of producers, trade auditing, and certification. It follows the ISO Standards for Certification Bodies (ISO 65). FLO's national branches certify products as well as run campaigns and inform consumers about fair trade products and where they can buy them. Several labeling schemes are in operation today. One of FLO's goals is the establishment of a single international fair trade label. This effort has received funding from the EU. A single global label is seen as important to provide consumers with clear information on what is and what is not fair trade labeled goods and to facilitate cross-border trade. Not all national labeling schemes agree that a single global label is necessary,[56] a criticism reminiscent of the views about the introduction of the EU-Flower.

There are other global fair trade actors. International Federation for Alternative Trade (IFAT) was founded in 1989 and has as its members alternative trading organizations and producer organizations in Africa, Asia, Europe, Latin and North America, and the Pacific. It is a global network designed to coordinate the different aspects of fair trade like information, business support, networking opportunities, market access, lobbying, and education. Over 50 countries are represented in this 160 member strong network.[57] NEWS (Network of European World Shops) was established in 1994 to coordinate the 2,500 world shops present in 13 member countries (Austria, Belgium, Denmark, Finland, France, Germany, Ireland, Italy, Netherlands, Spain, Sweden, Switzerland, and United Kingdom). World Shops give fair trade goods market access. As with many fair trade groups, NEWS conducts campaigns to raise consumer awareness about the relationship between their consumer choices and the situation of producers and workers in developing countries. The goal is to increase the market share of fair trade goods.[58]

Coffee is a recent example of a product used in campaigns to increase both awareness of fair trade and its market share. Some campaigns target institutional consumers' procurement policies, for example supermarkets, trade unions, public agencies, and social movements.[59] Others mobilize the support of individual consumers, for instance to join an e-petition movement.[60] The campaign has engaged fair trade supranational groups globally, their national branches, other organizations like Oxfam, the Migratory Bird Center, Rainforest Alliance, trade unions, the Red Cross youth movement, and even a young lawyer in Berkeley, California (Rick Young) who became a global celebrity for his initiative on the November 2002 ballot to allow only socially and/or environmentally conscious cultivated coffee to be served publicly in the city.[61] A special coffee campaign network, Responsible Coffee Campaign, targets American university campuses and offers information to the general public on the global coffee crisis.[62] Celebrities like Bianca Jagger are involved in the general coffee campaign. Television and movie star, Martin Sheen, has appeared on a public service announcement on the U.S. Transfair's website to encourage people to drink fair trade coffee.[63]

These examples show that fair trade is an issue that engages many different organizations not all of which are labeling schemes. It is becoming the core of several consumer-oriented groups like Ethical Consumer, Consumer's Choice Council, the non-sweatshop movement, and Clean Clothes Campaign (CCC). Ethical Consumer is the website of the Ethical Consumer Research Association, a not-for-profit organization founded in 1987. It characterizes itself as "the UK's only alternative consumer organization looking at the social and environmental records of the companies behind the brand names."[64] Its concerns are human, environmental, and animal rights. It publishes a magazine that contains practical guides for consumers, a database called Corporate Critic for checking the ethical and environmental performance of companies, and calls on consumers to participate in boycotts and use labeling schemes. The organization encourages consumers to buy ethically because it believes that individuals can play a role in the practical solutions to big problems and that individual action is necessary to counter the power of corporations.[65] The Consumer's Choice Council, founded in 1997 and based in Washington D.C., has the same basic goals. Through its network organization for 66 environmental, consumer, and human rights organizations from 25 countries, it promotes type I labels, reform of government procurement policy, and fair and sustainable trade.[66]

Both the CCC and non-sweatshop movement hold the same general belief about the important role that individual consumers can play in solving problems involving economic globalization and the division of resources between the North and South. However, their specific concern is the global garment industry. The CCC, a European network that represents over 200 nongovernmental organizations and trade unions in 12 European countries including France, Germany, Spain, and the Great Britain and India,[67] works closely with labor-related organizations, consumer organizations, researchers, solidarity groups, women's organizations, church groups, youth movements, and world shops in many regions of the world. It runs focused consumer campaigns on the "labour behind the label" whose goal is mobilizing the purchasing power of particularly young consumers. It is against boycotting. Its counterpart in North America is the anti-sweatshop movement, which includes a number of campaigns and movements like Sweatshop Watch, Behind the Label, Union of Needletrades Industrial and Textile Employees (UNITE), and United Students Against Sweatshops (USAS) with varying opinions on the benefits of boycotts.[68]

Organic food labels are a third kind of type I positive political consumerist endeavor. Organic food labels ensure that food is produced by farmers who use renewable resources and who conserve soil and water and also ensure that food is free of antibiotics, growth hormones, and commercial pesticides. Credible labeling schemes, reasonable prices for organic goods, and organic product availability are its central goals.[69] What makes this labeling scheme different from the eco-labels and fair trade labels is the role that producers and government had played in setting them up. Some organic labels, as branches of the international Ecocert, Australian Certified Organic, KRAV in Sweden, and Organic Trust in Ireland, have been started by producers (farmers, farmers associations, etc.). Others like USDA Organic and Danish Ø label have government as their initiators.[70] Initially consumers were only indirectly involved in their institutional design. Today most organic labeling institutions appeal in a variety of ways for consumer support, for instance through a consumer page on their websites. Unlike some eco- and fair trade labeling schemes, organic food labels cannot be characterized as advocacy networks that directly mobilize consumers to take action against unfair products and services. Rather they are professional certification institutions.

Organic farming and organic labeled foods are becoming big business. They are one of the fastest growing segments in the consumer goods market in many countries.[71] About 50 schemes are in operation in the world today.[72] Most of them are in Europe. A very professional umbrella organization, International Federation of Organic Agricultural Movements (IFOAM) from 1972, now has over 740 member organizations in more than 100 countries. An unspecified number of them are labeling schemes; 171 members state that they are involved with certification, and others are associations and networks concerned about the environmental quality of food.[73]

In different ways consumers have become more interested in organic food because of their concern over pesticide use, genetically modified organisms/engineered foods, irradiated food, and the mad cow disease.[74] Organic food can be considered a loosely organized movement including individual consumers worrying over the food they feed their families, environmentalists, farmers, citizens critical of global corporate influence, and people who care about the developing world. As such it includes both the private and public virtue tradition of political consumerism. Consumer, environment, and international-oriented humanitarian and religious organizations are part of it. It engages consultant firms, politicians, civil servants, scholars, journalists, and policy institutes.[75] Some of these groups conduct campaigns to raise consumer awareness about the need for organic labeling. Friends of the Earth has campaigned for "Real Food," the World Wildlife Foundation encourages citizens to mobilize against genetically modified foods, the global Pesticide Action Network creates consumer awareness about chemicals used on foods, and Organic Consumers encourages consumers to "help drive genetically engineered foods off the market, phase out industrial agriculture and convert to organic farming practices."[76]

Stewardship Certification Schemes

The newest kind of market-based beyond compliance labeling system is for common pool resources. Common pool resources differ greatly from agricultural and manufactured goods. They are resources owned by no one or by everyone so it is difficult to exclude people from appropriating them. At the same time they are finite in character, which means that they are easily abused and overused.[77] Philosophers, social scientists, and public figures call the misuse of common pool resources the tragedy of the commons. Water, air, marine life, and forests are good examples of common pool resources. Certification schemes have been developed for forest and marine resources.

The term stewardship is central for two of the schemes presented here. Stewardship is actors' responsibility to manage their life properly with due regard to the rights of others. These rights include those of other human beings as well as other living species. Stewardship institutions offer individual and corporate actors guidelines to promote environmentally appropriate, socially beneficial, and economically viable management of the world's forests and marine life without too much self-sacrifice. Users themselves develop rules for participant behavior, monitoring, sanctioning, and conflict resolution. The rules are created through deliberation, and they demand that participants learn the rules and practice them in the settings that stewardship constructs for them. They change how users perceive the costs and benefits of common resource use.

Stewardship is an example of transboundary governance and ecological modernization that has used the lessons of successful collective action well. It can also be seen as a kind of constitutional engineering because it requires that participants act rationally and decide to bind themselves to decision rules. This means that participants consciously and willingly construct a structural mechanism—a certification scheme—which limits their freedom of choice and action. A number of conditions must be in place to create a deliberative decisionmaking setting that avoids free riding and the individualism characterized by prisoner dilemma situations while promoting collective compliance of agreed-upon rules. An implicit base of stewardship projects is rational cooperative behavior and the logic of collective action. Involved actors must believe that time is ripe to use common pool resources in a different way. They must, thus, have reliable and valid information on the present general conditions of the resource and accept the calculations of experts about its future conditions. They must also believe that it is possible to improve the conditions through collective action and understand how their individual use—their footprints—affects common pool resources and creates a common problem for us all. Their incentive to participate is their own self-interest, that is, their dependence on the resource for their livelihood. As with many collective-action settings, it is important that big users—those with considerable economic and political assets—have a common understanding about how the tragedy of the common users affects them personally. They must also believe that they are in the same boat. It is crucial that the group of big users has this understanding because they form the core group for collective decisionmaking on stewardship. Users must also believe that other users are trustworthy, that they can be relied upon to keep promises and relate to one another with reciprocity.[78]

Like all forms of political consumerism, certification schemes for common pool resources must have the support of various actors or stakeholders for them to develop successfully. The demand for better common pool resource management was, as in the case of tropical-wood use, initially raised in consumer boycotts, which gave market actors the incentive to find ways of managing consumer discontent over the use of common pool resources. In other cases, environmental and social groups, displeased with the action taken by national and supranational governments, have pressured for more responsible production processes. A third initiative for market-based common pool resource management is international and regional agreements, which have been a platform for supporters of stricter standards and beyond compliance schemes.[79] A second characteristic that stewardship certification has in common with other forms of political consumerism is the importance of good organizational structure. It is important for common pool resource management that the institutional design is socially engineered and organizationally constructed to promote rational cooperation. The reason for this is, of course, the problem of free riding. The institutional design must safeguard against and discourage free riders. Mission, transparency, legitimacy, management, and stakeholders are key values here.[80] This section discusses two institutions of common pool resource management and market actor reactions to them. They are the Forest Stewardship Council (FSC) and Marine Stewardship Council (MSC).

Concern about tropical deforestation made sustainable forestry management a global political issue. The concern was expressed by consumers in tropical-wood boycotts, timber retailers, and distributors who were boycott targets, and at several meetings of the United Nations Conference on Trade and Development. Probably the first institution mandated to deal specifically with sustainable development of tropical forests was the International Tropical Timber Organization (ITTO), which was established by the International Tropic Timber Agreement in 1983.[81] Forest management was also an agenda item at the United Nations Conference on Environment and Development (the so-called Earth Summit) in 1993. An important topic for discussion at this meeting was the impact of ITTO commitments on developing countries and the need for nontropical timber producers to commit themselves to forest management. It was seen as problematic that the several different certification systems in operation simultaneously confused both consumers and producers. The Earth Summit suffered from governability problems and was unable to create a global forest convention. As a result, many environmental groups began to look for forums outside the state-sanctioned international ones for help in dealing with the problem of deforestation.[82]

Concern with deforestation, international government's inability to deal with the problem satisfactorily, and the confusion created by a plurality of certification schemes are the reasons for the FSC's establishment in 1993. The World Wide Fund for Nature (WWF) and other transnational groups decided to try and develop a market-based mechanism to influence forest landowners and forest companies to certify their products and consumers to buy them. Not surprisingly given the character of the problem and the need to reach an agreement among consumers, environmental groups, and producers, the process behind the adoption of the FSC Statues, Principles and Criteria, and Guidelines for Certifiers was chaotic and conflictual.[83] But it worked. Today the FSC has 567 individuals and organizations as members. It is actively endorsed by WWF, Greenpeace, Friends of the Earth, and national environmental associations.[84]

The FSC is an independent, nonprofit, nongovernmental organization with its headquarters in Mexico. Its goal is to provide consumers with reliable information about tropical and nontropical forest products. Reliable information comes in the form of the global and well-respected standard, Principles of Forest Management, a type I assessment of field-level forest management practices that includes social, ecological, and economic standards.[85] The stakeholders that established the FSC were timber users, traders, and representatives of environmental and human rights organizations from five continents.

Sustainable development forms the basis of the FSC principles, which are performance-based and broad in scope. Included among the criteria for certification are principles involving tenure and use rights, community relations, workers' rights, environmental impact, management plans, and monitoring and preservation of old growth forests.[86] The FSC program also requires the creation of regional or national working groups responsible for developing specific indicators and verifiers to apply the principles and criteria more locally.

The FSC presents itself as the only global certification organization "providing an incentive in the market place for responsible forestry."[87] It accredits certification bodies for forest management inspections. These inspectors are charged with the task of applying global forest management standards in accordance with local ecological, social, and economic circumstances.[88] They enforce rational cooperation. Local ecological circumstances concern harvesting timber and non-timber forest products in a way that maintains the forest's biodiversity, productivity, and ecological processes. Social considerations involve helping local people and society at large to enjoy long-term benefits of forest resources. This may include workers' rights and indigenous peoples. Economic viability implies that forest operations are structured and managed to ensure profitability without generating financial profit that is negative for the other two management criteria.[89] FSC accredited organizations also verify the chain of custody of certified forest products. Chain of custody evaluation is similar to the life cycle evaluations done by type I eco-labeling systems. It traces wood harvested in certified forests through the stages of transport, processing, and marketing to the finished product.[90]

Not all market actors are satisfied with the existence of one global certification scheme and want to create a countervailing power. Small woodland owners in Europe have criticized the FSC for its insensitivity toward the unique nature of the European woodlands. In 1999 they established a regional scheme, Pan European Forest Certification (PEFC). Today it has 18 members including a PEFC branch in both the United States and Canada. It differs from the FSC in two important ways. It is not an accreditation body but a coordinating one for mutual compatible national certification systems, and it states that it is designed with the interests of small, European woodland owners in mind.[91] Its principles are not as broad as the FSC's. Two competing national schemes that are not type I in character are the American Sustainable Forestry Initiative (SFI) and the Canadian Standards Association Forest Programme (CSA).[92] When compared to the FSC, the three schemes apply a narrower view of sustainable development, take forest owner's concerns as their point of departure, and believe that civil society does not have a good understanding of existing forest practices.[93] Together with other European, Asian, and global forestry actors, they are now attempting to create an international program for mutual recognition so they can develop a better international presence and compete more successfully with the FSC.[94]

The MSC was established in 1997 but began in 1996 as a joint initiative between the WWF and the multinational corporation Unilever "to harness market forces as an incentive to improve management of fisheries."[95] Its design is reminiscent of the FSC. It is an independent, nongovernmental standard setting, accreditation, and logo licensing organization operating as a not-for-profit registered charity. Its headquarters are in Great Britain. The MSC stakeholders are called signatories who are asked to take joint responsibility for the ocean's common pool resources. The signatories include fishermen's organizations, fish processors, fish buyers and food retailers, conservationists, and world financial leaders. Its mission statement is "to work for sustainable marine fisheries by promoting responsible, environmentally appropriate, socially beneficial and economically viable fisheries practices, while maintaining the biodiversity, productivity and ecological processes of the marine environment..."[96] Like the FSC its goal is to provide credible certification and accreditation services. It accredits type I certifiers to assess fishery products. At present its label appears on certain brands of Alaska salmon, lobster, herring, as well as processed fish and shellfish products. Like the FSC, it applies a chain of custody certification, which in this case consists of all parts of the supply chain from fishing vessels to the family's dinner preferences. Unlike the FSC, which focuses mostly on institutional consumers in the building trade, individual consumer recognition of the MSC logo in supermarkets is very important.[97]

SOCIALLY RESPONSIBLE INVESTMENTS

Socially responsible investing (SRI) is not a product labeling scheme, though it may evolve into one in the future. Rather it offers people advice and the opportunity to place their money in stock companies and stock funds that reflect their political and ethical values. Ethical or political consumerist investors may be individual citizens, civil society organizations, corporations, and government bodies. Many commentators view small investors' interest in the stock market and SRI as a new social movement and an innovative way to make a social and political statement.[98] It is also a good illustration of individualized collective action because it allows citizens to take part in politics in everyday subpolitical activities without joining a membership organization.

SRI is not well-researched in the social sciences. It roots are long and go back to at least the 1800s when Quakers withdrew investments in the slave trade and the early 1900s when other religious groups were concerned about temperance and fair employment conditions. It appeared again over 100 years later in the United States, which—interestingly enough given its relative weak commitment to eco-labels and the FSC—has had a particularly dominant position in this form of political consumerism. The social movement activism of the 1960s against the Vietnam War was played out on many fronts. While the public and media focused on street demonstrations and student activism, a more silent, private kind of activism took place in the form of negative responsible investing, that is, stock boycotts and divestment movements. Church groups and trade unions decided to protest practices they found abhorrent by divesting in certain stock companies. Citizens boycotted stock in companies that directly or indirectly supported the Vietnam War. Today this boycott activity is called negative screening. Scholars consider the negative screening during these war years as the beginning of the corporate accountability movement.[99]

Other citizens also began to think that it should be possible to invest in their values and not just divest because of their values. In 1971, the Pax World Fund, the first ethical investment fund, started to develop positive screening of companies for investment.[100] We can call this positive SRI. Other approaches were also tried. One idea that never really got off the ground was "Proxies for People," an envisioned national membership organization for primarily middle-class people wanting to use their economic standing to gain access to and influence over companies. The idea was for the organization to collect shareholders' votes and use them to influence company policy.[101] Another unrealized effort was Project on Corporate Responsibility, which the well-known consumer activist Ralph Nader hoped would create a political arena for public pressure on private business.[102] These two ideas would be realized in slightly different form in the coming decades.

Over the years, SRI became more institutionalized, legitimate, and mainstream. Changes in government policy on pension reform and financial fund establishment, as in the case of Sweden, the United Kingdom, and other European countries, opened the way for ethical funds to become established. More people invest in the stock market, and many of them believe that it is legitimate and justifiable to make money morally. Books now offer advice on putting money where your morals are, investing with your conscience, and making a difference in making money.[103] Thus, SRI offers an interesting combination of the public and private virtue tradition of political consumerism. The idea behind SRI is similar to ecological modernization discussed earlier. Both perspectives encourage social and environmental activists and businesspeople to participate in moneymaking business ventures that further sustainable development.

Today numerous funds profile themselves as ethical in character. In the United States many investment advisors author books that counsel concerned citizens on how to place their money ethically. Membership organizations in the form of ethical unit trusts that promote SRI are growing in number. Business and economic commentators and scholars write articles and reports on the profitability of social investment for individual investors and its impact on company profits. Social screening organizations rate individual companies on corporate social responsibility and institutional funds on whether they operate an SRI policy. This section discusses a few of the well-known ethical funds in existence today.

Friends Provident International, a mutual society with Quaker roots, is a financial service provider founded in 1832 in England. Since 1984 it has developed a profile in the ethical investment market in the United Kingdom. This is done in two ways. "Stewardship" is the first British range of retail ethical funds (unit trust, life assurance, and pension funds) that "only invest money in companies that have passed a strict positive and negative screening process regarding ethical, social, and environmental issues." It aims at avoiding investing in companies whose activities include weapons manufacture, environmental damage and pollution, trade with or operations in oppressive regimes, exploitation of developing countries, nuclear power, tobacco or alcohol production, unnecessary exploitation of animals, gambling, pornography, and offensive or misleading advertising. The second approach is "reo®" adopted in 2002, which stands for "Responsible Engagement Overlay." It is a process-oriented " 'across the board' approach to investment . . . to improve the social and environmental performance of the companies [Friends Provident] invest in."[104] Its focus is increased corporate awareness and improvement in the areas of environmental management, conservation, climate change, labor standards, human rights, bribery and corruption, governance, risk, and corporate social responsibility.

Other financial investors have been established specifically as political consumerist institutions. Council on Economic Priorities (CEP), Social Investment Forum (SIF), Ethical Junction, and New Economic Foundation are examples. The oldest, CEP, an American public research organization founded in 1969, unites consumers, investors, policymakers, and corporate managers in promoting and encouraging socially and environmentally responsible management of business.[105] In the late 1980s, it developed the Corporate Report Card, now a well-known rating system that grades over 200 publicly traded companies on a scale from A to F on six criteria: the environment; advancement of women and minorities; volunteerism and charitable donations; community outreach; family benefits for employees; and social disclosure. The Corporate Report Card is used extensively by such membership organizations as the SIF and Friends Providence.[106]

The SIF (established in 1991) exists in the United Kingdom and United States. It is a nonprofit organization associated with Co-op America and other civil society associations. It offers a listing of various kinds of socially responsible investment possibilities in its directory. Its strategy includes screening (inclusion or exclusion of corporate securities in investment portfolios based on social or environmental criteria), community investment (support to low-income communities), and shareholder advocacy (use of shareholders' voting power to influence company behavior).[107] The idea is reminiscent of "Proxies for People." Individual shareholders invest in approved mutual funds and allow the SIF to vote corporate proxy resolutions as a tool for corporate transparency and democracy.[108] The SIF and Co-op America have started the project Shareholder Action Network (SAN from the 1990s) to enhance shareholder advocacy through network creation and mobilization of citizens for action on investment concerns.[109] In a sense socially responsible investment actors play a role similar to political parties in parliamentary democracy because they represent, articulate, and aggregate interests and cast votes on the basis of them. They show how the political mechanism of voice has entered the marketplace.

SRI engages civil society in various countries. Interest groups and social movements have adopted SRI as their cause. A political arena for public pressure on private business is, therefore, being created. However, unlike the one envisioned by Ralph Nader, this one is global in orientation. Trade unions are increasingly investing in a political consumerist fashion, as illustrated by the American ALF-CIO's union-directed investment program for investing union pension funds and the British Transport Salaried Staffs' Association's ethical investment charter.[110] Civil society associations as Amnesty International, fair trade organizations, consumer organizations, and Friends of the Earth campaign for institutions and individuals to invest in a socially responsible way.[111] Ethical pensions are in particular the focus of their efforts. Organizations are now being established to assist institutional investors to find ethical placing for their pension funds, for example, British Ethical Investors and Ethical Investment Research Service catering to charities and churches and the 130-member pension fund Council of Institutional Investors.[112] People investing in particular funds have also organized campaigns to pressure them to focus more on SRI, as illustrated in the campaign resulting in the Ethics for Universities Superannuation Scheme (USS), one of the largest pension schemes in the United Kingdom.[113]

CHARACTERISTICS OF CONTEMPORARY POLITICAL CONSUMERISM

Unlike the other ways of regulating industry discussed at the outset of this chapter, the main inspiration for political consumerist institutions is civil society and the conscience of consumers. More research is necessary for richer comparisons, but it seems clear from the discussions in this book that contemporary political consumerism differs from its historical past. Today's version is more global in orientation, focuses on postmaterial or postmodern concerns, and possibly even represents the public virtue more than a private virtue tradition of political consumerism. The contemporary movement is more institutionalized than its historical cousins because it is increasingly based in labeling and certification schemes whose organizations are professional and resourceful bodies either created for specific political consumerist causes or embedded in the activities of established civil society associations. When compared to the past, current political consumerist activities also focus more on engaging the middle class to consider political values and virtues when using its economic resources in everyday settings. The reason for this is obvious. Middle-class economic power has grown tremendously in most countries.

Mainstreaming is another important characteristic. This is a natural consequence of the institution-building strategy employed by contemporary political consumerist actors. The goal of today's political consumerism is to embed and incorporate its ideas, products, and processes in political, societal, and economic life at the local, national, and global levels. For ordinary consumers in their daily lives, this means that political consumerist products should be desirable as well as easily available and affordable. An important prerequisite for developing political consumerism into ordinary consumer behavior and choice is, of course, the legitimacy of political consumerism as a tool in sustainable development. Good working relations with governments, corporations, and civil society associations are, therefore, a main goal of the political consumerist actors and institutions discussed in this chapter. They seek public legitimacy through this cooperation to build consumer awareness among ordinary consumers and they use consumer awareness as the basis for seeking public legitimacy.

What is particularly interesting about political consumerist institutions and actors is their character as brokers[114] that build bridges between consumers and business actors and institutions. The first step is to bring the different spheres together and create a shared basis for action, a common ground for voluntary action. Here political consumer policymakers have been very innovative in creating institutions and opportunities for "beyond compliance" policymaking. The different kinds of political consumerism discussed in this chapter show how a partnership is created among citizen-consumers, global companies, and in certain cases national and supranational governments. The terms stakeholder and stewardship capture this endeavor well. Stakeholder dialogue aims at opening up transnational corporations to more contemporary forms of profitability (profit-plus) and a broader understanding of their role in society. Concern about the future, as captured by the term stewardship, encourages all actors involved with market translations to take future responsibility for their actions and behaviors. An important implication of stake-holding and stewardship is that contemporary citizen-consumers are asked to shop smartly as a tool to encourage corporations to rethink their policy rather than to boycott them and their products. Boycotts, as found in this chapter, still play an important role in political con-sumerist endeavors, and we need to investigate them more thoroughly in terms of collective action, but when compared to the past it seems that they are perceived more as a way to create consumer awareness, release consumer and citizen political frustration, and possibly get corporations to the negotiating table rather than as viable and reliable problem-solving mechanisms. Perhaps this reflects the complexity of the global problems that characterize current forms of political consumerism. There is good reason to believe that contemporary political consumerism is less confrontational than its historical ancestors.

Mainstreaming can be broken down into a number of different goals. An important one is selling power, the mainstreaming of political consumerist products. The increasing number of labels, certification schemes, and opportunities for SRI imply that contemporary political consumerism focuses on the availability of products and services close to home and at neighborhood markets. A general goal is, therefore, larger market shares and broader citizen and consumer awareness of the availability and advantages of political consumerist products and services. Attention is directed at getting labeled products on store shelves and on information activities to convince consumers that food that is organically labeled, household chemicals carrying eco-labels, and fair traded products either do not cost much more than other products offered for sale at the neighborhood store or their extra costs are justified on the basis of their impact on global justice, fairness, and sustainable development. Many labeling schemes put great effort in convincing brand names and even supermarkets' own brands to undergo product labeling and certification evaluation. As shown in the fair trade case, they also engage in publicity campaigns to create public and consumer awareness of the politics behind products, which market studies find to be crucial for increasing the market share of labeled products.[115]

Efforts toward mainstreaming are also giving political consumerism an everyday, ordinary character. Political consumerism is becoming a form of everyday activism that can be expressed without exerting much effort and resources and without unwilling confrontation with other actors. The goal is a form of low-threshold collective action that can be performed on daily trips to the market for oneself and one's family. Exercising the public virtue tradition of political consumerism should not take much self-sacrifice. As such political consumerism is evolving away from an endeavor for social and political activists who identify themselves completely with public causes. Today political consumerism can appear as a form of serial identity (see chapter 1) that may be loosely coupled or completely decoupled from larger public engagements in politics and society in the form of membership in political parties and civic associations. Available survey data confirms that growing numbers of rather ordinary citizens engage in political consumerist actions.[116]

A measure of mainstreaming success is reactions of the business community. Many small and large corporations are now developing their own ethical profile in the form of codes of conduct, management systems, and labeling or certification schemes. At times business has created its own institutions as countervailing powers to check the public legitimacy given to the ones set up by consumers and civil society associations. Now even governments and influential civil society associations take notice of political consumerism. The United Nations, Amnesty International, Nordic Council, and EU all have political consumerism on their agenda.

Mainstreaming is also taking place internally in the world of political consumerism. Labeling and certification schemes tend to imitate the institutional design of other political consumerist schemes.[117] The eco-labeling institutional design has been a model for developing forest stewardship labels and even gender labeling schemes. Marine stewardship is patterned after forest stewardship. Codes of conduct are on occasion modeled on ILO conventions. Political consumer demand of information encourages institutionalization through imitation. Internal mainstreaming also implies the goal of cooperation and coordination among political consumerist actors and institutions. Figure 3.2 offers an overview of the political consumerist institutions discussed in this chapter and shows how they are forming global and regional networks, which bring together similar institutions in different countries. We also find that certain institutions are members of

Types of political consumerist institutions	Organizational mission	Product focus	Global (date of origin)	National (date of origin)	Regional examples (date of origin)
Eco-labels	Life cycle identification of products and services as less harmful to the environment than other similar products Rewards corporate environmental leadership	Household chemicals, detergents, shampoos, paper, office furniture and equipment, batteries, white goods, paint	Global Ecolabelling Network (GEN) (1994), Consumer's Choice Council (1997)	German Blue Angel (1978), U.S. Green Seal (1990), Japanese Eco Mark (1989), Swedish Good Environmental Choice (1992)	EU Eco-Label (EU Flower) (1992), Nordic Swan (1990)
Fair trade labels	Fair and direct trade relations, fair production conditions for producers from Third World countries Empowerment of Third World producers and workers	Coffee, chocolate, bananas, cocoa, tea, honey, textiles, sports balls	Fairtrade Labelling Organizations International (FLO-I) (1997), International Federation for Alternative Trade (IFAT) (1989),	Dutch Max Havelaar Quality Label (1988), Transfair U.S.A. (1998) and Canada (1994), U.K. Fairtrade Foundation (1993),	European Fair Trade Association (1990), Network of European World Shops (NEWS) (1994)

Figure 3.2 Political consumerist regulatory tools.

Source: The information is directly from the political consumerist institutions. See bibliography.

Types of political consumerist institutions	Organizational mission	Product focus	Global (date of origin)	National (date of origin)	Regional examples (date of origin)
	Cooperation strategy for greater equity in international trade		International Social and Environmental Accreditation and Labelling Alliance (ISEAL) (1998), Consumer's Choice Council (1997)	Swedish Föreningen för Rättvisemärkt (1996)	
Organic food labels	Food produced by farmers using renewable resources, conserving soil and water Food produced free of antibiotics, growth hormones, and commercial pesticides	Eggs, milk, meats, fruits, vegetables, bread, canned goods, cheese, soft drinks, farm input products	International Federation of Organic Agricultural Movements (IFOAM) (1972), International Social and Environmental Accreditation and Labelling Alliance (ISEAL) (1998),	Bio-Gro New Zealand (1983), Swedish KRAV (1985), Organic Food Federation in U.K. (1986), USDA Organic (2002)	Organic Trade Association (U.S.A., Canada, Mexico) (1985)

	Enhancement of biodiversity, biological cycles, and soil biological activity		Consumer's Choice Council (1997)
Forest certification	Chain of custody assessment of forestry use Sustainable forest management; improvement of the quality of life and relief of poverty for forest-dependent people and workers	Wood products, furniture	Forest Stewardship Certification (FSC) (1993), International Social and Environmental Accrediation and Labelling Alliance (ISEAL) (1998)
Marine certification	Chain of custody, well-managed and sustainable fishery	Fish, fish products, shellfish	Marine Stewardship Certification (MSC) (1997),

Figure 3.2—cont'd.

Types of political consumerist institutions	Organizational mission	Product focus	Global (date of origin)	National (date of origin)	Regional examples (date of origin)
	No overfishing or depletion of exploited populations, care for fishery ecosystem, effective management system respecting local, national, and international laws and standards		International Social and Environmental Accrediation and Labelling Alliance (ISEAL) (1998)		
Socially responsible investing	Integration of personal values and societal concerns with investment decisions	Not a labeling scheme Advice on investment placements	Shareholder Action Network (1990s), Ethical Investment Research Service (EIRIS) (1983), Friends Providence International (1984)	U.S. Pax World Funds (1971), U.K. and U.S., Social Investment Forum (SIF) (1991), U.S. Council on Economic Priorities (CEP (1969), Canadian Ethical Growth Fund, Ethical Funds (1986, 2000), Swedish Banco (1983)	European Sustainable and Responsible Investment Forum (EUROSIF) (2001), New Economic Foundation (1986)

Figure 3.2—cont'd.

more than one global or regional network, as exemplified by cross-memberships in FLO and IFOAM and the global network International Social and Environmental Accreditation and Labelling Alliance (ISEAL) established in 1998. The institutions also provide electronic links to each other on their websites for easy consumer navigation to other smart shopping sites, ideas, and products.

Mainstreaming coordination and cooperation takes other institutional forms as well. More general or umbrella coordinating political consumerist networks are establishing themselves. Some of them like Ethical Consumer discussed earlier offers not only online links to political consumerist institutions but also helps people to be informed about issues concerning, animals, peace, development and human rights, and the environment in the form of lists of web links to groups working on these questions. It is, thus, possible to become a cyber political consumerist and practice e-individualized collective action by purchasing ethical investments online, sending a statement in an E-mail to politicians, or buying animal-friendly goods online.[118] Another example is Ethical Junction, an online association dedicated to aggregating citizen-consumer interest in political consumerist issues. It characterizes itself as a "gateway to the ethical sector for people in the UK and Ireland, giving a focal point for a broad range of ethical issues and trading" and offers ethics to consumers online, that is, Internet assistance to find websites for ethical financial investment ideas, organic foods, and fair trade goods.[119] The Association of European Consumers, the Danish Active Consumer, and the Norwegian Ethical Consumption, work in a similar fashion.[120] These networks and organizations represent an integrative development in the field of political consumerism that connect different labeling schemes and web-based networks for consumers to exchange ideas, experience, and activism.

This new wave of the consumer movement has not gone unnoticed. It has been internationally recognized. The Right Livelihood Award (so-called Alternative Nobel Prize) has gone to Anwar Fazal (1982) who was the entrepreneur behind Consumer Interpol, International Baby Food Action Network, and Pesticide Action Network (1998), Alice Tepper Marlin at the Council on Economic Priorities (1990) for mobilizing consumer power for just and sustainable economic priorities, and the Japanese Seikatsu Club Consumer's Cooperative (1989) for creating a successful sustainable model of production and consumption for industrial society.[121]

A more encompassing mainstreaming transformation that is underway at present is the harmonization or synthesis of political consumerist institutional mission statements. The idea is represented by the Consumer's Choice Council's use of sustainability and sustainable development as its discursive frame to approach political consumerism in a comprehensive way. Sustainable development concerns ecology, economic development, and issues of democracy and social justice. It uses the sustainability frame in its coffee program: "Coffee is steeped in a number of social and environmental problems, including massive deforestation caused by the transition from shade to sun coffee; degradation of soils and water sources; extremely low wages and poor working conditions for farm workers on coffee estates; low prices paid to growers by commercial middlemen; and inequitable international distribution of the fruits of the gourmet coffee boom."[122] For this association, eco-labeling is a crucial step in providing consumers with the information they need to purchase products that are produced in more environmentally sustainable and socially just ways.

An integrating institution appealing to all stakeholders—not just consumers and civil society associations—is the Ethical Trading Initiative (ETI), an alliance of companies, nongovernmental organizations, and trade union organizations from 1998. Ethical trading targets both consumers and producers. Ethical trading is "a step towards sustainability" and encourages companies to deliver a "triple bottom-line" of environmental, social, and financial performance.[123] The key to ethical trade is responsibility-taking on the part of business, consumers, civil society, and government. At present only a few companies practice ethical trade, but the number is growing. The ETI has 28 companies listed as members. They include, The Body Shop International, Chiquita International Brands, Levi Strauss, and Marks and Spencer.[124] The Body Shop is probably the best-known ethic-based company.[125] Other examples include the Coalition for Environmentally Responsible Economies (CERES 2002).[126]

The institutions and actors behind mainstreaming of political consumerism and the synthesis of political consumerist endeavors hope that pressure from citizen-consumers, civil society, and multilevel government will encourage more companies to develop ethical trade toolkits and broaden the ethical niche in the marketplace. Their goal is global corporate citizenship practice and full citizenship for all people in the world. Their activities are an attempt to construct a framework for economic globalization that includes sustainability as its core element. It is noteworthy that they argue along a similar vein as Adam Smith who believed that the market needed to be structured by a normative framework that "operates in the context of prudence, cooperation, a level playing field of competition, and within a well-defined framework of justice."[127] Yet unlike Adam Smith they do not envision the market as framed in the container of the nation-state.[128] Rather they argue that the problems at hand require a framework that goes beyond national government and the domestic market. The envisioned framework, as exemplified by the collection-action efforts discussed in this chapter, requires more than consultation between government and industry. It needs to be the effort of global stakeholders—both individual and collective actors—that have stewardship and sustainability as their guiding light.

4

A Study of Political Consumerism Today: The Case of Good Environmental Choice in Sweden

Why Study Sweden?

This chapter looks closely at why people engage in political consumerism. What motivates them to get involved and who are they? How are current forms of political consumerism similar and different from the past? My answers to these questions come from a case study of green political consumerist activities in Sweden. Sweden was chosen because it is an unlikely place for political consumerism to take root. It is a hard case for political activism in the marketplace because the Swedish state is strong with a good record on environmental policymaking.[1] We are, therefore, inclined to assume that governability problems do not characterize Sweden. The country is also characterized as a strong social democratic welfare state that is proactive and problem-oriented,[2] which would lead us to believe that citizens do not need to turn to the marketplace to solve political problems. Even the strong political presence of the social democratic workers' movement, which as discussed in chapter 2 implies that production-oriented solutions are preferred over consumption-oriented solutions, adds to the argument that Sweden is an unlikely place for political consumerism. Swedes increasingly believe that they can influence the political system.[3] Sweden rates high on most measures of social capital,[4] and the more collectivist and corporatist political culture that characterizes Sweden does not point in the direction of individualized collective action.[5] Research results from chapter 2 show that the market becomes an arena for politics when the traditional political sphere is closed to groups and issues or when there are governability problems. This has not been the case in Sweden, which ranks high on most benchmarks of democracy.[6]

The puzzle is that four highly well-respected market-based labeling schemes—the Nordic Swan, TCO Development, KRAV, and Good Environmental Choice—are present in Sweden today. Government and particularly the Swedish state with the urging of environmental organizations played an important role in the establishment of the Nordic Council's Swan eco-label. It is noteworthy that government played a minimal role in the establishment of KRAV, TCO Development, and Good Environmental Choice, whose initiatives came from civil society. Why did environment-oriented civil society associations choose to use market-based tools to promote sustainable development? Why does it seem that Sweden against a well-grounded assumption is a likely place for political consumerism? Answers to these questions take their point of departure in the importance of civil society as a mobilizing force for political consumerism and the role played by the green movement in political consumerist endeavors. This chapter investigates how the political landscape changes of postmodernization, ecological modernization, individualized collective action, and even governance (see chapter 1) have turned Sweden into a likely place for political consumerism. It offers a case study of the eco-label Good Environmental Choice (*Bra miljöval*) established by the largest Swedish environmental association, the Swedish Society for Nature Conservation (*Svenska Naturskyddsföreningen*, SNF).

This case has been chosen for closer study because of its grassroots character. Consumer pressure and dissatisfaction motivated the SNF to engage in political consumerism. Good Environmental Choice is a type 1 labeling scheme whose base is citizen and consumer mobilization that is channeled by an environmental organization. It is a scheme that relies highly on responsibility-taking on the part of citizen-consumers. The issues involved are environmentally friendly shopping and local responsibility for global environmental problems. It is a scheme that requires the involvement of a variety of market actors and that takes government regulation and public policy as its point of departure for its more ambitious voluntary compliance criteria. It is genuinely Swedish and does not imitate an institutional design that has developed in other countries. International visitors come to Sweden to understand its workings.

IN COMPARISON WITH THE PAST

Contemporary Swedish political consumerism demonstrates how globalization, individualization, and the values of postmodernization are taking hold publicly. Concerns about human rights, labor rights, and particularly the environment and gender equality form the agenda of Swedish political consumerism today. This agenda shows how citizens and consumers are increasingly viewing it as partly their responsibility for protecting and improving their everyday lives and the common well-being of Swedes and people in other countries. Disillusionment with government efforts, distrust of established hierarchies, inability to use only government channels to solve newer political problems, self-interest, and a citizen need for self-activation and urgent action all play a role in contemporary Swedish political consumerist endeavors. Unlike many of the historical examples discussed in chapter 2, the blue-collar workers' movement has not been a dominant actor in contemporary Swedish political consumerist activities. The only trade union that is really present in political consumerism today is the whitecollar umbrella organization TCO, which established TCO Development.

Even though current Swedish political consumerist efforts reflect different values, they show some similarity with history. Three common traits are the importance of women and civil society associations as well as the focus on everyday problems with satisfying immediate everyday needs. Government is still important for boycotting and labeling networks. But a key difference between then and now is the kind of role that government plays in political consumerism. Contemporary efforts focus less on government as a policymaker—a producer of legislation and key structure in policy implementation—and more on its role as an actor who enables political consumerist endeavors by providing a platform in public policy, initial financial support (as in the TCO Development case), and its changes in procurement practices (as in the case of Good Environmental Choice). Government is now an important target for political consumerist activities because it is a large or institutional consumer of goods. It has immense consumer power. In Sweden it spends 300 billion crowns (ca. US$ 30 billion) per year on procurement goods.[7] It should, therefore, come as no surprise that government procurement policy is a focus of political consumerist struggles. As shown later in this chapter, once government decides to alter its consumer behavior it can change how business perceives the politics of products. Thus, when it comes to certain aspects of industrial regulation, the potential influence of government as a consumer may perhaps be greater than its influence as a producer of legislation, a development not unknown internationally.[8]

OPENING UP SWEDEN FOR GREEN POLITICAL CONSUMERISM

Good Environmental Choice was fully established as an eco-labeling scheme in 1992. A process tracking study of its establishment offered in this section shows how its development demanded flexibility on the part of its initiators, citizen engagement, willingness to explore unconventional alternatives and unusual cooperative partners, and an extremely good sense of political timing, that is, use of a policy window of opportunity. The general idea of promoting green political consumerism finds its origin in the dismay that many environmental activists feel with government and politics. They began to lose trust in political parties after the national referendum on nuclear power in 1980. Nuclear power was no ordinary political issue. It was divisive: Swedish citizens were highly engaged in it, and disagreement on whether Sweden should continue its nuclear power program even brought down a government in the 1970s.[9] The issue brought the conflict between the values of industrial society and postindustrial society to a head, and it divided people into two value-oriented camps. The decision of the highly pronuclear power alternative and the one that framed itself as a middle alternative to pool their election results after the referendum and declare the antinuclear power alternative the loser disillusioned these activists and made them dismayed with party politics. They began to shift their environmental involvement to other less routine, more elite-challenging, and even subpolitical channels. They had begun to mistrust the commitment of many of the political parties to the environmental issue and sought to do politics by other means.[10] Perceived government sluggishness in regulating industry as well as trends toward globalization, deregulation, and privatization prompted their search for and the use of new policy tools.[11]

Other important external events opened up a policy window for green political consumerist actions. Citizens in the 1985 parliamentary election, which is commonly characterized as the first green election in Swedish history, gave sufficient support for the Green Party to enter Parliament.[12] This was a signal to political actors that environmentalism was a viable political issue. A second policy window was Gro Harlem Brundtland's report from 1987, *Our Common Future*, which put sustainable development on the global political agenda. It signaled a new approach to environmentalism called ecological modernization (see chapter 1). This approach convinced environmental activists and market actors that economic growth and environmental protection need no longer be in conflict with each other and that it was necessary to develop new cooperative steering capacities that were problem-oriented. Other important events were the creation of the Swedish market-based labeling scheme for organic food KRAV in 1985, the presence of eco-labeling schemes in other countries, as well as discussions in the Nordic Council about establishing the Nordic Swan eco-label. Even the pressure from members of the SNF, the Swedish Cooperative Union (KF), and general consumers on supermarkets in the 1980s to develop a green profile should be included as part of the external circumstances within which Good Environmental Choice was embedded.[13] There was, in sum, good public awareness of environmental issues upon which the SNF could build its green political consumerist platform.

The SNF became involved with green political consumerism in the mid-1980s. Several important actions took place almost simultaneously from the late 1980s to early 1990s. This section discusses the most important actions. Its first political consumerist action was paper bleached with chlorine, and its concern was a response to citizen pressure for more environmentally friendly paper. It worked together with other environmental groups on the issue; among them were the remnants of the People's Campaign Against Nuclear Power. The issue had reached the political agenda, and the Minister of Environment along with the Swedish Environmental Protection Agency (*Naturvårdsverket*) was working on ways to decrease the amount of chlorine allowed to enter Swedish waterways.

To satisfy consumer demand and speed up the government process, the environmental groups decided in 1983 to publish a short book about acceptable and nonacceptable paper entitled in translation "Unbleached Paper for the Sake of the Environment" (*Oblekt papper för miljöns skull!* 1983). It was a simple book that included a list of acceptable paper mills that had a positive environmental impact. The book was edited, updated, and published in a more sophisticated edition in 1987.[14] Also in 1987 the Swedish Society for Nature Conservation and a small consumer-oriented environmental group (*Miljöförbundet*) called a boycott on paper bleached with what they considered to be excessive levels of chlorine. Both associations had previously and unsuccessfully lobbied government to pass legislation for stricter standards on chlorine use and called on industry to lower its use of chlorine voluntarily. Swedish paper industry officials told the environmental associations that more research and development was necessary before they would be able to change to green production methods. The organizations and their members did not want to wait until government finished its investigations or until business was ready to cooperate. They had a sense of urgency on this issue.

Paper was targeted because it is a mass product and its production was polluting the waterways. Also, a few smaller brands of paper were sufficiently "green" to be acceptable for a green consumers' list. The SNF mobilized its local chapter members to petition large institutional consumers (in particular local government) to purchase paper from companies on the green list. Together with the other environmental associations and with the help of government discussion on legislation, they convinced many municipal governments to change their procurement policy. The boycott, media publicity, and consumer demand for environmentally friendly paper forced Swedish paper mills into action. By 1988 Swedish paper mills had begun to change their production methods. This experience convinced the SNF that it could use the market as an arena for green politics and that procurement policy was a good target for action. Rather ironically, it found that its own procurement policy for paper for its magazine became a target of member criticism.[15]

The year 1988 is an important watermark for the association's campaign against chlorine-bleached paper. In early 1988 it sent out a press release to the editor-in-chiefs of all major publications that encouraged all Swedish newspapers, journals, and magazines to boycott Finnish chlorine-bleached paper, a less expensive and less environmental alternative to Swedish-produced paper. It encouraged procurement officers to buy Swedish environmentally friendly paper produced at Holmens Bruk, a small paper mill on the verge of financial ruin. It also mentioned that it was following its own advice and would no longer procure paper from Finnish manufacturers.[16] Larger Swedish paper manufacturers were not entirely negative to the boycott call against the export-oriented and therefore economically sensitive Finnish paper mills because they believed that the stricter environmental policy applied in Sweden gave them a competitive disadvantage. Perhaps they did not understand that they too could be the targets of future boycotts. In the small country of Sweden, this press release from the largest environmental association calling for a boycott and appealing to actors in the public sphere created a media storm. Almost every daily carried the story. Fearing a readership revolt and bad publicity, publisher after publisher announced immediate changes in their paper procurement policy.[17]

The boycott was an important victory for the environmental movement. It showed that smart shopping mattered and that it was conceivable that individual consumers—without mass organization, structured meetings, and work tasks carefully portioned out—could put demands on institutions to become environmentally friendlier. This was an important formative event of individualized collective action for the association. The environmental associations' members also answered the call. They mobilized locally and successfully lobbied their municipal governments, which began to use the simple book as a guide for procurement. Consumer pressure and change in procurement policy by institutional consumers acted as an incentive for business investments in environmental technology. As a result, government's environmental demands on paper mills were met earlier than expected. According to a SNF official, staff members at the association involved in the action made the assessment that there was a potential for consumer influence over the market that should be channeled to better the environment.[18]

The late 1980s and early 1990s were a very active, formative period for the SNF's involvement with green political consumerism. The association's president supported the effort, and the association began to employ people to work on green political consumer issues. SNF officials followed up the initial contact they had made in 1987 with institutions representing consumers. Cooperative activities intensified in the coming years. Government was also active. In 1988 its parliamentary commission presented a report on eco-labeling,[19] and SNF declared in its official comment on the report that it was willing, as suggested in the report, to play a central role in developing the labeling scheme.[20] Public release of the report intensified the general public debate and awareness on the issue. In 1989 the American consumer advocate Ralph Nader visited the SNF to discuss how he worked in networks with industry on concrete consumer problems.[21] The seminar was an eye-opener for the SNF, as Swedish environmental associations traditionally viewed industry as an enemy of the green cause that needs to be carefully regulated by government. We see here how ecological modernization began to take hold within the SNF.

Also in these years, the SNF successfully used political consumerism in two other instances. These actions show how the SNF began to institutionalize green political consumerism. Unlike earlier efforts, member input was restricted more to the role of consumers. They did not need to lobby institutional consumers partly because of the products it chose to politicize and partly because the paper boycott had given the SNF the public platform it needed to speak as a legitimate representative of green political consumer.

Its membership, the general consuming population, government, and industry respected its position.

Almost simultaneously the SNF began to work on making batteries and washing detergent more environmentally friendly. It lobbied producers of batteries to replace mercury with a less environmentally harmful substance, and once a more environmentally friendly (non-mercury) battery existed, it encouraged consumers to purchase it.[22] This was in 1990. In 1993 it continued to encourage readers of its magazine not to buy mercury batteries.[23] The SNF's engagement in the battery campaign, consumer response, as well as the ensuing media debate led to changes in production methods. The character of the battery market is an important factor explaining the SNF's success in negotiations with industry. Few battery producers are in existence, and all are dependent on global exports. They form a sensitive export-oriented economic market. Once they realized that green consumer sentiment was growing, they decided it best to adapt their production methods to greener standards. Soon afterward all batteries of certain categories sold in Sweden were mercury-free. Now many of these batteries sold globally follow the Swedish green standard.[24]

The next product to be politicized was washing detergent. At that time only 1 percent of the washing detergents on the market was environmentally friendly; manufacturers were hesitant to change their production methods. In a wise move that shows insight about boycott actions, the association targeted Lever, the leading laundry detergent manufacturer in Sweden, whose product Via comprised almost 10 percent of the Swedish market. It approached Lever and asked it to make its product more environmentally friendly but was told that change takes time. A few environmentally friendly detergent brands were on the market. They were put on a green list, and in 1991 consumers were encouraged to buy them and boycott Via. The boycott received considerable media publicity and engaged many consumers, but this did not convince Lever and other manufacturers to comply with the SNF demands. A break came when the three largest market retailers decided to boycott or not procure washing detergents that did not meet the SNF criteria. Consumer pressure and internal environmental concern explained their decision. Today Via does not carry the Good Environmental Choice eco-label but most of Lever's other detergents and those of other manufacturers now meet the original requirements set by the Society for Nature Conservation. At present over 90 percent of the washing detergents on sale in Swedish markets are eco-labeled either by Good Environmental Choice or the Nordic Swan.[25] Work on developing these initial requirements for substitute products during the boycott was an important experience in formulating and setting product criteria. This effort can be seen as the institutional origin of Good Environmental Choice.[26]

The final important internal event was the publication of the book, "Buy and Act Environmentally. An Everyday Handbook for a Better Environment" (*Handla miljövänligt! Vardagshandbok för en bättre miljö*) in 1988. The initial idea to publish a green political consumer guide came from different sources. Members had been asking for a green shopping list, and different people who knew each other from environmental activist networks began discussing green political consumerism. Unknown to SNF, there was even a book project in Great Britain going on at the same time.[27] What is particularly interesting for a theoretical theme of this book (the private virtue tradition of political consumerism) is that an important origin is a private discussion in an environmentally oriented family about where to buy safe food for the family's table. The woman in the family participated in a group that directly ordered ecological food from farmers. Her husband, a newly employed SNF official, who later coined the concept of "buy and act environmentally" (*handla miljövänligt*), believed that families should be able to purchase environmentally safe (i.e., organic) food at any local supermarket. In the theoretical language of this book, he was saying that there should not be a high threshold for everyday green political consumption. People should not be forced to engage in high levels of self-sacrifice to buy green products. He began to work closely with two environmental activists who already had been commissioned to write a practical guide for green consuming for SNF.[28] Thus, the private virtue tradition of wanting to find good products for one's family spilled over into civic engagement and provided a foundation for the public virtue tradition of political consumerism and the publication of a green political consumers' guide.

The book was published in a large edition (50,000 copies). About 9,000 copies were preordered before its publication. It was presented at a public conference on consumerism, where an additional 5,000 copies were sold. By February 1989, 45,000 copies had been sold, and the book was out-of-stock in a matter of three weeks. It received tremendous media and citizen-consumer attention. It took up two basic virtues of green political consumerism—smart shopping for environmentally friendly products and thriftiness in the consumption of goods. The book has been reprinted several times and has sold over 375,000 copies, which is quite extensive given the population of Sweden is less than 9 million people. Association members and consumers took the book with them when they purchased products at their local stores and even, on their own initiative, used it to create a local arena for discussions on green political consumerism and perform street-level, grassroots evaluations of the environmental profile of their neighborhood supermarkets. These spontaneous grassroots activities reflecting individualized collective action later became an important activity for the associational network "Buy and Act Environmentally" discussed later in this chapter.

As with the Brundtland report and other successful political consumerist activities, the book signaled that there was political agency in smart shopping to regulate industry. It also fell well in line with the dialogue on cooperative, shareholder ventures that had already been started between the SNF and KF (*Kooperativa Förbundet*).[29] In an internal policy memo, the SNF official who coined the phrase "act and buy environmentally" discussed how market-based activities fit into the larger environmental action framework. The memo begins with a discussion of the new wave of environmental consciousness particularly in Northern Europe and continues by stating "a dissatisfaction with the way politicians and public authorities deal with environmental questions has created extensive interest for individual environmental responsibility—many people ask themselves 'what can I do as an individual for a better environment.' "[30] In line with scholarly discussions on the need for new environmental regulatory tools or soft laws,[31] the official continued with a discussion of the need to regulate more dispersed sources of pollution generated by household waste, transportation, and energy production because production-oriented regulation of industrial waste could not manage or solve problems of environmental pollution. A solution suggested in the memo was individual environmental responsibility or reflexive consumerism.[32] Two obstacles were, however, noted: individuals needed guidance and industries lacked an objective measurement for environmentally friendly products.

These concerns opened up a window of opportunity for the SNF to continue its work on green political consumerism and develop an eco-labeling scheme. As stated in the memo: "[The SNF] has started a process and must now take measures to keep it on course and keep ourselves one step in front of industry, public authorities, and retailers. Never before have we been able to dictate the conditions for a segment of societal development. But this is exactly what we can do if we play our cards right and quickly formulate environmental criteria for important environmentally-harmful groups of products."[33]

Interesting arguments for the SNF involvement in green political consumerism are given in the policy memo. This kind of environmental work was said to have a positive clang. It encourages positive actions instead of telling members, the general public, and industry what not to do. It represents positive (buycotts) rather than negative screening (boycotts). It also represents an environmental activity that could involve everyone in a hands-on everyday way. And, as experience told the association, it leads to quick results that frequently are "beyond compliance" in character.

It is worthy to note that the policy memo also included self-interest arguments or what may be called a collectivist private virtue tradition of political consumerism. Green political consumerism and an eco-labeling system could promote the SNF as an environmental association. An SNF eco-label would put the association in the public limelight. Its name would appear on all approved products, which was a kind of free advertisement. An eco-label would also generate income for the association, help the association compete with other large environmental organizations with a consumer profile (e.g., WWF), and play a central role in member recruitment campaigns. "We should even see the essential background effort in this area as an investment in membership growth, because it lays the ground for the association to hold its forefront position in this new area of involvement and thereby makes it be attractive for even more people to become members."[34]

It was, as noted in earlier policy papers, important for the SNF to act quickly because government was dragging its feet on eco-labeling, and the Nordic Swan was not meeting SNF expectations.[35] The SNF was encouraged to use its knowledge and public legitimacy as well as the growing consumer interest in green political consumerist goods to help forge alliances, coalitions, and networks of actors from different segments of Sweden. Successful and effective green political consumerism required new kinds of cooperative ventures that build on a combination of private and public interests. This stakeholder approach is an example of ecological modernization because, if constructed properly, it could represent a win–win situation for all involved actors. The task was, then, to formulate an institutional design that convinced all stakeholders that it paid to cooperate.

GOOD ENVIRONMENTAL CHOICE TYPE I ECO-LABEL

Swedish supermarket retailers were internally and externally pressured to do something, and unlike their counterparts in many other countries and for reasons that deserve more academic study in the field of business and marketing, they understood relatively early that it was not in their interests to put up an adamant fight against green political consumerism. The KF, which owns a large chain of supermarkets (*Konsum*), was, due to member and customer pressure, increasingly concerned about the environment and found the book Buy and Act Environmentally a good and practical tool as did the other large chain ICA.[36] Both the KF and ICA were pushing for fast action, and they realized that they could not develop a publicly legitimate eco-labeling system on their own. They needed a trustworthy, independent monitoring institution. A cooperative endeavor with the three supermarket retailers in existence in Sweden, ICA, KF, and Dagab (the third supermarket retailer in Sweden now part of Axfood), gave the SNF the necessary economic resources to use its expertise in the natural sciences to develop criteria for labeling goods as environmentally friendly, with washing detergents heading the list. Together the four actors created a unit called Good Environmental Choice Daily Products (*Bra Miljöval Dagligvaror*). Unlike other schemes already in operation in other countries, their first label was put on shelves rather than products, a procedure that consumers found confusing and was later changed.

As citizen and consumer involvement in political consumerism and not institutional designing is a main theme of this book, the organizational development and design of Good Environmental Choice will only be discussed briefly. It was established as a separate organizational unit in 1992. The unit was placed in Gothenburg because the person to head the unit lives there. She was previously in charge of green political consumerism at the KF. The geographical distance between Stockholm and Gothenburg (approximately 500 kilometers) allowed the unit to develop a more independent profile.[37] Good Environmental Choice began to develop licensing or certification requirements and to assess products for certification. An important part of this kind of third party type I certification is transparency.[38] Manufacturers must reveal their secret formulas and allow their products to be tested in a life-cycle (cradle-to-grave) assessment, which includes production methods, packaging materials, and waste created from product use. As with other labeling and certification schemes, manufacturers apply for licensing and pay for product evaluation and licensing permission. Once they are approved they receive a limited-time license to use the Good Environmental Choice stamp of approval. There are two kinds of approval. Rank B sets minimum standards and the other (Rank A) gives manufacturers credit for going beyond the set standards. The unit uses the higher standard when it periodically reassesses the rankings to see whether it is practically feasible to make them stricter.[39] The unit is now self-financing. It is unique globally because it is not managed by government or a quasi-governmental body.[40]

The SNF made a number of very wise strategic and policy choices in its initial involvement with green political consumerism. These decisions show a great degree of adaptability and appropriateness, two key elements emphasized in the governance literature that are discussed in chapter 1. Also, as shown from studies of other eco-labeling schemes, they seemed to know that public awareness and consumer pressure were necessary for the labeling scheme's successful launching. Although they had some knowledge of other eco-labeling developments from the late 1980s,[41] the involved activists state that they were not aware of historical examples of labeling campaigns as the one discussed in chapter 2. Nor did they use the experience from the German labeling scheme Blue Angel to design their scheme institutionally or the American Council on Economic Priorities, which had earlier published its book "Smart Shopping," when they decided to commission the book "Act and Buy Environmentally" and establish the Good Environmental Choice unit.[42] The scheme was, therefore, made in Sweden.

POLITICAL AGENCY AND GREEN POLITICAL CONSUMERISM

Of particular interest for this book is the effect of green political consuming on political agency, that is, its role in renewing democracy and the political community. The historical examples discussed in chapter 2 show how a political consumer orientation opened up civil society for new issues, methods, members, and coalitions. Political consumerist concerns on the part of citizens led to the creation of spontaneous networks by people normally invisible in the political system. In the past, the collective action generated from private interests in what would generally be considered to be apolitical, everyday settings helped put issues of labor and food on the political agenda. Citizens and consumers also learned civic skills. Is it possible to see the same development in contemporary examples of political consumerism? Is there, as theoretically argued in chapter 1, political agency in consumer awareness and choice? Are people involving themselves in consumerist causes, joining political consumerist networks, and becoming empowered in them because of their everyday concerns as mothers, wives, husbands, and fathers? Is political consumerist activity affecting society, economics, and politics? The next three sections address the general question of political agency and impact. This section discusses how a green political consumerist agenda has affected the SNF and its members by opening up new ways of becoming involved in environmental issues. The next section focuses on the role of women as new environmental actors. In the final section, I offer general comments on the impact of the eco-label on Sweden in political, social, and economical terms.

The SNF is a mature, well-established social movement from 1909. As its name implies, nature conservation was the reason for its creation. As environmental pollution increasingly threatened nature conservation, the SNF began to focus on environmental issues. It called on government to regulate industrial pollution. In typical Swedish fashion, it wanted government action to target production.[43] Environmental public policy and nature conservation were the two main profiles of the association from the 1960s to the mid-1980s. During this period, its main agenda expanded from nature and particularly forestry conservation to such environmental concerns as energy production and traffic policy. It has opposed the use of nuclear power and encouraged the development of alternative sources of energy to replace both nuclear power and fossil fuels. Up until the decision to focus on green political consumerism, the association viewed industry more as a problem than part of environmental solutions. It sought government action to force industry to improve its environmental standards. An important organizational method of action was, therefore, pressure on government and political parties to enact environmental legislation to regulate industry. This "command and control" approach to the regulation of industry (see chapter 3) was complemented by public awareness campaigns. Carefully crafted issue campaigns were important here, and the SNF staff has traditionally included a number of journalists whose primary task is to create more public interest and awareness for environmental issues. Organizational action involved mobilizing citizens to join environmental associations, consider green issues in elections, and pressure group politics. Its focus was the political system.

If environmental concerns were the first paradigmatic change for the association, green political consumerism was its second. The SNF calls its political consumerist activities its third important method of action.[44] The paradigmatic shift means that it accepts the ecological modernization view of environmental change, no longer views industry as the main enemy, and no longer focuses all its attention on mobilizing citizens in issue campaigns as a part of lobbying government to adopt environmental legislation. Green political consumerism opened up a new arena, the market, for organizational activity. It also has given the association a new agenda and spirit, which helped to mobilize environmentally conscious citizens, some of whom became members. It has been estimated that green consumerism initially attracted 1,000 new members per week.[45] This is an example of the political agency of political consumerism. Figure 4.1 shows the SNF membership level over the past 25 years. As shown in survey date (see endnote 84), some of the increases in membership in the mid-1980s to early 1990s are attributed to the new green political consumerist focus. Unfortunately, the data does not allow us to assess the exact proportion of the increase and there is no other material to use as proxy measures.

Not all consumers and citizens reached by the SNF green political consumerist efforts (its book, boycott, and green lists) became members of the association. This is clear from a comparison of the number of members with the number of books sold, participants in boycotts, and users of green lists. Some engaged citizens, those very characteristic of individualized collective action, just used the green political consumer lists and chose products with the association's eco-label on their daily shopping trips or contacted the Good Environmental Choice unit if they found that manufacturers were using the eco-label improperly on products or in advertising or that new products deemed environmentally harmful were appearing on store shelves.[46] The focus on green political consumerism has created an everyday-maker market-based environmentalist movement that is not really visible if attention is solely directed at documenting membership fluctuations and the SNF's activities per se. This more individualized collective action environmental movement

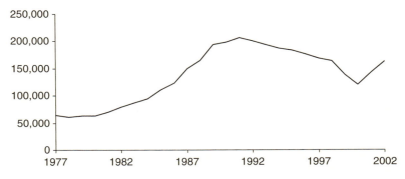

Figure 4.1   Membership in Society for Nature Conservation, 1977–2002.

shows the agency of political consumerism spurred on by the SNF's organization activity.

The political agency spinning off the eco-label and the smart shopping book has not always benefited the association directly. On occasion the SNF has viewed this individualized environmental collective activism as problematic because it is difficult to direct and control organizationally.[47] It is in part a kind of consumer mobilization that does not necessarily offer the SNF sufficient organizational paybacks, as envisioned in the policy paper discussed earlier. Membership levels, as shown in figure 4.1, have not increased steadily because of green political consumerism. In fact, they have even fallen because some people seem to be drawing the conclusion that membership does not do more to improve the environment than their everyday green political consumerist behavior (green shopping and recycling). Everyday individualized activism is, therefore, a threat to membership organizations that build their strength on collectivistic collective action. Another problematic aspect for the association is that local everyday-making environmental activism requires a core of dedicated, green political consumer activists. These people are not necessarily and easily socialized in organizational settings and do not always show loyalty to general organizational causes. They often find it difficult to work within established political homes like civil society associations, which they tend to view as sluggish, awkward, inflexible organizational structures unable to mobilize for spontaneous, urgent, and focused actions. Thus, there is, as discussed about boycotts, a wild side to Swedish green political consumerism that can be difficult to channel through established environmental organizations.

Basing environmental efforts on political consumerism may even be risky. It need not always represent a commitment to sustainable development. For example, research in psychology shows that people tend to have a fragmented view of political consumerist involvement. They are not loyal political consumers. Rather they buy some eco-labeled products but not others.[48] Price may be a factor here. The implication is that people not dedicated to environmentalism, through for example involvement in membership organizations, do not necessarily view political consumerism as a behavioral or an ideologically encompassing commitment. Instead it can represent a fragile serial identity. Nor does green political consumerism always translate into thrift in the use of nature's resources. Political consumers do not always think about consumer needs and sustainable consumption levels. Thus, the SNF is concerned that green buying and green activism are becoming separate environmental identities. The fear is that people believe that they do not need to think about sustainable development and their consumption patterns as long as they buy environmentally friendly goods. They can buy as much as they want as long as the products are eco-labeled.[49] Eco-labeling detached from other concerns can potentially disenable an ideologically driven environmental association.

A final problem that the SNF has experienced with its green political consumerist profile involves contacts within the global environmental movement. Some environmental associations believe that green political consumerism and ecological modernization are turning the SNF into an association that, because of its contacts with industry, no longer places tough environmental demands on the political system.[50] Particularly the Danish and German environmental associations have a skeptical view of the SNF's cooperative ventures with industry. They wonder at times whether conflict with industry is not the better route for environmental improvement.[51] They see the SNF as a "greenwash" organization (see chapter 5 for an explanation of the term). Problems of this kind have led to internal criticism and questions about the continued existence of Good Environmental Choice.[52]

At the same time, SNF officials are aware of the political agency embedded in green political consumerism. The SNF's efforts have made it feasible for members and nonmembers to take personal responsibility daily in implementing the general goals of the association and to see that their actions matter.[53] It has given the association a renewed identity and the opportunity to work in a new arena, the consumer market, which is becoming increasingly important as a central sphere for global political activity. An article in the organizational magazine *Sveriges Natur* explains the importance of individual environmental responsibility-taking in the present situation characterized by fast moving economic globalization and slow moving political globalization: "Our increasingly complex political steering of society is on the wane, and the market is taking over at the helm. The market is all of us—you and me—when we choose how to use our money."[54]

This insight explains why green political consumerism has over the years become a more important associational activity. By late 1980s it was one of the four central areas given priority.[55] The SNF is becoming representative of the new wave of the consumer movement mentioned in chapter 3 that focuses on issues of consumer behavior and sustainability. The number of green political consumerist issues discussed at the SNF council meetings has risen over the years, and it has grown in importance as a feature of the association's magazine, a notable change because the magazine reflects the priorities of the association. A 1991 study of what people read in *Sveriges Natur* showed that green political consumerism was becoming just as important as the traditional kind of articles on nature.[56] The magazine which has a National Geographic or nature conservation character has even included a political consumerist section for children as a way of teaching the relationship between consumer choice and sustainable development. Articles have taken up such issues as what to do about stopping fishermen from killing dolphins caught in tuna nets, how to assess soft drink packages, which form of transportation should be chosen for traveling different distances, and how to save on paper use.[57]

Green political consumerism is still a high priority. It has survived as an organizational priority even when the SNF has decided to narrow its thematic focus, not increase its allocation of the SNF budget, and members question whether market-based "beyond compliance" strategies can match state-oriented "command and control" policy in solving environmental problems.[58] It is viewed as a central aspect of sustainable development, and emphasis is put on the responsibility of each citizen to develop good environmental consumer habits, consider their ecological footprints, and practice a sustainable lifestyle.[59] More effort is made to tie in or mainstream green political consumerism with traditional activities of the association. Individuals are, for instance, encouraged to buy eco-labeled electricity because it saves otters when power plants are discouraged from damming more rivers,[60] to use paper sparingly, and to purchase eco-labeled paper because it helps save Swedish forests.[61] More traditionally SNF member networks and the Buy and Act Environmentally network are encouraged to work together in common projects.

The political agency of green political consumerism is shown in other ways as well. It has opened up new ways for members to participate in their association and reinforced the importance of the local associational base as an arena for member activity.[62] Members have been very innovative and spontaneous in their ways of revitalizing the local associational units and forging contacts between themselves and consumer market actors. Some of their activities are supermarket evaluations, yearly environmentally friendly weeks, and the national member network Buy and Act Environmentally.

Many local society chapters have participated in evaluating neighborhood supermarkets. Evaluating neighborhood supermarkets was started spontaneously by a few members dedicated to green political consumerism and is representative of more individualized collective action. The idea caught on, became institutionalized, and was an increasingly popular activity most probably because it gave members and nonmembers a concrete, everyday-making result-oriented task. Also, it engaged people from different walks of life and age groups.[63] At most 2,000 supermarkets were audited in one year.[64] Many local chapter activists have developed a good rapport with local supermarket managers. In certain areas, green political consumer activists have been invited into stores to answer questions and inform customers about eco-labeling.[65] The evaluation checklists formed the basis for awarding green supermarkets a diploma. Green political consumers checked supermarkets for environmentally friendly and environmentally dangerous products. In 1992 they were encouraged to pay particular attention to the presence of chlorine and the washing detergent Via on supermarket shelves. Consumers were encouraged to boycott these products, and supermarkets with these products received minus points in the evaluations.[66] Supermarkets that stopped selling chlorine were listed in the associational magazine in 1993 and 1994.[67] Over the years these grassroots, street-level evaluators have also counted the number of KRAV-labeled foods and Good Environmental Choice–labeled goods. Each year one or more supermarkets are chosen as Sweden's most environmentally friendly store. The storeowner receives a diploma at an awards ceremony. The local press and the SNF associational magazine cover the ceremony, which gives the stores good, free publicity. Manufacturers take note.[68] Supermarkets use the SNF diploma in their advertisements.

Interestingly enough, anyone—not just members—concerned with green political consumerism could use the Society's supermarket evaluation form. Not only is this kind of involvement low threshold in character because it does not require membership or meeting attendance, it shows how the SNF opened up its green political consumerist network for the general public. These individualized collective actors used the SNF as a base for their own environmental work. The high level of involvement in this activity initially overwhelmed Good Environmental Choice and forced it to develop more standardized green auditing techniques that include a life-cycle approach. The new more encompassing scheme is called Good Environmental Choice Supermarket Choice.[69] It was first used in 1998. Nine supermarkets received awards in 1999, and today the entire chain of Coop Forum stores are eco-labeled.[70]

Giving awards to the best supermarkets is not the only green political consumer member and nonmember activity. Environmentally Friendly

Weeks have taken place every year since early 1989. Each year has its own theme, one that has been agreed upon after deliberation within the unit. The slogans for the themes are carefully crafted to receive public attention. "Dethrone King Edward" was the 2002 theme slogan. King Edward is not the Swedish King but the name of a potato that requires the use of pesticides because of its sensitive nature. Examples of other yearly themes are Save the Forest's Life (a joint effort with the national SNF campaign on forests), why Swedes should eat lamb, the relationship between food consumption and the environment, the life cycle of bananas, unnecessary packages for supermarket goods, and the relationship between energy and food consumption.

In the time period of this case study (1980–2000), more people were involved in the yearly week than any other single SNF activity. Involved actors are consumers, SNF members, network members, journalists, politicians, and market actors. The week fills two purposes: it shows what individuals can do on an everyday basis for the environment and gives the SNF publicity. The week is well-orchestrated and planned well in advance. Local chapters decide for themselves how to set up the campaign week in their neighborhood. They request campaign materials from the Good Environment Choice unit. In the past, supermarket auditing was included in the week's activities. Most chapters participate in the yearly campaign week, and the local press covers the events.[71]

Consumer and member dedication to Good Environmental Choice has given it the support it needed to develop into a popular and respected green political consumerist institution that has expanded its expertise in product labeling. Now it has criteria for evaluating means of transportation and puts its seal of approval on environmentally friendly ones. The Swedish Railroad was the first means of transportation to apply and receive the eco-label.[72] It also has developed criteria for evaluating building maintenance and labels environmentally friendly producers of electricity. Deregulation in the energy field in 1996 opened up this area for environmental activity. Green electricity accounted for roughly 20 percent of all electricity production in 1998 and the sale of green electricity increased over 50 percent in the next few years.[73] Today it accounts for 10 percent of the selling market.[74] Reflecting a trend toward synthesis or harmonization discussed in chapter 3, the unit also cooperates with KRAV, TCO Development, discusses the environmental politics of coffee, bananas, and so on, and offers links to the fair trade movement. The Buy and Act Environmentally unit is involved in ventures to help other countries imitate its institutional design and develop green political consumerism. It has cooperative agreements today with Estonia and Poland.[75] The Good Environmental Choice label is even seen as a prototype in discussions on gender labeling in Sweden.[76]

The SNF's experiences with green political consumerism have also led it to view market actors as interesting cooperative partners and the market as a feasible arena for environmental policymaking. It has participated in working groups to develop Swedish forest stewardship certification criteria; a considerable proportion of productive Swedish forests (45 percent) are now classified as FSC forests.[77] Good Environmental Choice uses FSC forest materials as one of its criteria for labeling paper, and it includes FSC materials in its criteria for green electricity.[78] This is another way in which labeling schemes support each other. It has also begun to ask employees to put pressure on their companies to take greater responsibility for global warming. An Internet feature allows consumers to request information on environmental responsible investing, thus promoting SRI in Sweden.

The SNF has been effective in improving environmental standards with its market-based focus.[79] In some cases, as with certain mercury batteries, the environmental struggle is considered to have been won. These batteries are no longer an associational priority. The situation is different for other products like chlorine-bleached paper and household chemicals. Here the SNF sees the need for continued green political consumer diligence and associational pressure.[80] Manufacturers have also mobilized against eco-labeling schemes; there is concern at the Good Environmental Choice unit that the EU will push for a European standard based on the EU-Flower label, an eco-labeling scheme that the unit characterizes as confusing and ineffective, and that the WTO will make it more difficult for nationally based eco-labels to exist alongside regulations against barriers to free trade.[81]

This section shows that there is political agency in political consumerism, which can be harnessed by both individuals and groups. Even when consideration is given to its side effects, political consumerism has benefited the SNF. It has helped it hold its own in the ever-changing Swedish society and created a new profile for the association with an outreach broader than many of its traditional activities. Green political consumerism has facilitated partnerships with market actors and created new settings for dialogue with market forces at the global, national, regional, and local levels. Its everyday approach to solving environmental problems has appealed to new groups of citizens seeking low threshold, hands-on involvement with concrete issues that can be worked on in immediate, everyday ways and settings. Its local orientation encourages community building across regional and political lines. The consumer orientation put the SNF on the global map of non governmental organizations. Its success has been viewed as a role model for other national eco-labeling schemes. The eco-labeling scheme shows that political consumerism at least in certain settings and circumstances is a viable tool to manage environmental problems. The European Environmental Bureau, a nongovernmental organization working within the EU, offered the following assessment of Good Environmental Choice in 1999:

> Eco-labelling has made Sweden the world champion in environmental quality of cleaning agents used and the shining example of the effectiveness of eco-labelling at the same time. The Soap Industry has responded to the continuous pressure exerted by ever stricter eco-label criteria and has been very well able to cope with it. . . . After eight years 90 percent of all household detergents are labelled and the amount used has decreased by 15 percent. During this time, 45 percent of the used chemicals were replaced with less problematic ones and another 15 percent completely eliminated. . . . EEB would like the European Commission to insist on a much more meaningful policy . . . building upon Swedish experience, set stricter targets to be achieved within a given time-frame, and apply a transparent monitoring mechanism. . . .[82]

MIDDLE-CLASS WOMEN AS GREEN POLITICAL CONSUMER AGENTS

One of the most exciting results from the case study of Good Environmental Choice in the 1980s and 1990s is the impact of green political consumerism on creating new member activism in the SNF. Green political consumerism has not only empowered the SNF. It has also empowered members by giving them a new channel for involvement. The everyday-making approach has brought the SNF closer to local Swedish communities and residents in local communities closer to each other. It has encouraged partnership between members, local government, and local business. A relationship has been forged through the dialogue among these actors and their everyday involvements in concrete activities. This has created both a bridging kind of trust between different groups and an internal bonding trust within the SNF political consumerist network.[83]

A crucial group of members in these settings is middle-aged and middle-class women. The membership statistics discussed in the previous section show a dramatic increase in members in the 1980s and early 1990s, but unfortunately it is not possible to receive exact information on the number of women members. An estimate of the number of new women members is given in an attitudinal survey, which indicates that more women than men joined the SNF in these years. The survey indicates that many women became members because they wanted to work with green consumer issues.[84] The book "Act and Buy Environmentally," institutionalization of the eco-label, and creation of the Act and Buy Environmentally member network in 1990 gave them an institutional home for involvement in their issues. Before green political consumerism became an activity, women members were rather invisible in the SNF. Organizational tradition catered more to men. Men with a background in the natural sciences dominated the organization numerically, and their understanding of nature conservation had been given primacy in the association. Even the main issues of the association (forest conservation, energy production and use, and traffic problems) tended to reflect male priorities. Green political consumerism as an associational priority began to improve the visibility of women. By 2000 about 80 percent of all new members were women.[85]

The network Act and Buy Environmentally has given women an organizational setting for green political activism. In the period under study, the network was one of the most popular and successful networks in the association. Organizational networks allow members to work on their priority issues outside their local chapter because they bring together members interested in particular issues from all over the country. The Act and Buy Environmentally network is dominated by women. Material collected on it for the time period under study shows that an overwhelming number of its contact people are women.[86] Women members have used the green political consumerist network well. They are reported as stating that the network makes them feel useful, and, as indicated earlier, the local network branches are very active in promoting everyday green political consumerism in their local communities. Women in smaller communities have often been very involved, and they keep in touch with network members nationally via the Internet and intranet conferences.[87]

What is particularly interesting about these women is that they differ considerably from typical SNF members, and they follow a pattern of involvement for women found in other Nordic associations.[88] The SNF women active during the period of the case study are reported as being extremely interested in the network and are visible, active, and social in it. Social interaction in the network is an important priority, and they enjoy working together in groups for green political consumer causes. They would most likely score high on tests of such civic skills as organizing meetings and public speaking. This ability quite probably explains the popularity or success of the yearly Environmentally Friendly Week. At the same time they tend to be rather unconcerned about and uninterested in general SNF politics. As related by officials at the Good Environmental Choice unit and other SNF officials, these women are not interested in the Society's parliamentary affairs or procedural organizational democracy.[89] Their commitment to the organization is somewhat subpolitical, and they can be said to represent a special kind of late modern serial identity that allows them to focus on certain organizational activities while ignoring others.[90]

These women green political consumer activists fit many of the characterizations of postmodernization. They are consumer-oriented, concerned about the environment, unconcerned about organizational status, and uninterested in institutional hierarchies. The network is important for them because it gives them influence over their everyday lives and a forum for taking responsibility for future generations. They want this everyday influence but not organizational status or power. In this sense, they question the male priorities that have dominated the SNF.[91] Good Environmental Choice network women members can be contrasted to the typical male member who tends to be older in age, a loner, oriented toward the natural sciences, and more concerned about organizational status. His focus is also more on nature conservation per se and although a loner he is more involved with collectivist collective action, as reflected in concerns about organizational status. He may even question whether green political consumerism is really an environmental concern.[92]

SNF officials are aware of these differences and attempt to bridge them in various ways, for instance by formulating themes for the Environmentally Friendly Week that bring nature conservationists and green political consumers together in working groups. In the past they used amusing characterizations for the two groups. The men were called "beetle-bug geezers" (*skalbaggsgubbar*) for their focus on nature conservation and fragmented view of environmental life-cycle assessments. They were characterized as driving their cars out into the forest to look at bugs without reflection on the environmental effects of driving a vehicle powered by fossil fuels on the health of the bugs, the forest, and the environment in general.[93] The women were called "plastic-cup protesting women" (*plastmugstanter*) for their intense concentration on very concrete everyday use of products and everyday issues as leaving ecological footprints and impacting the global ecological balance. The differences between men and women that have come to the surface because of green consumerism in the SNF are reflected in the character of the Good Environmental Choice itself, which is dominated by women. Unlike other activity areas, most of the people on the unit staff are women, and most people who apply for positions at the unit are women.[94]

From this case study, it can be concluded that it seems that green political consumerism appeals more to women than men, as discussed in chapter 1, due to their different perceptions of environmental risks and that green political consumerism as a tool used by civil society associations seems to suit women more than men. This finding is substantiated by attitudinal research reported earlier, which shows women as predominant users of labeling schemes (see chapter 3).

MARKET-BASED BRIDGING AND BONDING: A NEW EVOLVING SWEDISH MODEL?

TCO Development, KRAV, the success of FSC in Sweden, and the Act and Buy Environmentally effort of the SNF shows clearly that political consumerism can be a new way of doing environmental politics in this small Northern European country. As such, it refocuses the venue of the political struggle from the political system to the marketplace. Environmental policymaking is no longer only the prerogative of legislative chambers, the offices of ministries and public agencies, and courtrooms. It concerns the manufacturing of products and corporate policy and is the prerogative of actors wanting to use the market as an arena for politics. Boycotts and labeling schemes politicize the manufacturing of products. The hands-on consumer involvement in the form of family shopping choices, dialogue with store managers, and yearly political consumerist weeks discussed in this chapter is a kind of market-based political lobbying at the most grassroots level imaginable. It involves daily routines performed by almost every person in society. And it shows that consumption is more than a private matter. The case study reported in this chapter illustrates well how private consumption has become a political issue.

The SNF's efforts are a particularly good example of the impact of consumer awareness and involvement in politicized market affairs. They show how green political consumerism can improve and enhance member involvement, lead to a renewal of civil society associations, and play an important part in environmental risk management. Political parties, the Cabinet ministry, business people, public agencies, and other civil society associations have taken notice.

Market-based environmental action in the form of the SNF eco-label and other efforts have facilitated new manufacturing practices and changed the chemical composition in batteries, papers, soaps, shampoos, detergents, cleaners, and so on in a more environmental direction, which are having a positive environmental impact. Its product selection is growing in size, and its eco-labeled products are now mainstreamed and sold in all large supermarkets and have a respectable and increasing market share. Most likely many shoppers do not even realize that they are choosing an eco-labeled product in their daily trips to the market.

Political consumerism is a controversial subject for the SNF. Some members argue that the main focus of the association should be on promoting a production-orientation "polluter pays principle." Others emphasize the importance of a consumption-oriented green political consumer strategy. More research is necessary on this and other examples of Swedish political consumerism as well as those from other countries to assess the involvement and impact of the SNF effort more fully. Also, the general political agency of political consumerism has yet to be determined. In particular, scholars should follow the efforts underway in the fair trade, no sweat movement, which is currently mobilizing considerable support among younger people and influencing global perceptions of free trade.

Yet with our current state of limited knowledge, it seems reasonable to conclude that the SNF effort is rather unique for Sweden and the rest of the world. Global actors see it as a unique civil society, member-driven, market-based labeling scheme. Many other national-based eco-labeling schemes are run by government and lack the public support of Good Environmental Choice.[95] Also, unlike most eco-labels currently in operation, it creates arenas for action. As discussed earlier, Act and Buy Environmentally has created arenas in local settings in towns and cities as well as a national network for members to come together to meet and discuss green political consumerism. This is its bonding function. It has also created new settings for political action in a time when citizens find conventional channels of participation less appealing.[96] It has opened up political space for women. The yearly buy and act environmentally weeks have created small, very local political consumer communities that express values held by other groups in Sweden and across the globe. The created arenas have given concerned citizen-consumers a site to express their postmaterialistic values and a setting for their subpolitical more individualized involvement, an opportunity that conventional politics has not yet been able to offer citizens. Also, as already alluded to and discussed further in the concluding chapter, these kinds of involvements are creating social capital and societal trust.

Another highly interesting aspect of the SNF's involvement in green political consumerism is the contacts that it has had with industry since the mid-1980s. Earlier in this chapter, these contacts were analyzed in terms of trends toward ecological modernization. The SNF played a brokerage or bridging role, which encouraged groups to build new coalitions with new steering capacities, as exemplified by the Good Environmental Choice eco-label. These contacts between opposites—environmental activists and industry officials—are reminiscent of the corporatist contacts between labor and capital that laid the basis for the Swedish welfare state.[97] Embedded in a Swedish context the contacts between the SNF and industry may even be seen as the initial efforts in creating a new Swedish model, the flagship of Swedish political culture.

Before the Swedish model became a way of characterizing the Swedish welfare state, it was used to explain the partnership or cooperation between labor and capital. Unions and employer associations did not agree on labor market issues, and they demonstrated their disagreements contentiously in strikes and lockouts. They knew that they as labor market actors were dependent on each other and began to realize that contentious behavior was not improving their respective situations. Cooperative endeavors began from the late 1920s. The formative event was the signing of the Agreement of Saltsjöbad, a cooperative venture between the dominant central organization for working-class labor, the Swedish Trade Union Council (LO), and the dominant central organization for employers, the Swedish Employers' Association (SAF). The agreement concerned the politics of products—unionization rights, unemployment, and business profits—and the state's need for labor peace to increase public revenues. It was a partnership among former enemies who had tested each other's strength in strikes and lockouts without any one side being declared a winner. State threats to intervene in the labor market with regulatory legislation encouraged these countervailing powers to sit together and have a meeting.[98] Organized capital and labor were both opposed to state intervention in the labor market. It was, therefore, in their self-interest to cooperate. These two strong labor market actors had different goals but labor peace was the means for them to reach their goals. The representatives of labor were concerned about unemployment and wages while those of capital wanted businesses to make a profit. Strikes and lockouts were counterproductive for these goals. Labor peace could lead to jobs, higher wages, profits, and public revenues in the form of taxes for the state. The Saltsjöbad agreement paved the way for decades of labor market peace that were duly noted internationally. Labor market actors from other countries began to visit Sweden to learn from the experience. The agreement also established cross-sphere cooperative ventures as a viable way to improve society.[99] The culture of cooperation that the agreement created became the hallmark of modern capitalism in Sweden. Its roots were the ability of conflicting powerful actors to bring themselves to a negotiating table. It was the Swedish model of first modernity (see chapter 1 for a discussion of the term modernity).

The establishment of Good Environmental Choice can be interpreted as an imitation or a reproduction of a key aspect of Swedish political culture, namely the bridging of interests of opposites through dialogue, deliberation, and mutual strength and respect. It is one of the key institutions in the creation of what I venture to call the Swedish Model of environmental peace. This "late modernity" Swedish model shows how cooperation among conflicting and powerful actors is creating compromise and stability in environmental affairs. The actors involved in these discussion rounds are different from those in industrial society times, whose orientation was production not consumption, and just like their predecessors, who did not always agree on all details and suggested ways of solving problems, they are willing to engage in deliberation together. One set of groups reflects the postindustrial values of green political consumers and environmental associations and represents a consumption orientation. They meet with another set of groups, the manufacturers and retailers catering to consumer society, to discuss the green politics of products. The state is also present, though its role differs somewhat from the one it played in the making of labor peace. It may threaten with "command and control" politics, and it also plays a supportive, parameter-defining function. Its environmental legislation sets an important normative parameter for the cooperative agreements, political parties supportive of the environmental cause are in Parliament and government, and the SNF has been able to use existing public policy as a baseline for its formulation of green criteria for labeling. Government policy has, thus, created a forum for discussion on green political consumerist endeavors, and it has had many of the SNF environmental issues, including chlorine-bleached paper and the greening of energy, on its political agenda. On occasion the state has granted financial support (seed money) to start green consumerist projects. At the same time, it has the ear of industry. Most importantly, it has given legitimacy to green consumerist market-based labeling schemes through both its own procurement practices as an institutional consumer and the praise it has given the SNF's eco-labeling and other schemes.

Although SNF officials recognize the support that government has given market-based environmental regulation, they have not always been pleased with the positive assessment given by government. They see this praise as a way for government to avoid taking political responsibility for serious environmental problems by passing the buck on the regulation of industry from hard law to soft law, that is, to voluntary compliance in negotiations between civil society actors and business institutions. Also, they express the belief that government should be responsible for operating eco-labels, not civil society,[100] as is common practice in most other European countries.[101] There is, as mentioned earlier, a strong commitment to political system–oriented environmental policy within the SNF that questions the power of consumer-oriented approaches.

In the long run, active government involvement in the first-modernity Swedish model of labor market peace was not a successful venture. It changed the balance of power among the labor unions and employers' associations, which politicized the labor market ideologically, led to legislative measures that irritated the interest of capital, which decided to take action to dismantle corporatism, and even weakened the grassroots base of labor.[101] Ecological modernization is also based on opposites finding common ground through dialogue, deliberation, and focused problem-solving. It is similar to the Swedish model because political values and market forces define its parameters. Time will tell if more active government involvement is necessary for the Good Environmental Choice eco-label or whether old regulatory tools (legislation) begin to replace new ones (market-based schemes). The parameters for a civil society generated and a market-based labeling scheme that is national in orientation are rapidly changing in the present decade of increased economic and political regional globalization of Europe. Perhaps the emerging late modernity Swedish model of environmental peace represented by the "Agreement of Good Environmental Choice" will need to be complemented or replaced by a more proactive governmental presence now that the parameters for market-based cooperative ventures are changing.

5

SHOPPING WITH AND FOR VIRTUES

WHY VIRTUES TODAY?

Virtues are generic benchmarks to help us navigate in the debates on what is good and bad, right and wrong, and who are them and us. They have always played a role in politics, community, and in economic and private life.[1] We use virtues as a basis for passing judgment on politicians, company owners, people we meet in brief but frequent daily encounters, and in family relations. Virtues and ethics are again a public focus because we sense that social, political, and economic interactions have changed and this threatens the roots and values embedded in our political, economic, and social communities. The shifts to globalization, individualization, postmodernization, risk society, and governance discussed in chapter 1 make us ponder about the quality of political, social, and economic life and make us aware that our communities are local, national, regional, and global in orientation. The shifts also imply that today more responsibility is put on individuals to formulate their own conceptions of right and wrong.[2] Good responsibility-taking requires the use of virtues.

An important finding reported in this book is that we now see a new sharing of responsibility for setting moral standards among the political, economic, and private spheres. A consequence of the political landscape changes—governance, globalization, individualization, postmodernization, and reflexive modernization—is that it is no longer possible to make sharp distinctions between politics, economics, and private life. This means that we as individuals cannot assume that we have taken sufficient responsibility for ensuring a good life and a sustainable future by voting in elections and paying fees to membership associations. The complexities of contemporary life have broadened the meaning of the term political. Our everyday conduct crosses the divide between politics, economics, and private life and, as reflected in the footprint metaphor, this crossover is increasingly important for our understanding of politics.

Virtues help people understand the importance of their everyday lives for other people's daily existence. Classic character virtues help people formulate their more individualized philosophy of life and apply their life philosophies in the different spheres in a coherent fashion.[3] These virtues appear in the phenomenon of political consumerism. This book has discussed in different ways how political consumerism is developing as an ethical guideline for citizens to take responsibility in our more complex, risk-filled, globalized world. Whether in the form of boycotts or buycotts, political consumerism brings virtues to the marketplace and into everyday consumer choices. Consumers in growing numbers shop with and for virtues. They make consumer choices on the basis of their virtues, and boycott and buycott campaigns encourage people to demand that virtues are present in marketplace transactions. Virtues are used to assess the politics behind the products sold in the global marketplace. But just like any other public or private activity, political consumerism is not necessarily only a virtuous phenomenon. The anti-Jewish boycott in the 1930s shows how vices can be practiced in shopping situations, and the Disney boycott illustrates well how political consumerist activities can include both virtues and vices. It is also the case that virtues can be understood differently. People may, as exemplified by the boycotts against Jewish merchants by African Americans, discussed in chapter 2, take their own situation as the point of departure for evaluating justice and fairness.

Yet what is interesting with the phenomenon of political consumerism is its normative stance that virtues should be embedded in market transactions. Democratic political consumerism is a virtue-practicing activity. As such, it is an example of *phronesis*: virtues in action in everyday settings.[4] Both classical and civic virtues are in play. We see the classical virtues of courage, uprightness, moderation, and fair-mindedness in many of the examples discussed in chapters 2–4. These classical character traits are crucial in situations in which citizens take more responsibility in their own hands. They are what Tocqueville would perhaps have called necessary virtues for the right kind of self-interest and what Shelly Burtt, the political philosopher discussed in chapter 1, would view as essential traits for a non-privatist understanding of self-interest. Scholars of postmodernization and reflexive modernization would define them as the core of individualization. Uprightness and fair-mindedness place self-interest in a broader context. They allow people to embed their concerns in societal and public concerns without requiring that they renounce their self-interests entirely. Uprightness and fair-mindedness are the basis of the private virtue tradition of political consumerism, which begins with the individual's own personal needs and activities to promote them.

Other classical virtues can be found in the phenomenon of political consumption. Empathy means that individuals identify with other persons or try to put themselves in the other person's situation. A more modern translation is perhaps solidarity and social justice, which imply that people contextualize their situation before making a final decision on actions. This action may, for instance, involve a shopping choice of sports shoes for their family. Empathy implies an act of balancing a self-orientation with an other-orientation in situations of choice. At times consumers need information to embed their choices in this fashion, which as discussed in chapter 3 can come in the form of labeling schemes and advice on socially responsible investing. Empathy, social justice, and solidarity are the basis of the public virtue tradition of political consumerism. In this tradition, consumers begin with concerns for the situation of other people and then attempt to find necessary products that reflect their concern for the plight of others.

Moderation is another classic virtue that we see in the phenomenon of political consumerism. It is an important fundament of the footprint metaphor of sustainable consumption. Perhaps the virtue of moderation is best expressed as the thriftiness side of green political consumerism. Chapter 4 discusses how Swedish consumers are taught that there are products not worthy of eco-labeling and that they need to make choices about how much of what to consume. Sustainable development, which can probably be viewed as a postmodern translation of the virtue of moderation, demands that people rethink their level of consumption.

A virtue that we increasingly find in political consumerist settings is patience, which too is a modernized version of moderation. Patience requires citizens to understand that their ethical expectations on the marketplace take time to implement. Their sense of urgency for individualized action may not have an immediate impact, but individual actions are still necessary for the process to continue in the right direction. Expectations may concern more environmental production methods, changes in corporate policy and practices, and even implementation of decided-upon criteria throughout an entire chain of production. Website after website stresses the need for consumers to persist in their actions even in the face of minor and major setbacks. The desire for fast results—impatience—is similar to the vice of greediness. Patience can, therefore, be seen as a kind of constant generosity with one's time, expectations, and financial resources.

Even other classical virtues come into play in political consumerism. Honesty implies that people tell the truth and do not hide their feelings and actions from other people. In political consumerism, it is perhaps not so much individual consumers who need to exercise the virtue of honesty. Rather producers of products and the institutions that run labeling schemes, stewardship certifications, and socially responsible investments must do so. Honest producers provide truthful information on the contents of their products, corporate policy, and in their marketing efforts. Honesty also implies that the producers follow the instructions of labeling schemes once they are certified and do not try to fool the public with less truthful claims about their products. Honesty in this setting is more a virtue that applies to those collective actors responsible for the politics of products. Dishonesty does not pay, as illustrated by the actions taken by political consumers against corporations and other political consumerist actors who have not really been truthful to their obligations. Poignant examples are found in the continued Nestlé boycotts and in criticism of Nike for its earlier claims that it had improved its offshore working conditions.

Transparency and trustworthiness are important character traits for corporations and political consumerist institutions. They are modernized versions of the virtue of honesty and the basis of their public legitimacy.[5] Transparency means that corporations must open their company doors to the interested public and give them information on the ingredients in their products and their production methods. Labeling schemes must publicize their evaluating criteria and ensure consumers that their criteria are legitimate. Often this means that they invite all shareholders to help formulate criteria, give the public access to information on their criteria, and do not have hidden ties with the producers to whom they grant labeling licenses. If political consumerist institutions call boycotts, they need to ensure the public that they have checked all the facts and make an honest assessment about the politics of the product. Their assessment of the situation must be trustworthy. Otherwise their goodwill or honest reputation will be tarnished, as Greenpeace learned the hard way in its 1995 boycott of the Shell Oil Company for its plans to destroy an oil platform at sea. Greenpeace was so eager to condemn Shell Oil that it overstated its case, that is, it did not have a complete factual basis for its claims. It conceded to what we may call here the temptations of the vice of greediness (impatience, eagerness, and wanting publicity) in its zeal to gain attention for its cause. Many boycotts lack in this and other virtues. Perhaps a lack of virtues explains why boycotts are so contentious and difficult to use as a tool in political consumerist collective action.

The virtue of wisdom is also found in political consumerism. Wisdom is a synthesis of other virtues, a kind of meta-virtue. Wise

people balance the virtues of courage, uprightness, fair-mindedne
moderation, honesty, and empathy in their total assessments of the
actions of individuals, groups, corporations, and states. A modern
name for wisdom is knowledge, in the meaning of enlightened understanding. Every political consumer requires knowledge about the politics of a product—what the problem is, why it is a problem, and how
smart shopping can solve it. Knowledge is even necessary for citizens
to assess adequately whether labeling schemes, socially responsible
investing, codes of conduct, and so on are advantageous for democracy and whether their positions on different consumer choice issues
form a cohesive whole. Enlightened understanding is also important
for citizens to evaluate if political consumerist campaigns advertised
on the Internet should be supported or whether they represent false
claims of justice and ethics. Knowledge is necessary to assess whether
political consumerist activities show signs of effectiveness or not.

Virtues form the basis of democratic political consumerism. An
important part of political consumerist activity is the teaching of
virtues and their practice in daily consumer choice situations. The
political consumerist institutions discussed in this book focus on
informing the public about the political and ethical implications of
the products they purchase on a daily basis. They dedicate a considerable part of their resources to awareness training so that people
understand the global politics of products. Special campaigns, like the
ones on coffee and clothing, are started to help consumers understand what their choice entails for our common global future. The
campaigns' emphasis on fair play, solidarity, and moderation show
how they reach out to virtues as a way of framing their messages.

Virtues are also important because new regulatory tools as political consumerism must base their activities and institutions in a moral
understanding that meets with stakeholders' approval. This book
shows how virtues are the backbone or common ground for mutual
understanding of problems. They provide the basic or generic argument for why involved but diverse actors need to come together
to discuss mutual concerns. They also show what character traits are
necessary for successful dialog among these actors.

Political consumerism is evolving into a way of doing politics
in our more globalized, postmodern, governance-oriented, and individualized world. Virtues are necessary to develop a market-based
platform for development that balances and respects the demands
of political, economic, and private life. They are crucial for positive
political consumerism whose basis is inclusive dialogue among all
stakeholders, who have tended to view each other as adversaries with

ests. Virtues form the roots for the growth of trustful
ic discussed in the next section. They are also impor-
ping new role responsibilities and actor categories, as
the terms citizen-consumer, corporate citizenship,
ible investors, and private governments (see chapter 1).

RESPONSIBLE SHOPPING, SOCIAL CAPITAL, AND TRUST

Participation in political consumerist activities contributes to the political community in two important ways. It builds bridges across different groups in society and bonds likeminded people more closely. Bridging and bonding are two forms of social capital. They create trust that facilitates cooperation among people.[6] Brokerage, as discussed in chapter 1, is similar to bridging social capital. Involved actors are encouraged to build new coalitions to develop new steering capacities. We see both bridging and bonding social capital in the historical examples with the housewives' revolts as perhaps the most poignant example, in the designing of contemporary political consumerist institutions, and in the case study reported in chapter 4. Ecological modernization has also at its core bridging or brokerage community-building in that it encourages actors to create networks with other actors generally viewed as holding opposing views regarding environmentalism and sustainable development. The shareholder approach to problem-solving does this as well because all involved actors are encouraged to participate in discussions on how to identify common problems and participate in managing them.

Citizen involvement in political consumerism is initiated by everyday self-interest (private virtues) or concern about the everyday consumption of goods on our common well-being (public virtues). Collective action is needed to bring together actors representing the private virtue tradition of political consumerism with those representing the public virtue tradition. A good example is the collective action needed to develop forest stewardship certification as discussed in chapter 3. The actors representing the private virtue tradition of political consumerism were forest owners, furniture manufacturers, and the like. The actors representing the public virtue tradition were environmentalists and humanitarian groups. Once collective action united or bridged their private and public virtues a bond of trust was established and it became possible to develop the political consumerist institution of forest stewardship certification. This community building or coalition building reinforces the legitimacy or trustworthiness of the certification scheme because it is has as its base the virtues of honesty, uprightness, and fair-mindedness. Then it is up to everyday consumers to use these arrangements as consumer's guide. Consumer involvement is more like individualized collective action because consumers do not need to join together in groups to satisfy their own shopping needs, be they public or private in nature. All they need to do is rely on the labeling scheme.

Use of labeling schemes is not the only form of everyday political consumerism at the grassroots level. Political consumerist networks and movements encourage more active involvement on the part of citizens and consumers. People use political consumerism as a way to satisfy their need for social and political engagement. Social capital is present in these instances. The historical examples and the case study show the importance of social capital for political consumerism and the importance of political consumerism for social capital. Thus, political consumerism both needs and generates social capital.

Social capital can be viewed in different ways. A general, well-accepted view used in this book is the features of social organization that can improve the efficiency of society by facilitating coordinated actions.[7] Examples of such features that can be found in the literature are trust, norms, and networks. Social capital is frequently measured by membership and involvement in civil society associations.[8] Scholars believe that social capital is created in such groups and that they are necessary for cooperation among citizens for involvement in politics, society, and economics.[9] Social capital is, thus, necessary for democratic and sustainable development.[10]

An important finding from chapter 4 is that the presence of environmental associations was essential for the promotion of green political consumerism in Sweden. Research on other eco-labeling schemes' successes reports the same finding.[11] These associations were able to put green political consumerism on the civil society and political agenda and were able to help create public awareness about the environmental politics of products because they could mobilize their members in new cooperative ventures. The SNF was able to use its legitimacy in the environmental field—social capital at the aggregate level—to develop a green political consuming standard perceived as legitimate and trustworthy by large groups of people. Good Environmental Choice is also an example of a globally unique effort in political consumerism because it is entirely based in civil society. Most other schemes include state institutions as founding members. The case study reports how successful use of political consumerism builds upon the already accumulated and institutionalized social capital found in established civil society associations. In fact, the presence of social capital in Swedish civil society is an important explanation for the development of political consumerism in the country. Otherwise, as discussed in chapter 4, we would assume that a country with a strong proactive social democratic state would not need to use the market as an arena for politics. Thus social capital plays an enabling role in political consumerism. It is a platform for activity. This is a common finding in studies on social capital and political participation, which verifies theoretical discussions on the direction of the causal link between social capital and citizen engagement.[12]

What is interesting about political consumerism as illustrated in the examples in chapters 2–4 is that it also creates social capital. It is a platform for social capital. This means that the causal link between political consumerism and social capital goes in the opposite direction than the one described above and found in most studies. Political consumerism links individual citizens and actors together into newly created networks and institutions to pursue their self-interests or public interests. This is different from the brokerage function of social capital because they were not established groups with accumulated social capital that were bridged together into cooperative ventures. Neither does it just strengthen bonds among likeminded individuals. We see in chapters 2 and 4 how political consumerism creates cooperative settings, behaviors, and trust. Both the private and public virtue traditions play a role here. People were brought together because of family and public concerns. Qualities of the phenomenon of political consumerism such as its low-threshold character, blurring of the public/private divide, use of the market as an arena for politics, and concentration on products as political problems explain its ability to create social capital. Worries about consumer goods give people a reason to come together at their local supermarket, in civil society meeting rooms, and in online settings. People create bond with other people when they find that their private worries are shared by others. This creates a new identity, a serial identity as consumers caring about genetically modified food and chemical pesticides on potatoes. Political consumerism opens up new public space for citizens to base their cooperative endeavors in everyday concerns of what and where to shop. They do not need to be socialized into an association's ideology or apply for formal membership. Rather, cooperative efforts develop from everyday concerns and in more concrete, everyday, practical ways. These kinds of efforts, as shown in the chapters in this book, cross conventional political and social cleavages and they tie people together closely. In doing so, they create forums and networks for social interaction and trust. The forums may be completely new in the sense that they are independent from established political homes or new arenas within them.

Everyday political consumerism as well as the highly rational action-based constitutional community-building efforts illustrated by labeling schemes foster collaboration among bonding groups who are normally locked in conflict relationships or who have difficulty in understanding how collective action can benefit them personally. In the case of forestry labels, the opposing groups include indigenous peoples, environmentalists, forest owners, and furniture producers. For Good Environmental Choice such old adversaries as consumer and producer associations started joint projects. Even individual consumers and individual retailers have stopped mistrusting each other and work jointly to improve product assortment in the local supermarket. In the historical examples we found that women from different regions, social classes, religions, political persuasions, and ethnic groups formed networks to satisfy their everyday family needs. These examples show how political consumerism creates bridging social capital among diversified groups of people.

The trust-building and community-building function of political consumerism deserves more scholarly attention. We need to study more closely whether the creation of social capital by political consumerism is developing new actor categories and possibly new spheres of action, an issue raised in a later section in this chapter. We also need to penetrate further the role of women in the creation of political consumerist social capital. From the case study we learn that middle-class women play a crucial role in the creation of social capital through everyday political consumerism.

There are different ways of understanding the relationship between women and social capital in political consumerism. The first is the network character of political consumerism and women's attraction to networks as a form of action. As shown in the case study and in other research,[13] women find network structures a very appropriate and comfortable way to be involved in political, economic, and social life. Networks are based on dialogue and interaction, a kind of activity that research shows suits women well.[14] Networks can be contrasted with a more male-oriented activity like the signing of contracts, which also builds trust but does so in a regulated legal fashion, and formal organizational democracy. Networks are relevant for social capital because their informal character creates interpersonal trust. Theoretical and empirical research shows a close relationship between interpersonal trust building and more generalized or abstract trust,[15] which in my theoretical framework implies cross-sphere cooperation. The second explanation takes its point of departure in women's sensitivity to environmental risks, which as discussed theoretically in chapter 1 and studied empirically in chapter 4 means that they have a lower threshold for environmental problems than men. Women react more negatively to the use of pesticides and other poisonous substances on goods needed for their family. This triggers their engagement in green political consumerism. A third probable explanation is the time women (as opposed to men) spend on shopping for daily needs and the kind of responsibility they assume as opposed to men for the well-being of their families. This time allocation characterizes many countries.[16]

POLITICAL CONSUMERISM CRITICIZED

Political consumerism is controversial participative activity. As discussed in chapter 1, scholars find it questionable. But instead of arousing their academic curiosity as a "gold mine" for theoretical, methods-oriented, and empirical research, many scholars react politically. For some reason, they believe that scientific studies of political consumerism are political statements in themselves. This reaction is particularly common among American social scientists. They condemn the phenomenon of political consumerism as a right-wing, left-wing, or inconsequential political activity. This is indeed a surprising academic response given the American examples discussed in this book and the richness of the phenomenon as an area of study for the social sciences. Political consumerism and the market as an arena for politics should be studied in the current research focus on new forms of citizen involvement in politics and society and community building. Other important areas for research are outlined in the appendix.

Political consumerism is a political phenomenon that we have yet to study, interpret, and analyze fully. It provokes strong reactions for a variety of reasons. We do not know how to place it ideologically on a left-right continuum of political struggle, and it may well be the case as with other forms of more postmodern reflexive involvements that it cannot be placed in any one ideological camp. Political consumerism questions our conventional conceptions of the public/private divide. It takes a clear stand for an integration of the public and private sphere, as illustrated by the footprint metaphor used in sustainable development. That our private wants and desires as expressed in consumer choice have public significance is a controversial standpoint for many people. It signals a kind of individualized responsibility-taking for common well-being that challenges political ideological conceptions of the political. It means that politics is more than the doings of the political system and representative democracy, implying that private attitudes, choices, and behavior may have important political content and concern other people. Political consumerism is, thus, controversial because it opens up more of our own lives to public and political thought and inspection and sanctions the role of individuals as legitimate political agents. Conservatives, neoliberals and others with ideological affinities on the Right find this standpoint both unreasonable and provocative. Yet it forms the basis of feminist thought and is playing an increasingly important role in academic thinking on sustainable development.[17]

A second hot issue is the political consumerist standpoint that the political and economic spheres are not separate entities working according to different logics of action. Critics argue that the mixing of spheres is deludingly dangerous because it leads to a loss of an actor's sense of direction and rationality. Mixing morality and the market is creating a crossbreed capitalist, corporate actor, and consumer who "arrogates for itself a political role, which is bad for business and bad for politics."[18] Proponents of political consumerism, along with their predecessor in the public interest movement in the United States, argue that we cannot choose whether or not to view corporations or consumers as pure economic actors because the power of business in the world today has politicized them. Corporations are political because they can exercise influence over political systems and political relations in countries across the globe. Private corporations have, therefore, evolved into political actors and institutions. As alluded to in chapter 1, they are now a new actor category, private governments, and need to exercise new actor characteristics, corporate citizenship, and business ethics. These new actor and characteristic categories imply the need for corporations to internalize the same democratic demands placed on government. Political consumerism and the public interest organizations argue that transparency, accountability, justice, responsibility, and citizen participation are virtues that apply to private corporations. They do not condemn market capitalism and acknowledge that private corporations and self-interest have a role to play in societal betterment. The same reasoning applies to individual citizens, who are encouraged to be socially responsible investors, another new actor category that amalgamates previously separate categories from the spheres of economics and politics. Political consumerists argue that citizen concern for their own private lives can be used in a beneficial way for society at large. Privately oriented virtues have, thus, a public role to play, or as stated by political scientist David Vogel: "In reality, the only way that one can really live as a 'public citizen' is to make a living at it; the public-interest movement has succeeded so well, in part because it has been able to make defense of the 'public interest' into a source of private, economic gain, however modest."[19]

Political consumerism provokes controversy in other ways as well. A third criticism is that it is flight from politics. People holding this view consider it an ersatz for proper democratic politics and engagements, whose focus is the political system and government regulatory policy. They raise two basic criticisms that relate to the theoretical discussion in chapter 1 on the government/governance distinction and subpolitics/individualized collective action. Scholars who subscribe to the government approach of politics emphasis the need for government action in the form of "command and control" public policy and state economic intervention. They are wary of effort to use the market as an arena for politics because it can be read as a stance against strong government. They fear that political consumerism will encourage governments to float responsibility to other actors and spheres, thus weakening the political system and government as the basis of politics and democracy.[20]

Findings in this book show that public policy is an important platform for political consumerist institutions. The institutions use existing public policy as a floor to construct their "beyond compliance" criteria. In some cases political consumerist institutions have developed because government is seen as slow in acting on market-based problems and has floated its responsibility. Civil society actors have mobilized to find ways of solving or managing serious problems because of these governability weaknesses. Good Environmental Choice is an example. In other cases, the findings show that government alone has not been able to deal effectively with the transboundary problems created by common pool resource exploitation and economic globalization. Governments have not been able to act together. Their collective-action problems prompt the creation of market-based voluntary institutions, as forest stewardship certification and fair trade labels, which set up voluntary regulatory frameworks that can be applied globally. The political consumerist institutions established for this reason have created cooperation among diverse actors as a proxy or perhaps replacement for supra-governmental action.

Not only has it been argued that political consumerism allows and perhaps encourages government's flight from politics (proactive behavior and making tough decisions). It is said to encourage citizens to exit politics and established political homes by enticing them to satisfy their interests and needs for political action in market-oriented buycotts and boycotts. This occurs because political consumerism gives people the sense that they are participating politically but in reality they are only shopping as individuals to satisfy private needs and wants. The argument is that smart shopping cannot begin to rectify the wrongs committed by multinational companies or make the world greener, better, and more just. It is a quick fix for a sense of political urgency expressed by politically impatient people and just another public relations trick used by private industry to convince citizens to continue to buy "new" products.[21] Political consumerism is an example of the fall of public man and the self-obsessive nature of consumer society, which turns citizens away from the political sphere and what in chapter 1 was called collectivistic collective action.[22] Political consumerist individualized collective action in the form of smart shopping, boycotts, and Internet activism is an excuse for citizens to insulate themselves from contact with the political system and established political homes. For civil society the result is disastrous. "Bowling alone" is the metaphor now used to capture this fall of public man.[23]

But is "emailing alone"[24] as illustrated by the Nike Email Exchange really evidence of the fall of the public person? The findings in this book show that this position lacks sufficient substantiation and is, therefore, not the only way of assessing political consumerist actions, actors, and institutions. Findings from chapter 2 emphasize how political consumerism gives simple folks a political tool to civilize capitalism[25] and create regulatory mechanisms in areas where the state is unable or does not want to act effectively. It empowered marginalized citizens politically. American scholars analyze the importance of what we in this book call political consumer activity in the United States by pointing to the relative weakness of the political sphere and its actors when compared to the economic sphere and its actors. This is reported clearly in historical studies of the use of political consumerism by the American labor movement.[26] Boycotts are still an important tool for American trade unions. Preliminary results also show that political consumerism is used in countries lacking a good democratic foundation. Nigeria is an example. Disempowered, suppressed Nigerian citizens use boycotts and other market-based activities as a way to express their discontent with Shell Oil and their government.[27] Findings in this book also emphasize how in certain cases, as with the Swedish Society for the Conservation of Nature, political consumerism has revitalized established political homes. It has given them a new method to work with their issues and attracted new members to the association. In the cases of the civil rights movement and United Farm Workers' Union in the United States, it has led to increased negotiating strength. Finally, available survey data reports that political consumers are also involved in more established political homes and are interested in politics.[28] Their market-based efforts do not, therefore, signify the fall of the public person. Rather political consumerism is frequently a complement to other forms of civic engagements. From these examples, it can be concluded that political consumerism is, in certain circumstances, a welcome development in democracy.

More specific criticisms of political consumerism concern its accountability, orientation, and effectiveness. The arguments are that political consumerism lacks the accountability mechanisms necessary for it to be considered a democratic new form of regulation, has a Northern or Western bias harmful for developing countries, and is not an effective way to regulate industry. "Who guards these guardians?" is a question commonly raised about political consumerist institutions' accountability.[29] The claim, as discussed in chapter 3, is that political consumerist institutions will only be trustworthy and legitimacy if they allow themselves to be scrutinized publicly. Exactly what democratic accountability means for market-based institutions is a matter of debate. Scholars must begin to formulate benchmarks that can be used to evaluate the quality of political consumerist institutions and to study whether the same benchmarks used to assess public institutions can be applied to market-based ones. Basic requirements are organizational transparency and receptivity, the application of the character virtues discussed earlier. They are applied by the type I labeling schemes discussed in this book. These schemes make available information on their assessment criteria, organizational set-up, and apply a shareholder approach to criteria development and formulation. An important research question is whether they do so sufficiently and whether they fulfil other requirements of democratic accountability that can and should be placed on them.

Political consumerism is criticized for applying universal (read Western) standards and rights on workers, manufacturers, and producers in developing countries. This is a common criticism of all action originating in the West or North that apply to the South or developing countries. It needs to be taken seriously and studied systematically. Child labor may in certain circumstances, for example, be a better alternative for children than poverty and prostitution and our attempts to eradicate it through our consumer choices may, in the short run, worsen their situation.[30] Many political consumerist institutions acknowledge this problem. However, their stand is that if a country has ratified international agreements and treaties on human, workers', and women's rights—for whatever reason—it must live up to its commitments. Here political consumerist buycott institutions show their superiority over boycotts actions, which have difficulty in modulating the impatience of moral outrage. Frequently, labeling schemes involve local-based producers and workers in their discussions on criteria and have constructed a process-oriented approach to improvement, which recognizes and praises attempts toward betterment, ratcheting up, and realizing human and workers' rights and environmental standards.[31]

Rather ironically, the need for a process-oriented approach to sustainable development sensitive to local needs and conditions has led to the third serious criticism. Critics claim that political consumerism is an ineffective way of regulating business and solving or managing problems of sustainable development. It is words, rarely deeds, and definitely not outcomes. For its proponents, political consumerism is effective if it shows progress toward goal attainment. Its point of departure is incremental change, a position that is in stark contrast to the claims of its critics who believe that the global market capitalist system must be revamped entirely by governments who step in with forceful regulatory tools to change its contours and incentive structures. Many anti-globalists as well as some scholars believe that the only way to develop economic, ecological, and social sustainability is by changing drastically the structure of market capitalism.[32] For them, mixing money and morality in political consumerist acts and institutions cannot have a sustainable impact.[33] Incremental change allows companies to pretend they are working for sustainable development while all they are doing is corporate marketing.

The metaphors greenwash, bluewash, and sweatwash have been coined to summarize this position.[34] They mean that corporations whitewash their facades to appear cleaner, more just, and environmental while their policies and practices remain unchanged. The Oxford English Dictionary defines greenwash as disinformation disseminated by an organization so as to present an environmentally responsible public image. Bluewash is direct criticism of the UN's Global Compact. It refers to transnational corporations wrapping themselves in the UN's blue flag without having changed their policies and practices to enhance sustainability.[35] Sweatwash describes companies that divert attention from their factories' offensive

practices by offering token acknowledgment to sustainable development in their words and deeds. Critics of corporate commitment to
sustainable development argue that sustainable development cannot be
based on mixed motives: global humanitarianism and human rights
cannot be blended successfully with the corporate profit-motive.
Money and morality do not mix. Corporate citizenship, business ethics,
and corporate social responsibility are window dressing. Such attempts
as the Global Contract, labeling schemes, and Amnesty Business, as
well as ecological modernization are, to use a favored word from this
discourse, hogwash. The outcome of cross-sphere cooperative ventures cannot be sustainability only public relations. Like neoclassical
economists, they see political consumerism as a dangerous delusion.

Political consumerism's assessment of problems and option alternatives reflects a different logic of action and change. It is characterized
by ecological modernization, a view that sustainable development is
a long haul with a multitude of small steps. Any assessment of its
effectiveness must take into consideration the multitude of decisions
and actions involved in changing corporate, citizen, consumer, and
government mentality on what in chapter 1 was called the responsibility for the responsibility of our common future.[36] The assessment of
which sphere and which actors are responsible for the outcome of various decisions and behaviors must consider the entire political consumerist process—from words to deeds to outcomes. The steps in the
process toward effectiveness need to be operationalized properly in
order to be useful in the assessment. They concern how well political
consumers have been able to formulate problems, set the public
and corporate agenda on these issues, influence the thoughts and
discourses of other actors, influence actor's institutional rules and procedures, change government and company policy (goals, distribution
of resources, strategies of implementation), influence the behavior of
states, multinational corporations, and the like, and show concrete
results in terms of problem solution and outcome resolution. A complete assessment requires a cross-disciplinary approach in the social sciences (see the appendix).

This book offers a few preliminary results on the effectiveness of
political consumerist actions and institutions. It reports that political
consumerist boycotts and buycotts are proving instrumental in refor-
mulating problems. Fair trade actors and institutions are problema-
tizing clothes, shoes, and food produced in developing countries.
Consumer, government, civil society, and corporate awareness of
the problems are higher today than in the past. This is changing
the discursive practices of corporations. A look at the homepages of

Nike, Nestlé, H & M, Ikea, Shell Oil, and others show this. A more penetrating assessment is necessary to establish whether corporate efforts are a genuine step toward change or simply greenwash, bluewash, and sweatwash.

Most likely it is too early to make a definitive academic assessment, as changes in mentality, behavior, and practice are process-oriented transformations that take time. However, scholars should begin to develop measures of effectiveness and start their assessments. They should also give consideration to what can be seen as a reasonable time frame for effectiveness.

Findings in this book report that in certain instances political consumerist institutions (eco-labels and FSC) have been instrumental in managing problems by creating public awareness, changing business production processes, and decreasing environmental pollution. They are showing positive outcomes. However, this should not be construed as concluding they have or are alone solving the complex problems of their mandate. Other actors and institutions are necessary. Finally, it is necessary to compare an assessment of the effectiveness of "beyond compliance" political consumerist institutions with "command and control" public policy. How effective are government regulatory tools in the same policy field?

Market-Based Political Responsibility, New Actor Categories, and Great Transformations

Historically, as Pierre Bourdieu reminds us, the economic field constituted itself within the framework of the national state.[37] Market actors relied upon the nation-state for normative, financial, and physical support. Within this territorially based supportive unit, the market could unify itself and flourish. A harmonization took place that, as shown in Karl Polanyi's work *The Great Transformation* as well as Adam Smith's *The Wealth of Nations*, needed the deliberate and rational action of actors other than the corporate class. National government was crucial in the framing activity. It embedded the economic sphere in the framework of the national political sphere. We can say that it acted as a socializing agent. Domestically based corporations became part of the national identity and national interest. Automobile manufacturers like General Motors, Volvo, and Damlier Benz capitalized greatly on this, both economically and morally. Embeddedness was a win–win situation for politics and economics. The moral framework set up nationally created an economic sphere for economic actors who could regulate themselves by following their self-interests.

Today we emphasize the disembeddedness of economic institutions from territorially based social, moral, political life (the nation-state framework), as exemplified in the American outcry when Nike decided to move its production units offshore.[38] Scholars recognize the dismantling of the political framework for capitalism in their distinctions between economic and political globalization. Benjamin Barber explains:

> Markets have escaped the boundaries of eroding national frontiers and become global, but governing organizations have not. This has created a perilous asymmetry: Global economics operation in an anarchic realm without significant regulation and without the humanizing civic institutions that within national societies rescue it from raw social Darwinism. National boundaries have become too porous to hold the economy in, but remain sufficiently rigid to prevent democracy from getting out and civilizing the larger world. We have globalized our economic vices—crime, drugs, terror, hate, pornography, and financial speculation—but not our civic virtues. The result has been a growing tension between the beneficiaries of globalization and just about everyone else, a tension symbolized by the unrest in Seattle [in 1999] and in Washington, D.C., and London [winter 2000].[39]

Globalization has furthered the disembeddedness of corporations from their national setting. Efforts are now underway to create a new norm complex, a new embeddedness, to reunite politics and economics globally. Political consumerism is playing a central role in this creation process. It teaches consumers to practice virtues by buying products that do not promote objectionable market practices. It asks them to understand material products as embedded in a complex social and normative context, which this book calls the politics of products. Political consumerism is one of the agents in transforming the logic of production and consumption. It brings production issues via the politics of products into our homes and political consumerist actions and institutions make the business of consumption a public agenda item for policymaking, collective bargaining, and company boards. Political consumerism actors and institutions force us to rethink the role we play as consumers and, therefore, the forms and methods for citizen influence in society at large.

Perhaps we are witnessing a great transformation whose point of departure is globalization from below[40] and whose goal is to give the market a global moral framework based on sustainable development.

Unlike Adam Smith's and Karl Polayni's times, the current restruc-
turing and transforming involves less state action. People individually
and collectively are playing a role as framework-makers. They are
increasingly becoming active agents in shaping this global framework
for economic, political, and social actors.[41] Their reflexivity (individualized responsibility-taking and subpolitical involvement in postmodern risk society) is forming them anew as citizen-consumers by
de-differentiating their public role as citizens and private role as consumers. Reflexive citizens are "discovering ways to creatively amalga-
mate previously separate practices, life experiences and meanings
across political, economic and cultural institutions."[42] Globalization
from below urged on by reflexive individualized responsibility-taking
citizenship is blurring the public/private divide and merging the
spheres of politics and economics.

New terms have been coined to capture the great transformation
of people into global reflexive transboundary actors. They are called
citizen-consumer and ethical consumers while their cross-sphere
behavior is classified as political consumerism, ethical consumption,
and socially responsible investing. Their new roles and actions are
encouraging other actors to join in. Corporate citizenship and private
governments are terms coined to capture the new role of business in
our cross-sphere world. They are urged to behave according to corporate social responsibility, ethical trade, and fair trade. Many of these
terms have been used in this book. The actor category citizen-
consumer assumes that consumers think publicly when they make
consumer choices. Corporate social responsibility, private governments, and corporate citizenship proclaim that business corporations
are political actors and as such need to follow public morals in their
words and deeds. They need to apply the same virtues and values as
democratic (public) institutions in their policies and practices. Socially
responsible investing and fair trade reflect an acknowledgment that
money can be made morally and that making money morally makes a
difference politically and economically. All the terms represent ideas
that both recommend and reflect the collapse of the traditional
spheres of activity and thought that have governed our lives for
centuries.[43] They call on us to consider new centers of responsibility-
taking in our more individualized and globalized world, and they
argue that actors can make a difference.

We need to ponder whether these discursive markers indicate the
beginning of a new great transformation. Are the new actor categories and ideas packed with sufficient agency to function as transforming drivers? Do they really address the contemporary challenge

of developing sustainability economically, socially, and ecologically? Or are they just attractive in theory but extremely difficult in practice?[44] The new actor categories and responsibilities reflect a change in orientation from production to consumption as the focus of political work and economic life. They establish consumption as a cohesive sphere that integrates politics and economics and collapses the public/private divide. Consumers, consumer choice, and consumption are topics high on the global political and scholarly agenda because they reflect "a recognition that although the *structural* driver of our current system is capital accumulation and profit, the *transforming* driver may well life elsewhere, namely in the sphere of consumption."[45] The new actor categories may be, as argued by a growing number of scholars, consultant, and activists, the best option open for creating new cooperative thinking on how best to live on our small planet.[46]

Appendix

The Political Business of Consumerism: A New Research Agenda for the Social Sciences

Why Study Political Consumerism?

The phenomenon of political consumerism addresses different problems of the business of consumption. It targets industrial pollution or what may be called the sustainable politics of products by evaluating goods according to their life cycle impact—from production methods, substances, and conditions to consumer choice to waste disposal. It calls into question consumer purchasing behavior and, thus, involves the more diversified negative effects of everyday consumer routines and choices and levels of consumption on sustainability.[1] Political consumerism challenges corporations to integrate human rights, workers' rights, and women's rights in their company policies and practices. It raises a warning finger against risky production methods involving genetic modification and asks all of us to consider how we use common pool resources. Research shows that many sustainability problems are difficult to regulate through public policy because they represent diversified negative effects not easily targeted in legislation and are transboundary in nature. Other reasons pointed out in research are disagreement among decisionmaking actors on the nature of the problems, need for problem-solving, and extent of intervention in the market necessary to solve problems. There are political, ideological, coordination, and collective-action issues involved with solving the problems of sustainability. Moreover, the effects of political consumerism or its outcomes are questioned and still unknown.

Fair trade, ecological, and common pool resource problems are a particular focus of the new political consumerist regulatory tools now being developed. As discussed in chapter 3, these tools are voluntary compliance schemes, which make them different from the command and control tools of public policy. Some of them are national in scope while others are regional and global in orientation. The tools differ in character, but they all reflect trends toward reflexive modernization. The people who have taken the initiative to establish them believe that the only way to solve complex problems is through cooperative endeavors that in one way or another involve government, civil society, private industry, and individual consumers from the local to the global level. Some writers even go so far as to call citizen involvement in these issues local foreign policy.[2]

Political consumerism is controversial. It evokes emotions and political responses that are seldom grounded in empirical findings, which at present are few in number. It divided citizens into two camps, those for and against, and provokes scholars to define their view of the world in either actor-oriented or structuralist terms. Misunderstandings must be cleared up and opinions need to be based on factual findings. There is an obvious, evident, and immediate need for social science research in the field.

RESEARCH CHALLENGE

For social scientists, the research challenge is to study the role of individual citizens, networks of citizens, and institutions in the development and effectiveness of new market-oriented regulatory tools for sustainability. This general research challenge can be divided into different components that involve the expertise of several disciplines in the social sciences. Political consumerism can be studied philosophically, theoretically, and empirically. Due to its controversial nature, it is of particular importance to study the development of political consumerism empirically.

This book shows the richness of the phenomenon of political consumerism for the social sciences. It builds on and interprets existing knowledge and has produced theoretical and empirical knowledge on the phenomenon. While researching the book, I began to note areas where we lack sufficient knowledge to evaluate the phenomenon scientifically. From my notations, the following list of the most important topics for empirical research has been formulated.

Development of new regulatory tools for sustainability. We need research on the characteristics and motivations of the actors who promoted new regulatory tools. Where do the ideas come from? Who took the initiative? Available research shows that these actors include corporations, governments, civil society associations, the academic community, and individual citizens. Media coverage has also been important. Why have these actors decided to develop and invest resources in these new tools? Do they consider public policy, national, regional, and global government as unable to deal with sustainable problems in a satisfactory manner?

Citizen and consumer support. Available research from Great Britain shows that individual consumers support new regulatory tools if they distrust corporations.[3] A Danish survey finds political consumers to have trust in political institutions, to be interested in politics, and involved in civil associations.[4] Do these finding apply to other countries as well? How should we analyze these survey findings? How do consumers assess their role in sustainable development? Do they believe that their efforts have an impact and are an effective way of managing sustainable risks globally? Who are political consumers? How should they be characterized in terms of socioeconomic and demographic factors like gender, generation, education, ethnicity/race, income, and social class? Institutional consumers (governments, nongovernmental organizations, and private corporations) who have procurement policies are also an interesting area of study. What role do procurement policies play in political consumerism?

Institutional designs of new regulatory tools. An important research topic is the study of their structure, norms, cognitive frameworks, and resources. A few relevant research issues are as follows. How should we classify the schemes in terms of transparency, relationship with the companies evaluated or certified, accountability, and definition of sustainability? What is the input of government, business, and civil society, consumers in them? Are the regulatory schemes similar in nature or do they differ in set up? Do they compete or cooperate with each other? What tendencies toward mergers, mainstreaming, and harmonization are there?

Probably one of the most challenging research tasks is to assess the *effectiveness of the new market-based regulatory tools.* An assessment of effectiveness involves several different research agenda items: limitations, scope of applicability, necessary preconditions for success, and outcome assessment. First, are there limitations on the application of new regulatory tools? Limitations may concern national, regional, and international legal frameworks that constrain the development and product scope of such new regulatory tools. Research shows that trade regulation, and particularly international trade regulations, restricts certain kinds of policymaking because trade barriers are illegal. National protectionism also tends to craft trade policy and practices. How do trade regulations and protectionism affect the institutional design, scope, and effectiveness of new regulatory tools like labeling schemes?

Second, what is the scope of new regulatory tools? Efforts to establish gender labeling in Europe are, for instance, devoting considerable time in deciding what can be gender labeled and how well eco-labeling practices can be applied to the field of gender equality.[5] The question is, therefore, whether life cycle product assessments are more feasible for certain product groups and issues and inappropriate for others.

Third, are market-based new regulatory tools more effective in certain market settings than others? Available research on eco-labeling and forest certification finds that characteristics of the market and public awareness of the problems and the schemes are important for success and effectiveness.[6] Closed domestic markets are least likely to consider labeling schemes. Markets that are export-oriented and particularly those catering to foreign markets in political settings with high levels of political consumer awareness have a proclivity to participate in political consumerist labeling schemes. Also, markets that are net importers of raw materials are more open to political consumerism. Other market characteristics as the structure of industry (number of competing firms, ownership structure, and interest representation) can play a role in business' interest in political consumerism.[7] An important question for further research is whether the same market characteristics apply to the other political consumerist schemes as well and whether market characteristics vary in importance in different political consumerist product areas.

Fourth, how should effectiveness be measured? An assessment of effectiveness should consider the entire political consumerist process—from words to deeds to outcomes.[8] The general aspects that need to be assessed are at least six in number. (1) How well have political consumerist activities succeeded in formulating the problem that they are created to serve? Do other actors have its understanding of the problems? Have they succeeded in convincing other actors (consumers, groups, organizations, corporations, politicians, governments) that their formulation of the problem is the correct one? Is it used by other actors as an interpretative frame? (2) How well has political consumerism succeeded in setting the agenda on the issues it is concerned with? Do its ideas, actions, and demands come up in other settings, for instance in civil society, the multileveled political system, and in corporate boardrooms? (3) Is political consumerist activity influencing the discourses of other actors involved in the problem? Do we, for instance, find that corporations refer to problems defined by political consumerism in their advertisements, on their home pages, in their yearly reports, and in discussions with consumers, shareholders, politicians, and other actors? (4) Is political consumerist activity influencing corporate rules, procedures, and policies? Do we see changes in written corporate policy on its goals, distribution of resources, strategies of implementation, employment policy, working environment politics, and the like? (5) Are corporations changing their practices and behavior due to political consumerist activities? Are words becoming deeds? Are changes announced in corporate policy being implemented throughout the entire commodity chain? What kinds of changes in behavior are observable? (6) Is political consumerist action solving problems? Is it creating positive outcomes in the situations considered as problematic? What kinds of problems are being solved?

A fifth crucial research area concerns comparisons between the effectiveness of new regulatory tools and older regulatory tools. The newer "beyond compliance" tools take government regulation as a point of departure and create partnerships among market actors willing to go further than required by law. Are voluntary compliance schemes more successful in creating cooperation for policy goals than traditional "command and control" public policy? Are market actors more willing to cooperate in them than with government? How should the effectiveness or ineffectiveness of political consumerist activities be compared with the effectiveness or ineffectiveness of traditional regulatory tools? Are there significant differences when domestic settings are compared with global settings? Is political consumerism successful in developing international regimes? Or are they characterized as temporary measures until political globalization and proper legal authority becomes well established?

Comparative studies of political consumerism. This book shows that we need many more case studies to compare the historical roots of political consumerism to be able to generalize about the connections between the historical and contemporary phenomenon. Case studies from different countries that examine the same historical or contemporary political consumerist occurrence will also help us understand national differences and how ideas are transmitted across country borders. Contemporary studies should include as well regional, international, and global examples. Case studies comparing the development of a particular political consumerist event within a particular country will give us knowledge on internal differences and show whether and why there are domestic strongholds of political consumerist activism. Aspects for comparison involve both actors and structure. Relevant actor categories are consumers, government, industry, civil society associations, and media. Relevant structural aspects are characteristics of the political system, the market, civil society, media, and individuals. Whether the studies are historical or contemporary in orientation they should emphasize the role of information technology in mobilizing consumers for collective action.

Need for cross-disciplinary approach. Comprehensive study of political consumerism requires a cross-disciplinary approach. The analytical tools developed in one academic discipline alone cannot assess its nature, qualities, and potential. Studies on the different stages and aspects of effectiveness, for instance, need to be conducted by political scientists who use analytical frameworks from policy research, market and communication scholars who focus on corporate imaging, students of organizational theory and business administration who study institutional design, and economists who emphasize economic relationships and cost–benefit analysis. Issues regarding citizen and consumer participation are the field of political science, sociology, and social psychology. Political and social philosophers, historians, economic historians, and scholars of the history of ideas can offer important insights into the significance of political consumerism and begin to answer the question if it represents a great transformation.

NOTES

PREFACE

1. See the report by the Instituttet for Fremtidsforskning and Elsam, *Den politiske forbruger* (Copenhagen: Elsam, 1996).
2. These disciplinary differences were quite apparent at the May/June 2001 meeting of the International Seminar on Political Consumerism. Some of them are discussed in Mads P. Sørensen, *Den politiske forbruger—en analyse af ideen og fænomenet* (Aarhus: Department of the History of Ideas, 2002).

1 WHY POLITICAL CONSUMERISM?

1. Jonah Peretti with Michele Micheletti, "The Nike Sweatshop Email: Political Consumerism, Internet, and Culture Jamming," in Micheletti et al., eds., *Politics, Products, and Markets. Exploring Political Consumerism Past and Present* (New Brunswick, NJ: Transaction Publishers, 2003).
2. Andrew Ross, ed., *No Sweat. Fashion, Free Trade, and the Rights of Garment Workers* (New York: Verso, 1999); Archon Fung et al., *Can We Put an End to Sweatshops?* (Boston: Beacon Press, 2001); and Eldon Kenworthy, *Responsible Coffee Campaign: Organic, Sustainable, Fair-Traded Issues* [online], 1997, www.planeta.com/ecotravel/ag/coffee/campaign/campaignb.html.
3. Herbert McClosky, "Political Participation," in Sills, ed., 1968, 252; and Nancy Burns et al., *The Private Roots of Public Action. Gender, Equality, and Political Participation* (Cambridge, MA: Harvard University Press, 2001), 20 f.
4. Mathis Wackernagel Mathis and William Rees, *Our Ecological Footprint. Reducing Human Impact on the Earth* (Gabriola Island, BC, Canada: New Society Publishers, 1996).
5. Ulrich Beck and Elisabeth Beck-Gernsheim, *Individualization* (London: Sage Publications, 2001), 45.
6. Michele Micheletti et al., eds., *Politics, Products, and Markets. Exploring Political Consumerism Past and Present* (Rutgers, NJ: Transaction Publishers, 2003), xiv.
7. This is my experience from presenting papers, giving talks, and discussing political consumerism at the American Political Science Association, European Consortium of Political Research, and other conferences where

American scholars have been present. Not all American scholars hold these attitudes, and they were not voiced at the International Seminar on Political Consumerism.

8. This is a common interpretation based on Easton's writings. See David Easton, *A Framework for Political Analysis* (Englewood Cliffs, NJ: Prentice Hall, 1965); and Jørgen Goul Andersen, *Politik og samfund i forandring* (Copenhagen: Förlaget Columbus, 1993), 11–15.

9. Easton, 59–75.

10. B. Guy Peters and Donald J. Savoie, eds., *Governance in a Changing Environment* (Montreal and Kingston: McGill-Queen's University Press, 1995).

11. Jan Kooiman, "Governance and Governability: Using Complexity, Dynamics and Diversity," in Kooiman, ed., *Modern Governance. New Government-Society Interactions* (London: Sage, 1993).

12. Renate Mayntz, "Governing Failures and the Problem of Governability: Some Comments on a Theoretical Paradigm," in Kooiman, ed., *Modern Governance. New Government-Society Interactions* (London: Sage, 1993). 11–16 ibid., 35 f, 43–8.

13. Compare with David Vogel, "The Corporation as Government. Challenges and Dilemmas," *Polity* 8 (1975): 17.

14. See Benjamin Cashore et al., "Legitimizing Political Consumerism: The Case of Forest Certification in North America and Europe," in Micheletti et al., eds., 2003, 182.

15. Kelly Kollman and Aseem Prakash, "Green by Choice?: Cross-National Variation in Firms' Responses to EMS-Based Environmental Regimes," *World Politics* 53 (April 2001).

16. Cashore et al., 182–7 and Andrew Jordan et al., "Consumer Responsibility-Taking and Eco Labeling Schemes in Europe," in Micheletti et al., eds., 2003, 162–3.

17. C. W. Anderson, *Pragmatic Liberalism* (Chicago: University of Chicago Press, 1990); and James G. March and Johan P. Olsen, *Democratic Governance* (New York: The Free Press, 1995), 28.

18. Ronald Inglehart, *Modernization and Postmodernization. Cultural, Economic, and Political Change in 43 Societies* (Princeton: Princeton University Press, 1997).

19. Laura Westra and Patricia H. Werhane, eds., *The Business of Consumption: Environmental Ethics and the Global Economy* (Lanham, MD: Rowman & Littlefield, 1998).

20. Gert Spaargaren, *The Ecological Modernization of Production and Consumption* (Ph.D. diss., Landbouw: Landbouw Universiteit Wageningen, 1997), 14.

21. Árni Sverrisson, "Translation Networks, Knowledge Brokers and Novelty Construction: Pragmatic Environmentalism in Sweden," [online] *Acta Sociologica* 44 (4) (2001), http://www.tandf.co.uk/journals/tfs/00016993.html.

22. Robert D. Putnam, *Bowling Alone. The Collapse and Revival of American Community* (New York: Simon and Schuster, 2000).

23. Boris Holzer and Mads Sørensen, *Subpolitics and Subpoliticians*, Arbeitspapier 4 des SBF 536 Reflexive Modernisierung (Munchen: University of Munich, 2001).

24. Ulrick Beck, "The Reinvention of Politics: Towards a Theory of Reflexive Modernization," in Beck et al., eds., *Reflexive Modernization. Politics, Tradition, and Aesthetics in Modern Social Order* (Oxford: Polity Press, 1994), 7, 31–2, 43–9;" and Ulrich Beck, *The Reinvention of Politics. Rethinking Modernity in the Global Social Order* (Oxford: Polity Press, 1997), 99 ff.

25. Michael Power, *The Audit Society. Rituals of Verification* (Oxford: Oxford University Press, 1997), 1–4 ; and Kristina Tamm Hallström, *Kampen för auktoritet: standardiseringsorganisationer i arbete* (Stockholm: School of Business, EFI, 2000), ch. 15.

26. Power, 1997, 5, 122.

27. Ibid., 5.

28. Cashore et al., 190–6.

29. Jonathan Purkis, "The City as a Site of Ethical Consumption and Resistance," in O'Connor and Wynne, eds., 1996.

30. Hazel Henderson, "New Markets, New Commons, New Ethics: A Guest Essay," *Accounting, Auditing & Accountability Journal* 4 (3) (1991): 72.

31. Kenworthy.

32. Bente Halkier et al., *Institutional Determinants of Consumer Trust in Food: Six Country Studies*. Working paper for the workshop in the EU project "Trust in Food" in Copenhagen, June, 2001.

33. Margaret Scammell, "The Internet and Civic Engagements: The Age of the Citizen-Consumer," *Political Communication* 17 (2000): 352.

34. Frank R. Baumgartner and Bryan D. Jones, "Agenda Dynamics and Policy Subsystems," *The Journal of Politics* 53 (4) (1991), 1045.

35. Margaret E. Keck and Kathryn Sikkink, *Activists Beyond Borders. Advocacy Networks in International Politics* (Ithaca: Cornell University Press, 1998), 44–5, 158–9, 205, 209; and Baumgartner and Jones, 1047.

36. One E-mail message read: "Thank you for your quick response to my inquiry about my custom ZOOM XC USA running shoes. Although I commend you for your prompt customer service, I disagree with the claim that my personal iD was inappropriate slang. After consulting Webster's Dictionary, I discovered that 'sweatshop' is in fact part of standard English, and not slang. The word means: 'a shop or factory in which workers are employed for long hours at low wages and under unhealthy conditions' and its origin dates from 1892. So my personal iD does meet the criteria detailed in your first email. Your web site advertises that the NIKE iD program is 'about freedom to choose and freedom to express who you are.' I share Nike's love of freedom and personal expression. The site also says that 'If you want it done right…build it yourself.' I was thrilled to be able to build my own shoes, and my personal iD was offered as a small token of appreciation for the sweatshop workers poised to help me realize my vision. I hope that you will value my freedom of expression

and reconsider your decision to reject my order." Peretti together with Micheletti (2003) contains the entire email exchange.

37. Michael Power, "The Politics of Brand Accounting in the United Kingdom," *European Accounting Review* 1 (1992): 41.

38. Meredith M. Fernstrom, "Corporate Public Responsibility: A Marketing Opportunity?" in Bloom and Smith, eds., *The Future of Consumerism* (Lexington, MA: Lexington Books, 1986), 202–4" and Minna Gillberg, *From Green Image to Green Practice. Normative Action and Self-Regulation* (Lund: Lund Studies in Sociology of Law, 1999), 173 f.

39. Vogel, 17 ff.

40. Global Compact at unglobalcompact.org., 2002.

41. Amnesty International, *Socially Responsible Investment Campaign* [online], www.amnesty.org.uk/business/campaigns/sri.shtml, 2002.

42. Renée Andersson, "Enfrågerörelser," talk for the conference "Politikens nya villkor," 2002.

43. Peretti together with Micheletti, 128, 133, 136–7.

44. Sidney Tarrow, *Power in Movement: Social Movements and Contentious Politics* (Cambridge: Cambridge University Press, 1998).

45. Albert O. Hirschman, *Exit, Voice, and Loyalty Responses to Decline in Firms, Organizations, and States* (Cambridge, MA: Harvard University Press, 1970).

46. Albert O. Hirschman, *Shifting Involvements. Private Interest and Public Action* (Princeton, NJ: Princeton University Press, 1982), chs. 6–7 and ibid., 4, 15.

47. See for instance Naomi Klein, *No Logo. No Space, No Choice, No Jobs.* (London: Flamingo, 2000), ch. 2; older literature represented by Vance Packard, *The Hidden Persuaders* (Harmondsworth: Penguin, 1981); and Herbert Marcuse, *One Dimensional Man* (London: Sphere, 1964).

48. Slater, Don, "Consumer Culture and the Politics of Need," in Nava et al., eds., 1997, 51.

49. Mica Nava, "Consumerism Reconsidered. Buying and Power," *Cultural Studies* 5 (2) (1991): 165.

50. See Scammell, 354.

51. On agency see Piotr Szrompk, *Society in Action. The Theory of Social Becoming* (Cambridge: Polity Press, 1991), 99.

52. Beck, "The Reinvention," 129.

53. Compare with P. Kotler, "What Consumerism Means for Markets," *Harvard Business Review* May–June (1992).

54. Pekka Sulkunen, "Introduction," in Sulkunen et al., eds., 1997, 13.

55. Herman R. van Gunsteren, *A Theory of Citizenship. Organizing Plurality in Contemporary Democracies* (Bolder, CO: Westview Press, 1998), 29.

56. Anne Phillips, "Who Needs Civil Society? A Feminist Perspective," *Dissent* (Winter 1999): 59.

57. van Gunsteren, 12.

58. Philip A. Titus and Jeffrey L. Bradford, "Reflections on Consumer Sophistication and Its impact on Ethical Business Practice," *The Journal of Consumer Affairs* 30 (1) (1996): 175.

59. Compare Georgia L. Stevens, "Linking Consumer Rights with Citizen Roles: An Opportunity for Consumer Educators," *The Journal of Consumer Education* 12 (1994), 1–2.

60. Magnus Linton, *Veganerna—en bok om dom som stör* (Stockholm: Atlas, 2000); and Adrienne Sörbom, *Vart tar politiken vägen? Om individualisering, reflexivitet och görbarhet i det politiska engagemanget* (Stockholm: Almqvist & Wiksell International, 2002).

61. Michele Micheletti, "Why More Women? Issues of Gender and Political Consumerism," in Micheletti et al., eds., 2003.

62. Per E. Gustafson, "Gender Differences in Risk Perception: Theoretical and Methodological Perspectives," *Risk Analysis* 18 (6) (1998); and Kathryn Harrison, *Too Close to Home: Dioxin Contamination of Breast Milk and the Political Agenda*. Paper for ECPR, Copenhagen, April 14–19, 2000.

63. Cecilia Solér, *Att köpa miljövänliga dagligvaror* (Stockholm: Nerenius & Santérus Förlag, 1997).

64. Shelley Burtt, "The Politics of Virtue Today: A Critique and a Proposal," *American Political Science Review* 87 (1993).

65. Gerald Delanty, *Citizenship in a Global Age. Society, Culture, Politics* (Buckingham: Open University Press, 2000).

66. For a discussion see Dietlind Stolle and Marc Hooghe, "Consumers as Political Participants? Shifts in Political Action Repertoires in Western Societies," in Micheletti et al., eds., 2003.

67. Saul Alinsky, "Proxies for People. A Vehicle for Involvement. An Interview with Saul Alinsky," *Yale Review of Law and Social Action* 1 (Spring 1971): 64.

68. Solér, 64, 181–4.

69. Burtt, 361.

70. Compare Nina Eliasoph, *Avoiding Politics. How Americans Produce Apathy in Everyday Life* (Cambridge: Cambridge University Press, 1998).

71. See Anthony Downs, *An Economic Theory of Democracy* (New York: Harper & Row, 1957).

72. Putnam, 122–4.

73. Dingwix Zhao, "Ecologies of Social Movements: Student Mobilization During the 1989 Prodemocracy Movement in Beijing," *American Journal of Sociology* 103 (6) (1998); and Michael Suk-Young Chwe, "Structure and Strategy in Collective Action," *American Journal of Sociology* 105 (1) (1999).

74. Mancur Olson, *The Logic of Collective Action. Public Goods and the Theory of Groups* (Harvard: Harvard University Press, 1975).

75. Peter Hedström, "Contagious Collectivities: On the Spatial Diffusion of Swedish Trade Unions, 1890–1940," *American Journal of Sociology* 99 (5) (1994): 59 ff.; and Mark Granovetter, "Threshold Models of Collective Behavior," *American Journal of Sociology* 83 (6) (1978).

76. Hirschman, 1982.

77. Dag Wollebæck and Per Selle, *Det nye organisajonssamfunnet. Demokrati i omforming* (Bergen: Fagbokforlaget, 2002), 216; Olof Petersson et al.,

Demokrati och medborgarskap. Demokratirådets rapport 1998 (Stockholm: SNS Förlag, 1998), ch. 3, 147 ff.; Pippa Norris, ed., *Critical Citizens. Global Support for Democratic Government* (Oxford: Oxford University Press, 1999), ch. 13; Michele Micheletti, *Civil Society and State Relations in Sweden* (Aldershot: Avebury, 1995), 21 ff., ch. 6, 127–41; and Putnam, chs. 2–3.

78. Manuel Castells, *The Rise of the Network Society* (Oxford: Blackwell, 1997); Vivien Lowndes, "Women and Social Capital: A Comment on Hall's 'Social Capital in Britain,' " *British Journal of Political Science* 30 (3) (2000); and Robert Wuthnow, *Loose Connections. Joining Together in America's Fragmented Communities* (Cambridge: Harvard University Press, 1998). See also Michele Micheletti and Dietlind Stolle, *Political Consumption. Politics in a New Era and Arena.* Research Project funded by the Swedish Council of Research, Stockholm, Sweden, 2001.

79. Scott Lash, "Individualization in a Non-Linear Mode," foreword to Beck and Beck-Gernsheim, *Individualization* (London: Sage Publications, 2001), 2; and Beck and Beck-Gernsheim, ch. 4.

80. Norman Blaikie, *Designing Social Research. The Logic of Anticipation* (Cambridge: Polity Press, 2000), 180–1.

81. See the discussion on political participation and representative democracy in Jan Teorell, *Political Participation and the Theories of Democracy. A Research Agenda.* Paper for the Annual Meeting of the American Political Science Association, San Francisco, CA, 2001.

82. Micheletti, 1995, 21.

83. Olson, chs. 1–2; Micheletti 1995; and Michele Micheletti, *Organizing Interest and Organized Protest. Difficulties of Member Representation for the Swedish Central Organization of Salaried Employees (TCO)* (Stockholm: Stockholm Studies in Politics No. 29, 1985), ch. 1.

84. Peretti with Micheletti, 128–36.

85. See Bente Halkier, "Consequences of the Politization of Consumption: The Example of Environmentally Friendly Consumption Practices," *Journal of Environmental Policy and Planning* 1 (1999).

86. Eva Sørensen, "Brugeren og demokratiet," *Grus* 53 (1997): 96.

87. For a good overview of the concept of subpolitics see Holzer and Sørensen, 3–6, 10–17.

88. Holzer and Sørensen, 11–13.

89. Beck and Beck-Gernsheim, 45.

90. Beck, 1997, 101.

91. Ibid., 128.

92. Henrik P. Bang och Eva Sørensen, "The Everyday Maker: A New Challenge to Democratic Governance," *Administrative Theory and Praxis* 21 (3) (1999); and Sørensen, 1997.

93. Niels Nørgaard Kristensen, "Brugerindflydelse, politisk identitet og offentlig styring," *Nordisk Administrativt Tidsskrift* No. 1 (1999).

94. Beck and Beck-Gernsheim, 24, 43 ff.

95. Sørensen, 96.
96. Compare with Delanty, 3 ff., 46, 130–6.
97. Iris Marion Young, "Gender as Seriality: Thinking about Women as a Social Collective," *Signs: Journal of Women in Culture and Society* 19 (1994).
98. The quotations are from ibid., 723 and 728 respectively.
99. Chantal Mouffe, *The Return of the Political* (London: Verso, 1993), 71.
100. Karol Edward Sołtan, "Civic Competence, Attractiveness, and Maturity," in Elkin and Sołtan, eds., *Citizen Competence and Democratic Institutions* (University Park, PA: Pennsylvania State University Press, 1999), 18.
101. David Trend, "Democracy's Crisis of Meaning," in Trend, ed., *Identity, Citizenship, and the State* (NY: Routledge, 1996), 15; and van Gunsteren, 29.
102. See Delanty, ch. 9.
103. Beck, 1997, 92.
104. Zygmunt Bauman, *Life in Fragments* (Oxford: Blackwell, 1995), 4 ff.

2 HISTORY OF POLITICAL CONSUMERISM

1. David Miller, "Consumption as the Vanguard of History. A Polemic by Way of an Introduction," in Miller, ed., *Acknowledging Consumption. A Review of New Studies* (NY: Routledge, 1995).
2. N. Craig Smith, *Morality and the Market. Consumer Pressure for Corporate Accountability* (London: Routledge, 1991), 146.
3. Monroe Friedman, "On Promoting a Sustainable Future Through Consumer Activism," *Journal of Social Issues* 51 (4) (1995): 198–9.
4. Lawrence B. Glickman, "Born to Shop? Consumer History and American History," in Glickman, ed., *Consumer Society in American History. A Reader* (Ithaca, NY: Cornell University Press, 1999), 2.
5. T. H. Breen, "'Baubles of Britain': The American and Consumer Revolutions of the Eighteenth Century," *Past & Present* No. 119 (May 1988): 104.
6. T. H. Breen, "Narrative of Commercial Life: Consumption, Ideology, and Community on the Eve of the American Revolution," in Glickman, ed., 113 ff.
7. Breen, 1988, 76–7.
8. Glickman, 2.
9. Margaret E. Keck and Kathryn Sikkink, *Activists Beyond Borders. Advocacy Networks in International Politics* (Ithaca, NY: Cornell University Press, 1998), 41–51.
10. Mary King, *Mahatma Gandhi and Martin Luther King Jr. The Power of Nonviolent Action* (Paris: UNESCO Publishing, 1999), 49.
11. Judith M. Brown, *Gandhi's Rise to Power. Indian Politics 1915–1922* (Cambridge: Cambridge University Press, 1972), 202–5, 312 ff.; Judith M. Brown, *Modern India. The Origins of an Asian Democracy* (Delhi: Oxford University Press, 1985), 174, 207–18; and

R. C. Majumdar et al., *An Advanced History of India* (London: Macmillan & Co., 1960), 950.

12. Subhas Chandra Bose, *Swadeshi and Boycott* (Calcutta: Liberty Newspapers Limited, 1931), 34–5.

13. John Bohstedt, "Gender, Household and Community Politics. Women in English Riots 1790–1810," *Past and Present* 120 (1988).

14. Annelise Orleck, " 'Who are that Mythical Thing Called the Public': Militant Housewives during the Great Depression," *Feminist Studies* 19 (1993): 156.

15. Iris Marion Young, "Gender as Seriality: Thinking about Women as a Social Collective," *Signs: Journal of Women in Culture and Society* 19 (1994): 735.

16. Orleck, 149, 156.

17. Ibid., 157.

18. Ibid., 156.

19. Mica Nava, "Consumerism Reconsidered. Buying and Power," *Cultural Studies* 5 (2) (1991): 165.

20. Erik Giertz and Bengt U. Strömberg, *Samverkan till egen nytta. Boken om konsumentkooperativ idé och verklighet i Sverige* (Stockholm: Prisma, 1999), 62–4.

21. Andreas Follesdal, "Political Consumerism as Chance and Challenge," in Micheletti et al., eds., 2003; and Monroe Friedman, "Using Consumer Boycotts to Stimulate Corporate Policy Changes: Marketplace, Media, and Moral Considerations," in Micheletti et al., eds., *Politics, Products, and Markets. Exploring Political Consumerism Past and Present* (New Brunswick, NJ: Transaction Publishers, 2003).

22. Yvonne Hirdman, *Magfrågan. Mat som mål och medel. Stockholm 1870–1920* (Stockholm: Rabén & Sjögren, 1983), 215 f.

23. Ibid., 234, 274–5.

24. Yvonne Hirdman, "Den socialistiska hemmafrun," in Åkerman et al., eds., *Vi kan, vi behövs! Kvinnorna går samman i egna föreningar* (Stockholm: Akademilitteratur AB, 1983), 48.

25. As quoted in ibid., 45, my translation.

26. Ibid., 48 f.

27. *Kvällsposten* (local Swedish newspaper), "Husmödrarnas mjölkkrig blir ett politiskt hot," February 27, 1972.

28. His comment in Swedish was "Ni är ju totalt urblåsta, er behöver vi inte lyssna på" (as quoted in Per Gahrton, "Aktuella frågor: Feldt, Helén och matpriserna") *Sydsvenska Dagbladet (Snällposten)*, March 2, 1972.

29. Michele Micheletti, *Civil Society and State Relations in Sweden* (Aldershot: Avebury, 1995), ch. 6.

30. Franck Cochoy, "Industrial Roots of Contemporary Political Consumerism: The Case of the French Standardization Movement," in Micheletti et al., eds., 2003; and Andrew Jordan et al., "Consumer Responsibility-Taking and Eco Labeling Schemes in Europe," in Micheletti et al., eds., 2003.

31. Justice William J. Brennan in a dissenting opinion 1990 as quoted in Frank
    I. Michelman, *Brennan and Democracy* (Princeton: Princeton University
    Press, 1999), 80 f. I want to thank my good friend and colleague Andreas
    Follesdal at the University of Olso for showing this quote to me.

32. Peter Aléx, *Den rationella konsumenten. KF som folkuppfostare
    1899–1939* (Stockholm: Brutus Östlings Bokförlag Symposion, 1994),
    55, 62 f.; and Lawrence B. Glickman, "The Strike in the Temple of
    Consumption: Consumer Activism and Twentieth-Century American
    Political Culture," *The Journal of American History* 88 (1) (2001): 105.

33. Aléx, 164 ff.; and Dana Frank, *Purchasing Power. Consumer Organizing,
    Gender, and the Seattle Labor Movement 1919–1929* (Cambridge:
    Cambridge University Press, 1994).

34. Kathryn Kish Sklar, "The Consumers' White Label Campaign of the
    National Consumers' League 1898–1919," in Strasser et al., eds.,
    *Getting and Spending. European and American Consumer Societies in the
    20th Century* (Cambridge: Cambridge University Press, 1998).

35. Ibid., 18.

36. As quoted in ibid., 27.

37. Ibid., 18.

38. Lawrence B. Glickman, *A Living Wage. American Workers and the
    Making of Consumer Society* (Ithaca, NY: Cornell University Press,
    1997), 93–128.

39. See Frank, 115.

40. Ibid., 6.

41. Monroe Friedman, *Consumer Boycotts. Effecting Change through the
    Marketplace and the Media* (New York: Routledge, 1999), 47–65.

42. Robert D. Benford and Danny L. Valadez, *From Blood on the Grapes to
    Poison on the Grapes: Strategic Frame Changes and Resource Mobilization
    in the Farm Worker Movement.* Paper for the Annual Meeting of the
    American Sociological Association, San Francisco, CA, August 21, 1998.

43. As quoted in ibid., 8.

44. Kech and Sikkink, 43–5, 204.

45. Friedman, *Consumer Boycotts*, chs. 5–6.

46. King, *Mahatma Gandhi*, 126; and Friedman, *Consumer Boycotts*,
    96–107.

47. Cheryl Goldberg, "Don't Buy Where You Can't Work," in Glickman,
    ed., 244 ff.

48. Lizabeth Cohen, *Making a New Deal. Industrial Workers in Chicago,
    1919–1939* (Cambridge: Cambridge University Press, 1990), 154.

49. Friedman, *Consumer Boycotts*, 116 ff.

50. Ibid., 107 ff.

51. Boycott Crown Oil, www.boycottcrownoil, 2000.

52. Peter Wallensteen, *A Century of Economic Sanctions: A Field Revisited*
    (Uppsala: Department of Peace and Conflict Research, Uppsala
    University, 2000); and Follesdal et al., "Conclusion," in Micheletti et al.,
    eds., *Politics, Products, and Markets. Exploring Political Consumerism*

Past and Present (New Brunswick, NJ: Transaction Publishers, 2003), 295–7.

53. Friedman, *Consumer Boycotts*, 8.
54. Divest Now, *Divest from Israel* [online], www.princetondivest.org, harvardmitdivest.org, ucdivest.org, 2002.
55. Naomi Bromberg Bar Yam, "The Nestlé Boycott. The Story of the WHO/UNICEF Code for Marketing Breastmilk Substitutes," *Mothering* (Winter 1995).
56. Kathryn Sikkink, "Codes of Conduct for Transnational Corporations: The Case of the WHO/UNICEF Code," *International Organization* 40 (1986); and Bar Yam, 59–60.
57. Bar-Yam, 60–1; Sikkink, 834–7; and Keck and Sikkink, 1998, 14, 21 ff., 131, 159, 204 ff.
58. International Baby Food Action Network, *Don't Be a Mug—Give Nescafé The Boot. Stop Bottle Baby Deaths—Boycott Nestlé* [online], www.babymilkaction.org/pages/boycott.html., 2002; and *Information page on the Nestle Boycott* [online], shell.ihug.co.nz/~stu/nestlmilk.htm, 2002.
59. Kech and Sikkink, 1998, x.
60. David Black, "The Long and Winding Road: International Norms and Domestic Political Change in South Africa," in Risse et al., eds., 1999, 80.
61. B. Vivekanandan, *International Concerns of European Social Democrats* (Basingstoke: Macmillan, 1997), 11, 115; Kofi Annan, *Dag Hammarskjöld and the 21st Century. The Fourth Dag Hammarskjöld Lecture* (Uppsala: Dag Hammarskjöld Minnesfond, 2001); John Bierman, *Raoul Wallenberg. En hjälte i vår tid. Biografi om "mannen som räddare 100 000 judar," hans liv, kamp och försvinnande* (Stockholm: AWE/Geber, 1982).
62. Annika Forsberg, *Meet Sweden* (Stockholm: ISAK, 1995); Kim Salomon, *Rebeller i takt med tiden. FNL-rörelsen och 60-talets politiska ritualer* (Stockholm: Rában Prisma, 1996); Mats Örbrink, *FNL-rörelsen i Sverige: en historik* (Stockholm: DFFGs skriftserie, 1973); and Micheletti, 1995, ch. 6.
63. Micheletti, 1995, 182–6.
64. Åke Magnusson, *Konsumentbojkott—ett användbart vapen? Om kooperationen och Sydafrikafrågan* (Kooperativ Information No. 5. Stockholm: KF, 1974).
65. Magnusson, 10–14.
66. Ibid., 23–4.
67. Ibid., 24.
68. For a discussion of successful boycotts see Friedman, "Using Consumer," 47–50.
69. Terence Prittie and Walter Henry Nelson, *The Economic War Against the Jews* (London: Secker & Warburg, 1978).
70. Smith, 157 f.
71. Ibid., 158, 162 f.

72. Ibid., 161 f.
73. Elisabeth Liljedahl, *Stumfilmen i Sverige—kritik och debatt. Hur samtiden värderade den nya konstarten* (Stockholm: Svenska Filminstitutet, 1975); Georg Branting, "Ansvaret. Slutkapitel i SACO-Vanzettidramat," in Höglund and Mehr, eds., 1927; Svenska Sacco-Vanzetti Försvarskommittén; *Sacco-Vanzetti rörelsen i Sverge. Redogörelse för Svenska Sacco-Vanzetti försvarskommittens verksamhet* (Stockholm: Svenska Sacco-Vanzetti försvarskommittén, 1928); and Monica Andersson, *Sacco Vanzetti—en politisk rättegång* (Förening BHS Småskrifter No. 6. Borås: Föreningen BHS publicerar, 1976).
74. *Encyclopædia Judaica Jerusalem*, "Boycott, Anti-Jewish" (Jerusalem: Keter Publishing House, 1971), 1278 ff.
75. Ibid., 1279.
76. The advertisement declared "Svensk vara bör köpas av svenskar hos svenska affärsmän! Medverka icke till den internationella judiska storfinansens exploatering av svenska arbetare och företag!" It appeared in a newspaper on February 24, 1934. Unfortunately, I do not have the name of the newspaper. I want to thank Orsi Husz at the Department of History, Stockholm University, for calling my attention to this advertisement. Such advertisements could be found in most local Swedish newspapers in the 1930s.
77. Cheryl Goldberg, "Political Consumer Action: Some Cautionary Notes from African American History," in Micheletti et al., eds., 2003, 64–7.
78. Disney Boycott, *Your Official Disney Boycott Site*! http://www.laker.net/webpage/boycott.htm, 2002.
79. For instance, Leah Hollbrook, *Disney, Inc., Feeling the Wrath of Southern Baptist* [online], www.siue.edu/ALESTLE/library/summer 1997/jun.25.97/Disney.hml.
80. *Picture of a Protest Demonstration Including the Sign "Disney Funds Abortion, Sodomy, Violent Films"* [online], Disney Boycott—Your Official Disney Boycott Site! http://www.laker.net/webpage/Boycott.htm, 2002.
81. Joseph K. Elster, *Letter to Disney* [online], www.geocities.com/CapitolHill/1555/Disney1.html, 1996.
82. David Miller, "The Case Against Disney: Twenty-Three Reasons (and Counting) to Beware of the 'Magic Kingdom' " [online], *The Ethics and Religious Liberty Community*, www.erlc.com/Culture/Disney/ 1997/case.htm.
83. *African-Americans Boycottt Disney* [online], www.laker.net/ webpage/African.htm, 2002; and Muna Salam, *Disney's Unholy War on African Americans and Muslims* [online], www.arabmedia.com/octnov97farakhan.html, 1997.
84. Disney Boycott, *Your Official Disney Boycott Site*! http://www.laker.net/webpage/boycott.htm, 2002.
85. Salam.

86. Friends of Al-Aqsa, *Urgent Action: Campaign 2. Disney Promotes Israeli Occupation* [online], www.aqsa.org.uk/activities/campaign2.html, 2002.

87. Jenni "Emiko" Kuida, "Why You Should Boycott Disney," *The Rafu Shimpo*, June 24, 1997 [online], www.kuidaosumi.com/JKwriting/ Disney.html; *Disney's Child Labor and Union Busting*, www.laker.net/webpage/aadisneylabor.htm, 2002; and Angelfire, *Labor Law Breakers and Their Crimes. Abuser List* [online], www.angelfire. com/nd/NoahWeb/labor.html.

88. Glickman, "The Strike," 102.

89. Goldberg, 2003, "Political Consumer," 79.

90. Axel Raphael and Eliel Löfgren, *Blockad, bojkott och svarta listor. Två möte-suttalanden i andledning af hr Hilderbrands motion om ändring af 3§ 11:0 Tryckfrihetsförordningen* (Stockholm: A. B. Nordiska Bokhandeln, 1908); Frank, 115 f.; *Aschehong og Gyldendals Store Norske leksikon* (Oslo: Kunskapsforlaget, 1986), 441 f.; and Brennan in Michelman, 80 f.

91. Vance Packard, *The Hidden Persuaders* (Harmondsworth: Penguin, 1981); Betty Friedan, *The Feminine Mystique* (Harmondsworth: Penguin, 1965); Herbert Marcuse, *One Dimensional Man* (London: Sphere, 1964); and Stuart Ewen, *All Consuming Images* (New York: Basic Books, 1988).

92. Frank, 4 ff., 40.

93. Meg Jacobs, " 'Democracy's Third Estate': New Deal Politics and the Construction of a 'Consuming Public,' " *International Labor and Working-Class History*, special issue on Class and Consumption 55 (Spring 1999): 27 ff.

94. Robert S. Lynd, "The People as Consumers," *Recent Social Trends in the U.S. Report of the President's Research Committee on Social Trends. Volume II* (New York: McGraw-Hill Book Company, Inc., 1933); Robert S. Lynd, "The Consumer Becomes a 'Problem,' " The Ultimate Consumer. A Study in Economic Illiteracy," *The Annals of the American Academy of Political and Social Science* 173 (May 1934); Robert S. Lynd, "Democracy's Third Estate: The Consumer," *Political Science Quarterly* 51 (1936).

95. J. G. Brainerd, ed., "The Ultimate Consumer. A Study in Economic Illiteracy," *The Annals of the American Academy of Political and Social Science* 173 (May 1934).

96. As quoted in Jacobs, 37.

97. Lyman Briggs, "Services of the National Bureau of Standards to Consumers," *The Annals of the American Academy of Political and Social Science* 173 (May 1934): 154 f.

98. See Edith Ayres, "Private Organizations Working for the Consumer," *The Annals of the American Academy of Political and Social Science* 173 (May 1934).

99. David Vogel, "The Corporation as Government. Challenges and Dilemmas," *Polity* 8 (1975): 33.

3   CONTEMPORARY FORMS AND INSTITUTIONS

1. Ronald Inglehart, *Modernization and Postmodernization. Cultural, Economic, and Political Change in 43 Societies* (Princeton: Princeton University Press, 1997), 313; Environics International, *The Environmental Monitor. Global Public Opinion on the Environment. 1999 International Report* (Toronto: Environics International, 1999), available at www.environics.net/eil/articles/green; *The Economist*, "How Green is Your Market?" January 8, 2000, 76; Roger Cowe and Simon Williams, *Who are the Ethical Consumers?* (London: The Co-operative Bank, no date).

2. This is an interesting development because it goes against "exit" as the conventional economic mechanism for consumers to influence the market, as eloquently explained by Albert O. Hirschman in his book *Exit, Voice, and Loyalty. Responses to Decline in Firms, Organizations, and States* (Cambridge, MA: Harvard University Press, 1970). See also Laura Westra and Patricia H. Werhane, eds., *The Business of Consumption: Environmental Ethics and the Global Economy* (Lanham, MD: Rowman & Littlefield, 1998).

3. Paul Smith, "Tommy Hilfiger in the Age of Mass Customization," in Ross, ed., 1999, 249.

4. Compare with Minna Gillberg, *From Green Image to Green Practice. Normative Action and Self-Regulation* (Lund: Lund Studies in Sociology of Law, 1999).

5. ISO, *What are Standards* [online], www.iso.ch/infoe/intro.htm.

6. W. Lee Kuhre, *ISO 14020s. Environmental Labelling-Marketing. Efficient and Accurate Environmental Marketing Procedures* (Upper Saddle River, NJ: Prentice Hall, 1997); Kristina Tamm Hallström, *Kampen för auktoritet: standardiseringsorganisationer i arbete* (Stockholm: School of Business, EFI, 2000); and Nils Brunsson and Bengt Jacobsson, eds., *The World of Standards* (Oxford: Oxford University Press, 2000).

7. Minna Halme, "Environmental Issues in Product Development Processes: Paradigm Shift in a Finnish Packaging Company," *Business Ethics Quarterly* 5 (4) (1995); Minna Halme, *Environmental Management Paradigms Shifts in Business Enterprises: Organizational Learning Relating to Recycling and Forest Management Issues in Two Finnish Paper Companies.* (Tampare: University of Tampare, Finland, 1997); Gillberg 119–29, 141–50, 157–69, 178–90.

8. Kelly Kollman and Aseem Prakash, "Green by Choice?: Cross-National Variation in Firms' Responses to EMS-based Environmental Regimes," *World Politics* 53 (April 2001).

9. European Environmental Bureau, *Position of the EEB on the Commission's Proposal for the Revision of the EMAS Regulation* [online], www.eeb.org/activities/position_of_the_ebb_on_proposal_htm, 1999.

10. Social Accountability International, *A General Introduction* [online], www.cepaa.org, 2000.
11. Ann-Katrine Roth, *EQ 2000. Kvalitetssäkring av jämställdhetsarbete* (Stockholm: Jamställdhetskonsult/E(uro)Quality, 1998).
12. Ans Kolk and Rob van Tulder, "Child Labor and Multinational Conduct: A Comparison of International Business and Stakeholder Codes," *Journal of Business Ethics* 36 (2002): 292; Codes of Conduct [online], www.codesofconduct.org, 2002; and European Commission, *Green Paper. Promoting a European Framework for Corporate Social Responsibility* (Brussels: COM (2001) 416 final, 2001). Examples of nongovernmental organization-formulated codes are Amnesty International's Human Rights Principles for Companies and Clean Clothes Campaign Code of Labor Practices for the Apparel Industry. Governmental codes include the International Labor Organization (ILO) Tripartite Declaration of Principles Concerning Multinational Enterprises and Social Policy, United Nation's Global Company, and U.S. Department of Commerce Model Business Principles. Samples of company codes are Ben and Jerry's Statement of Mission, the Body Shop's Reasons for Being, and Nike Code of Conduct. Examples of industry codes are Apparel Industry Partnership (AIP) Workplace Code of Conduct, Canadian Business for Social Responsibility (CBSR) Guide, and World Federation of the Sporting Goods Industry Model Code. Union sponsored codes are International Confederation of Free Trade Unions (ICFTU) Basic Code of Labor Practices, and International Federation of Building and Wood Workers (IFBWW) Model Framework Agreement. University codes are United Students Against Sweatshops (USAS) Provisional Statement of Principles and Duke University's Code of Conduct for Licensees. For more information on these examples see Codes of Conduct.
13. Bob Jeffcott and Lynda Yanz, *Codes of Conduct, Government Regulation and Worker Organizing* (Toronto: ETAG, 2000).
14. Office of Consumer Affairs, *An Evaluative Framework for Voluntary Codes* [online], http://strategis.ic.gc.ca/SSg/ca01227e.html, 2000, 2.
15. Kolk and Tulder, 298.
16. The adjectives "positive" and "negative" as well as "successful" and "effective" referring to boycotts are used in varied and at times contradictory ways in the literature on boycotts. My use of the terms negative and positive political consumerism have been developed from a report on political consumerism from the Danish Institutt for Future Studies, and I follow Monroe Friedman's distinctions regarding successful and effective boycotts in assessing the potential of political consumerism as a force for political change. See Institutt for Fremtidsforskning and Elsam, *Den politiske forbruger* (Copenhagen: Elsam, 1996), 8–9 and Monroe Friedman, "Using Consumer Boycotts to Stimulate Corporate Policy Changes: Marketplace, Media, and Moral Considerations," in Micheletti et al., eds., *Politics, Products, and Markets. Exploring Political*

Consumerism Past and Present (New Brunswick, NJ: Transaction Publishers, 2003), 47–50.

17. Benjamin Cashore et al., "Legitimizing Political Consumerism: The Case of Forest Certification in North America and Europe," in Micheletti et al., eds., 2003, 189.

18. See Naomi Klein, *No Logo. No Space, No Choice, No Jobs* (London: Flamingo, 2000); and Grant Jordan, *Shell, Greenpeace and the Brent Spar* (Basingstoke: Palgrave, 2001).

19. Monroe Friedman, *Consumer Boycotts. Effecting Change through the Marketplace and the Media* (New York: Routledge, 1999).

20. Ralph Nader et al., "Shopping for Innovation. The Government as Smart Consumer," *The American Prospect* 11 (Fall 1992).

21. Friedman, ibid., ch. 20; and Pippa Norris, *Democratic Phoenix. Reinventing Political Activism* (Cambridge: Cambridge University Press, 2002), 198.

22. Simon Zadek, "Consumer Works!" *Development. Journal of the Society for International Development* 41 (1) (1998): 7 [online], zadek.net/consuminworks.pdf, 7.

23. Margaret Scammell, "The Internet and Civic Engagements: The Age of the Citizen-Consumer" [online], *Political Communication* 17 (2000), 353–4; and Friedman, "Using Consumer, Friedman.... Consumer, 52–4; and W. Lance Bennett "Branded Political Communication: Lifestyle Politics, Logo Campaigns, and the Rise of Global Citizenship," in Micheletti et al., eds., *Politics, Products, and Markets. Exploring Political Consumerism Past and Present* (New Brunswick, NJ: Transaction Publishers, 2003), 112–20.

24. AFL-CIO, *AFL-CIO National Boycott List* [online]. Union Label and Service Trades Department, www.unionlabel.org/donotbuy/Default. htm, 2002; Consumers Against Food Engineering, www.cafemd. org/cafe.htm, 2000; and CorpWatch, *CorpWatch Bulletin Board* [online], http://www.corpwatch.org/bulletins/PAM.jsp, 2002.

25. Co-op America, *Co-op America's Boycott Action News* [online], www.boycotts.org/, 2002.

26. See e.g., Co-op America, *Co-op America's Boycott Organizers' Guide* [online], www.coopamerica.org, 2002.

27. Jordan; and Third World Traveller, *Shell Oil in Nigeria*, http://www. thirdworldtraveler.com/Boycotts/ShellNigeria_boycott.html, 2002.

28. International Peace Bureau (IPB), "IPB Calls for Boycott of French Goods," *Wise News Communique* June 30, 1995 [online], www. antenna.nl/wise/435/4293–4.html; *Los Angeles Times*, "British to Boycott French Wine Until Weapons Testing Stops," also published in *The Tech* 155 (39) (1995): 3 [online], http://www.tech.mit.edu/ V115/N39/brit.39w.html; Peacenet, *Campaign Against Nuclear Testing*, July 12, 1995 [online], http://nativenet.uthscsa.edu/archive/ nl/9507/0415.html; Peacenet, *Physicians Condemn French Nuclear Testing*, September 6, 1995 [online], http://nativenet.uthscsa.edu/

190 NOTES

archive/nl/9507/0415.html; Alex Bryans, "Boycott to Protest French Nuclear Testing," *Peace and Environmental News*, September, 1995 [online], http://perc.ca/PEN; and Mother Earth, *News Conference and Action Launches FME's International Boycott against French Nuclear Testing*, Press Release [online], November 18, 1995, www.mother earth.org/archive/archive/boycot/pr01.html. A list of nongovernmental organization supporters includes Greenpeace International, Friends of the Earth, Peace Action, Physicians for Social Responsibility, Women's Action for New Directions, Campaign for Nuclear Disarmament, for Mother Earth, International Physicians for the Prevention of Nuclear, National Peace Council, Physicians for Global Survival, National Test Ban Coalition, Vision National Project, Women's International Peace Initiatives, and Women Strike for Peace.

29. Friedman, "Using Consumer," 54–60.
30. Co-op America, *Co-op America's Boycott Organizers' Guide* [online], www.coopamerica.org, 2002; and Friedman, *Consumer Boycotts*, ch. 2.
31. Gene Watch, www.genewatch.org/News/labeling.htm, 2002; Genetics Forum, *Food Briefing Paper* [online], www.geneticsforum.org.uk/foodfact.htm, 2002; Greenpeace, *Shopper's Guide to GM* [online], www.greenpeace.org.uk, 2002.
32. Cashore et al., 184–7; and Andrew Jordan et al., "Consumer Responsibility-Taking and Eco-Labeling Schemes in Europe," in Micheletti et al., eds., 2003, 162–3.
33. Arthur Edmond Appleton, *Environmental Labelling Programmes. International Trade Law Implications* (London: Kluwer Law International, 1997); and Gary Cook et al., *Applying Trade Rules to Timber Ecolabeling. A Review of Timber Ecolabeling and the WTO Agreement on Technical Barriers to Trade* (Geneva: Center for International Environmental Law (CIEL), 1997).
34. Cowe and Williams, 29.
35. Jordan et al., 176–7 and Cashore et al., 194–6.
36. Benjamin Cashore, "Legitimacy and the Privatization of Environmental Governance: How Non State Market-Driven (NSMD) Governance Systems Gain Rule Making Authority," *Governance Journal* 15 (October 4, 2002).
37. Jordan et al., 166–74. Jakob Klint, *Max Havelaar-mærkede produkter— en undersøgelse af forbrugeren og storkunden* (Copenhagen: CASA, 1997); and *Miljömärkt*, "Sveriges mest kända miljömärke," magazine for the Nordic White Swan Eco-Label, No. 3, 1998.
38. Members of Global Ecolabelling Network (GEN) include Australia, Brazil, Canada, Croatia, Czech Republic, Denmark, EU, Germany, Greece, Hong Kong, Hungary, India, Israel, Japan, Korea, Luxembourg, New Zealand, Taiwan, Spain, Sweden, Thailand, United Kingdom, and the United States. For more information see www.gen.gr.jp/members.html. Other countries with type 1 schemes are Austria and the Netherlands.

39. For information see Global Ecolabelling Network at www.gen.gr.jp.
40. Jordan et al., 163–7.
41. Ibid., 163.
42. D. J. Caldwell, *Ecolabeling and the Regulatory Framework: A Survey of Domestic and International Fora* (Washington, D.C.: Consumer's Choice Council, 1998), 3; and Jacquelyn Ottman, *The Debate over Eco-Seals: Is Self-Certification Enough?* [online] (J. Ottman Consulting, 1998), http://www.greenmarketing.com/articles/ama_Mar-2-98.html.
43. See Jordan et al.
44. EU-Flower, *EU Eco-label*, http://europa.eu.int/comm/environment/ecolabel, 2002; and Swan (Nordic Swan eco-label), www.svanen.nu, 2002."
45. TCO Development, 2002, *This is TCO Development*, www.tco developmentl.com/i/omtcodevelopment/index.html.
46. Simon Zadek and Pauline Tiffen, *Dealing with and in the Global Economy: Fairer Trade in Latin American. Sustainable Agricultural and Development Experiences* [online]. TNI On-Line Archives, http://www.tni.org/achives/tiffen/tiffzad.htm, 2.
47. Oxfam,www.oxfam.org.uk/fairtrad/whyft.htm, no date; and Fairtrade Labeling Organization, *Fairtrade: A Better Deal*, www.fairtrade.net/better_deal.html, 2002.
48. Probably the best-known proponents are Simon Zadek and Pauline Tiffen. See Zadek and Tiffin, "Dealing with," Simon Zadek and Pauline Tiffen, " 'Fair Trade': Business or Campaign?" *Development. Journal of SID (Society for International Development)* 3 (1996); and Simon Zadek, *Trade Fair* [online], http:/www.zadek.net/tradefair.pdf.
49. EFTA, *Fair Trade: Let's Go Fair. Fair Trade—History, Principles and Practices* [online], www.eftafairtrade.org/Document.asp?DocID = 33&tod = 152942, 2002.
50. Eduard Douwes Dekker, *Max Havelaar of de koffijveilingen der Nederlandsche handelmaatschappij* (Amsterdam, 1917).
51. Max Havelaar Foundation, www.maxhavellar.nl/eng.
52. Paul D. Rice and Jennifer McLean, *Sustainable Coffee at the Crossroads* (Washington D.C.: Consumer's Choice Council, 1999), 52–3.
53. Directorate-General for Agriculture, European Commission, *The Common Agricultural Policy. Attitudes of EU Consumers to Fair Trade Bananas* (Brussels: European Commission, 1997).
54. Network of European World Shops, *European Commission on Fair Trade* [online], www.worldshops.org/fairtrade/communication4.htm; European Commission, *Green Paper. Promoting a European Framework for Corporate Social Responsibility* (Brussels: com (2001) 416 final).
55. Others include Austria, Belgium, Denmark, Italy, Norway, Ireland, Finland, Luxemburg, the Netherlands, Sweden, and Switzerland.
56. *FLO News Bulletin*, "International Fairtrade Certification Mark," No. 6 (April 2002): 3–4.
57. International Federation for Alternative Trade (IFAT), *IFAT the Global Network for Fair Trade* [online], www.ifat.org/dwr/home.hml, 2002.

58. Network of European World Shops, www.worldsshops.org, 2002.
59. For instance, one of the largest unions in the Swedish Trade Union Council (LO) now purchases fair traded coffee. See "Rättvist kaffe på Metall," *LO Globalt*, November 4, 2002 [online], www.lo.se.
60. Oxfam has run an e-petition campaign entitled "The Big Noise." The rock stars Bono and Chris Martin and as well as such distinguished international policymakers as Archbishop Desmond Tuto, his holiness Dalai Lama, and U.N. Secretary General Kofi Annan have signed the e-petition. Over one million people have signed it as of June 2003. See Oxfam, "Make Trade Fair," www.maketradefair.org, 2003."
61. Rick Young, "Green Coffee," *Fault Line* June 10, 2002 [online], www.faultline.org/news/2002/07/coffee.html.
62. See Oxfam, www.oxfam.org.uk, 2002; Smithsonian Migratory Bird Center, *Shade Grown Coffee* [online], http://natzoo.si.edu/smbc/Research/Coffee/coffee.htm, 2002; and Responsible Coffee Campaign, *Wake Up and Smell the Coffee* [online], http://www.planeta.com/ecotravel/ag/coffee/campaign/campaign.html, 2002.
63. See the video on the Transfair USA's website, www.transfairusa.org, 2002.
64. Ethical Consumer, *Welcome to Ethical Consumer* [online], www.ethicalconsumer.org, 2002.
65. Ethical Consumer, *Why Buy Ethically? An Introduction to the Philosophy Behind Ethical Purchasing* [online], www.ethicalconsumer.org/aboutetc/why_buy_ethically.htm, 2002.
66. Consumer's Choice Council, www.consumerscouncil.org, 2002.
67. The other countries are the Netherlands, Flanders Belgium, Walonia Belgium, Italy, Sweden, Portugal, Austria, and Switzerland. See www.cleanclothes.org/contacting.htm, 2002.
68. For information on this student organization see Lisa Featherstone and United Students Against Sweatshops, *Students Against Sweatshops* (London: Verso, 2002).
69. International Federation of Organic Agricultural Movements, *Information about IFOAM* [online], www.ifoam.org/whoisifoam/general.html, 2002.
70. Ecocert Belgium, www.ecocert.be/ecopresenteng.html, 2002; Organic Trust, *The Organic Trust Symbol* [online], www.iol.ie/~organic/trust.html, 2002; USDA Organic, *The National Organic Program. Organic Food Standards and Labels: The Facts* [online], www.ams.usda.gov/nop/Consumers/brochure.html; Biological Farmers Association, *The Australian Certified Organic* [online], www.bfa.com. au, 2002; and KRAV, www.krav.se.
71. Organic Trade Association, *Organic Consumer Trends 2001* [online], www.ota.con/consumer_trends_2001.htm, 2002; New Economics Foundation, *The Naked Consumer. Why Shoppers Deserve Honest Product Labelling*. Report January, 2001 (London: New Economics Foundation), 3–5.

72. See KRAV, *Foreign Certification Bodies Recognized by KRAV* [online], www.krav.se, 2002.

73. Personal communication with Laurence Leduc, IFOAM, November 7, 2002.

74. For instance, GeneWatch and the Consumer's Choice Council 2002.

75. For instance, Friends of the Earth, www.foe.org.uk/campaigns/food_and_biotechnology, 2000.

76. Friends of the Earth, *Real Food. Campaign* [online], www.foe.org.uk/campaigns/real_food/issues/food_for_all, 2002; World Wildlife Foundation U.K., *Wildlife Benefits from Organic Farming* [online], www.wwf.org.uk, 2002; Pesticide Action Network International, *PAN International Campaigns* [online], www.pan-international.org/campaignsEn.html, 2002; and Organic Consumers Association, *Campaigning for Food Safety, Organic Agriculture, Fair Trade and Sustainability* [online], www.organicconsumers.org, 2002.

77. Elinor Ostrom, *Self-Governance and Forest Resources* [online] (Jakarta, Indonesia: Center for International Forestry Research (CIFOR). Occasional Paper No. 20, 1999), http://www.cgiar.org/cifor; and Aseem Prakash, "A New-Institutionalist Perspective on ISO 14000 and Responsible Care," *Business Strategy and the Environment* 8 (1999): 232–6.

78. Ostrom, 4–6; and Elinor Ostrom, *Governing the Commons. The Evolution of Institutions for Collective Action* (Cambridge: Cambridge University Press, 1990).

79. Cashore et al., 182; and Jonathan Peacey, *The Marine Stewardship Council Fisheries Certification Program: Progress and Challenges* [online], www.msc.org, 2.

80. Cashore, "Legitimacy," 509–13.

81. International Tropical Timber Organization, *What is the International Tropical Timber Agreement?* [online], www.itto.or.jp/inside/about.html, 2002.

82. Steven Bernstein and Benjamin Cashore, "Globalization, Four Paths of Internationalization and Domestic Policy Change: The Case of Eco-forestry Policy Change in British Columbia, Canada," *Canadian Journal of Political Science* 33 (1) (2000); and Steven Bernstein and Benjamin Cashore, "The International–Domestic Nexus: The Effects of International Trade and Environmental Politics on the Canadian Forest Sector," in Howlett, ed., *Canadian Forest Policy: Regimes, Policy Dynamics and Institutional Adaptations* (Toronto: University of Toronto Press, 2001).

83. Ostrom, *Self-Governance*, 8–10.

84. FSC, *Frequently Asked Questions* [online], www.fscoax.org/principal.htm, 2002.

85. Rachael Crossley, *A Review of Global Forest Management Certification Initiatives: Political and Institutional Aspects* [online], http://www.forestry.ubc.ca/concert/crossley.html, 1996, 3.

86. Cashore et al., 182, 185.
87. Forest Stewardship Certification, *Welcome to the Forest Stewardship Council* [online], www.fscoax.org/index.html, 2000.
88. Forest Stewardship Certification, *FSC Process Guidelines for Developing Regional Certification Standards* [online], FSC A.C. document 4.2, www.fscoax.org/html/ 4–2.html, 2000.
89. Ibid.
90. Cashore, et al., 185.
91. The Pan European Forest Certification, www.pefc.org, 2000.
92. Cashore, 506–9.
93. For details see Cashore et al., 184.
94. International Forest Industry Roundtable, *Proposing an International Mutual Recognition Framework* [online], report edited by James Griffiths, www.sfms.com/recognition.htm, 2001.
95. Peacey, 1.
96. Marine Stewardship Certification, www.msc.org/homepage.html.
97. Cathy Wessells et al., *U.S. Consumer Preferences for Ecolabeled Seafood: Results of a Consumer Survey*, unpublished report (Rhode Island: Department of Environmental and Natural Resource Economics, University of Rhode Island, 1999); and Marine Stewardship Council, *Chain of Custody Certification. Questions and Answers* [online], www.msc.org, 2000.
98. Samuel Case, *The Socially Responsible Guide to Smart Investing. Improve Your Portfolio as You Improve the Environment* (Rocklin, CA: Prisma Books, 1996); David Vogel, "Tracing the Roots of the Contemporary Political Consumerist Movement: Marketized Political Activism in the U.S. in the 1960s," in Micheletti et al., eds., 2003, 93–5.
99. David Vogel, *Kindred Strangers. The Uneasy Relationship between Politics and Business in America* (Princeton: Princeton University Press, 1996).
100. PAX World Funds, *The History of Pax* [online], www.paxfund. com/matures.htm, 2002.
101. Saul Alinsky, *Rules for Radicals. A Practical Primer for Realistic Radicals* (New York: Vintage Books, 1971).
102. Vogel, *Kindred Strangers*, 117.
103. A sample of advice books on the subject includes Scott Fehrenbacher, *Put Your Money Where Your Morals Are. A Guide to Values-Based Investing* (Nashville: Broadman and Holman Publishers, 2001; Amy Domini, *Socially Responsible Investing. Making a Difference in Making Money* (Chicago: Dearborn Trade, 2001); Hal Brill, *Investing with Your Values. Making Money and Making a Difference* (Gabriola Island, BC: New Society Publishers, 2000); John C. Harrington, *Investing with Your Conscience. How to Achieve High Return Using Socially Responsible Investing* (New York: Wiley, 1991); and Alan J. Miller, *Socially Responsible Investing. How to Invest with Your Conscience* (New York: New York Institute of Finance, 1991).

104. The quotations are from Friends Provident, *Welcome to the Socially Responsible Investment Web Site*, www.friendsprovident.co.uk/steward-ship/bottom.jhtml; jsessionid=CSO4WY4Z.

105. Council on Economic Priorities, 1998, *The Corporate Report Card. Rating 250 of America's Corporations for the Socially Responsible Investor* (New York: Dutton Book, Penguin Putnam Inc., 1998), ix.

106. Social Investment Forum, *What is the Social Investment Forum?* www.socialinvest.org/areas/general/whatisSIF.htm, 2000; and Friends Provident, *Friends Provident. Stewardship Newsletter* No. 8 (Winter 1999/2000) [online], www.friendsprovident.co.uk/portal/aboutus.html.

107. Social Investment Forum.

108. Ibid. and Shareholder Action Network, *Shareholder Activity as a Tool for Corporate Transparency and Democracy* [online], www.foe.org/international/shareholder/toolsfordemocracy.html.

109. Shareholder Action Network, *Take Action* [online], www.share holderaction.org/action.cfm.

110. AFL-CIO, *The AFL-CIO Investment Program* [online], www.aflcio.org/publ/estatements/feb2001/investmentprogram.htm,2 001; and Transport Salaried Staff' Association, *TSSA Ethical Investment Charter*, www.tssa.org.uk/news/jnl/9912/ethics.htm, 1999.

111. Amnesty International, *Socially Responsible Investment Campaign*, www.amnesty.org.uk/business/campaigns/sri.shtml, 2000; Friends of the Earth (FOE), *FOE Calls for Ethical Pension Information* [online], Press Release, March 28, 2001, www.foel.org/uk; Rättvisemärkt, *Samarbete för etiska placeringar!* [online], press release November 23, 1998, www.raettvist.se/press63.htm; Ethical Consumer, *Welcome to Ethical Consumer*, www.ethicalconsumer.org, 2002; and Co-op America, *Invest Responsibly* [online], www.coopamerica.org, 2002.

112. Ethical Investment Research Service (EIRIS), *About EIRIS*, www.eiris.u-net.com, 2000; Ethical Investors, *Services for Charities. Retirement Planning* [online], www.ethicalinvestors.co.uk/charity_ retire.htm, 2002; and Council of Institutional Investors, www.cii.org.

113. Russell Sparkes, "Social Responsible Investment Comes of Age [online]," *Professional Investor*, June 2002, http://www.uksif.org/publications/article-2000–06/contents.shtml.

114. See Árni Sverrisson, "Translation Networks, Knowledge Brokers and Novelty Construction: Pragmatic Environmentalism in Sweden," *Acta Sociologica* 44 (4) (1999).

115. Compare with Directorate-General for Agriculture, European Commission, *The Common Agricultural Policy. Attitudes of EU Consumers to Fair Trade Bananas* (Brussels: European Commission, 1997), 4.

116. Political consumers have not been studied sufficiently and caution should be exercised when evaluating the available statistics. It is diffi-cult to compare the different data sets with each other. The most

comprehensive study of political consumers to date is a study from the Danish Study of Power and Democracy. This study underscores the importance of education (particularly junior college and university education) as the main explanation for political consumerist involvement, a common result for interpreting varying levels of political participation in a population. In terms of political ideology, Danish political consumers tend to have slight Left leanings and a global political identity. Thus, far leftist or rightist political ideology does not show up as a special characteristic of political consumers. Neither are they rich people. Rather, they are middle-income people who trust the political system and are interested in politics. See Jørgen Goul Andersen and Mette Tobiasen, *Politisk forbrug og politiske forbrugere. Globalisering og politik i hverdagslivet* (Aarhus: Magtudredningen, Aarhus Universitet, 2001) and their chapter in English, "Who are these Political Consumers Anyway? Survey Evidence from Denmark," in Micheletti et al., eds., 2003. A Swedish survey shows that a majority of Swedes (69%) believe that they can influence society by purchasing goods and services from companies that are ethical role models, that they (77%) have personal responsibility for societal development when s/he purchases goods and services from companies, and believe (71%) that their consumer choice is a better vehicle than legislation to influence the ethical behavior of companies. See SIFO, *Vad händer med Sverige* (Stockholm: SIFO, 2001). These two surveys also tend to emphasize the role of women and young people. Available market studies from the United States, Sweden, and Denmark find that women stand out as users of organic food labels, the Max Havelaar fair trade label, and eco-labels for seafood and are more concerned than men about genetically modified food and pesticide use on food. See LUI Marknadsinformation AB, *Konsumentundersökning om ekologiska produkter/KRAV* (Stockholm: LUI, 1999), 3; LRF and Ekologiska Lantbrukarna, *Vägen till marknaden. Ekologiska produkter. En underlag för kommunikation om ekologiska produkter med konsumenternas önskemål och kunskaper som grund* (Stockholm: LRF, 2001), 21; Klint, 28; and Wessells et al. Consumer political activists confirm the importance of women and underscore that middle-class women are the focal group for all new political consumerist efforts. They are seen as the people with the interest and means for this kind of political involvement. See interview with Chad Dobson, Head of Consumer's Choice Council, Washington D.C., 2000. A market study commissioned by The Co-operative Bank in the United Kingdom on ethical consumerism in Britain shows that the group called "active consumers," a group similar to political consumers, are defined by their attitudes to and behavior on ethical issues and not by standard socio-demographic criteria: Cowe and Williams, 2.

117. For an interesting discussion on institutional imitation see Paul J. DiMaggio and Walter W. Powell, "The Iron Cage Revisited: Institutional Isomorphism and Collective Rationality in Organizational Fields," *American Sociological Review* 48 (1983); and Kerstin

Sahlin-Andersson, "Imitating by Editing Success. The Construction of Organizational Fields," in Czarniawska and Sevón, eds., *Translating Organizational Change* (Berlin: Walter de Gruyter, 1996).

118. Ethical Consumer, *Links*, www.ethicalconsumer.org/links.htm, 2002.
119. Ethical Junction, www.ethical-junction.org.
120. Association of European Consumers, *Responsible Consumption. Position Paper* [online] October, 2002, www.consumer-aec.org; Danmarks Aktive Forbrugere, www.aktiveforbrugere.dk; and (Norwegian) Etiskforbruk, www.etiskforbruk.no.
121. Right Livelihood Award, *Award Recipients 1980–2000* [online], www.rightlivelihood.se, 2002.
122. Rice and McLean, 4.
123. Mick Blowfield and Keith Jones, *Ethical Trade and Agricultural Standards—Getting People to Talk* [online] (Greenwich: Natural Resources Institute, no date), 8.
124. Ethical Trade Initiative, www.ethicaltrade.org, 2002.
125. For information on The Body Shop see Simon Zadek et al., eds., *Building Corporate Accountability. Emerging Practices in Social and Ethical Accounting, Auditing and Reporting* (London: Earthscan Publications LTD, 1997), 105–10. For a general discussion on the problems involved with ethical business see Paul Kennedy, "Selling Virtue: Political and Economic Contradictions of Green/Ethical Marketing in the U.K.," in Micheletti et al., eds., *Politics, Products, and Markets. Exploring Political Consumerism Past and Present* (New Brunswick, NJ: Transaction Publishers).
126. Coalition for Environmentally Responsible Economies (CERES), www.ceres.org, 2002.
127. Patricia H. Werhane, *Adam Smith and His Legacy for Modern Capitalism* (Oxford: Oxford University Press, 1991), vii f.
128. Compare with Ulrich Beck and Elisabeth Beck-Gernsheim, *Individualization* (London: Sage Publications, 2001).

4   A Study of Political Consumerism Today: The Case of
      Good Environmental Choice in Sweden

1. Andreas Duit, *Tragedins institutioner. Svenskt offentligt miljöskydd under trettio år* (Stockholm: Stockholm Studies in Politics, Department of Political Science, Stockholm University, 2002), ch. 2.
2. Bo Rothstein, *Just Institutions Matter. The Moral and Political Logic of the Universal Welfare State* (Cambridge: Cambridge University Press, 1998); and Diane Sainsbury, *Gender, Equality, and Welfare States* (Cambridge: Cambridge University Press, 1996).
3. Swedes have a rather negative view of the political system when measured by questions about the responsiveness of Members of Parliament to the opinions of ordinary citizens and their proclivity for vote maximization. See Sören Holmberg, "Down and Down We Go: Political

Trust in Sweden," in Norris, ed., *Critical Citizens. Global Support for Democratic Government* (Oxford: Oxford University Press, 1999), 107. However Swedes increasingly believe that politicians pay attention to demands placed for instance by local civil groups and groups of people. See Olof Petersson et al., *Demokrati och medborgarskap. Demokratirådets rapport 1998* (Stockholm: SNS Förlag, 1998), 51. Survey research also shows that Swedes tend to have trust in the welfare state. See Stefan Svallfors, "Kan man lita på välfärdsstaten? Risk, tilltro och betalningsvilja i den svenska välfärdsopinionen 1997–2000," in Fritzell and Palme, eds., *Välfärdens finansiering och fördelning* (Published as a parliamentary investigation in SOU 2001: 57), 357–90.

4. Dietlind Stolle, *Communities of Trust: Social Capital and Public Action in a Three Country Comparison in Sweden, Germany and the United States* (Ph.D. diss., Princeton: Princeton University, Department of Political Science, 2000).

5. Michele Micheletti, *Civil Society and State Relations in Sweden* (Aldershot: Avebury, 1995). It can also be mentioned that corporatist countries like Sweden have better environmental performance. See Duit, 61.

6. Bo Rothstein, ed., Demokrati som dialog. SNS-demokratiråds 1995 års rapport (Stockholm: SNS Förlag, 1995).

7. Statskontoret, "Översyn av offentlig upphandling" [online], www. statskontoret.se/dagensforvaltning/nyheterna/artiklar/199.shtml, 2000.

8. Ralph Nader et al., "Shopping for Innovation. The Government as Smart Consumer," *The American Prospect* 11 (Fall 1992); Trevor Russel, ed., *Greener Purchasing. Opportunities and Innovations* (Sheffield: Greenleaf Publishing, 1998); and European Commission, *Public Procurement in the European Union: Exploring the Way Forward* (Brussels: European Union, 1996).

9. Sören Holmberg and Kent Asp, *Kampen om kärnkraften: en bok om väljare, massmedier och folkomröstningen* (Stockholm: Liber, 1984).

10. Micheletti, 103–6.

11. SNF, Information from the website "Bra miljöval," www.Snf. se/hmv/bmv_artikel.htm; Svante Axelsson, "Miljömärkning—ett tecken på misslyckande," *Bra Miljöval magasin* No. 1 (1999); and Helena Norin, Handling officer, Good Environmental Choice, interview January 12, 2000.

12. Peter Esaiasson, *Svenska valkampanjer 1866–1988* (Gothenburg: Gothenburg Studies in Politics No. 22, Department of Political Science, Gothenburg University, 1990).

13. SNF, *Anteckningar från uppvaktning hos Margot Wallström angående ett svenskt miljömärkningsystem.* August 21, 1989.

14. Göran Bryntse et al., *Oblekt papper—för miljöns skul* (Stockholm: Svenska Naturskyddsföreningen, 1987).

15. The politics of paper products continued to play an important role in the SNF and for green political consumers. Association members became concerned about the paper on which the SNF magazine, *Sveriges Natur* (Sweden's Nature) was published. They sent letters and printed protest postcards to the SNF as well as a number of other associations who published magazines for their members. The postcards had been printed in a magazine for another environmental association. Some of the letters even offered expert advice on paper quality. A letter writer who lived close to a paper mill asked how the SNF could legitimately criticize paper mills for polluting the waterways when it used chlorine-bleached paper. He also compared the paper in *Sveriges Natur* with the paper used by a large supermarket chain. See Walter Tinnacher, "Angående: Tidskriften 'Sveriges Natur,' " February 21, 1987. Members and the interested public could read an article discussing the choice of paper quality in the April 1987 issue of the magazine, but the article did not silence their criticisms. Many of them still considered the SNF a hypocrite. The SNF took notice and changed the paper for its magazine in 1988. Discussion between members and the SNF regarding its use of paper for the magazine continued into the 1990s. See e.g., "Papperet är glättat med klorfritt," *Sveriges Natur* No. 3 (1991): 13; "Vi lyssnar på medlemmarna," *Sveriges Natur* No. 2 (1992): 15; "Optiskt vit," *Sveriges Natur* No. 4 (1993): 11; and "Läs kritiskt!" *Sveriges Natur* No. 5 (1993): 11.

16. SNF, *Information från Svenska Naturskyddsföreningen.* Press release on Finnish chlorine-bleached paper, 1998; and Lars Vaste, Information head at the Swedish Society for Nature Conservation, interview December 13, 2000.

17. For example, the large publisher, Liber, released two press statements. See "4 miljoner Liber-böcker på miljövänligt paper," March 4, 1988, and "Miljövänliga Liber-böcker minska klorutsläpp i våra sjöar," March 14, 1988.

18. Anders Friström, staff member of the Swedish Society for Nature Conservation and one of the people who started the Good Environmental Choice process in the 1980s, interview January 16, 2001.

19. SOU 1988: 61. *Miljömärkning av produkter.*

20. SNF, Yttrande över betänkandet "miljömärkning av produkter" (SOU 1988: 61).

21. Friström, interview.

22. "Köp bara miljöbästa batterier," *Sveriges Natur* No. 1 (1990): 12–15; and "Miljövänliga veckan," *Sveriges Natur* No. 4 (1990): 42

23. *Sveriges Natur,* "Köp inte!" No. 4 (1993): 26–30.

24. SNF, *Alla bra miljöval märkta produkter* (Stockholm: SNF, 1997); and Vaste.

25. SNF, *Historien om Bra Miljöval* [online], www.snf.se, 2002 and Magnus Boström, *Den organiserade miljörörelsen. Fallstudier av Svenska Naturskyddsföreningen, Världsnaturfonden, WWF, Miljöförbundet Jordens Vänner, Greenpeace och Det Naturliga Steget* (Stockholm: Score, 1999), 19.

26. Friström, interview.

27. John Elkington and Julia Hailes, *The Green Consumer's Supermarket Guide. Shelf by Shelf Recommendations for Products Which Don't Cost the Earth* (London: Gollancz, 1989).

28. Friström, interview.

29. Vaste.

30. Anders Friström, *PM om marknadsorienterat miljöarbete.* February 6, 1989, 2 (my translation).

31. See Andrew Jordan et al., "Consumer Responsibility-Taking and Eco Labeling Schemes in Europe," in Micheletti et al., eds., 2003, 162–3.

32. Magnus Boström, *Miljörörelsens mångfald* (Lund: Arkiv förlag, 2001), 180.

33. Friström, *PM*, 3.

34. Friström, *PM*, 13.

35. Anders Friström, *Anteckningar från uppvaktning hos Margot Wallström angående ett svenskt miljömärkningssystem*, August 21, 1989; Fredrik Holm, *Förslag till aktiviteter med anledning av diskussionen på TEM*, April 10, 1989; and Fredrik Holm, *Minnesanteckningar från seminarium om miljömärkning mm på TEM-gården i Sjöbo April 6–7*, April 10, 1989.

36. Norin, 2000; Friström, *PM*; Friström, *Anteckningar*; and Boström, *Den organiserade miljörörelsen*, 19–23.

37. Eiderström.

38. Arthur Edmond Appleton, *Environmental Labelling Programmes. International Trade Law Implications* (London: Kluwer Law International, 1997), 22–6.

39. SNF, *Alla bra miljöval märkta produkter* (Stockholm: SNF, 1997)

40. For comparisons see Appleton, 8. The unit also publishes a consumer guide that lists items approved in two rankings. The consumers' guide, which can also be accessed through the Internet, lists now over 500 products in the following fields: laundry detergents; stain removers and bleaches; cleaners; toilet cleansers; dishwasher detergents; dishwashing detergents; soap and shampoos; paper; diapers and similar products; textiles; electricity supplies; passenger (i.e., public) transport, and goods transport. The unit states that it only labels necessity products used in large quantities and with a significant environmental impact. Products used in large quantity with a negative environmental impact that are not seen as necessary—e.g., fabric softeners and private transportation in automobiles—do not qualify for assessment. Deregulation of the electricity industry has made it feasible to label electricity produced by non-fossil, renewable sources as green electricity. See SNF, Information from the website "Bra Miljöval-registret," www.snf.se/bmv/bmv-register/index.cfm, 2003; and Norin.

41. Holm, *Förslag*; and Holm, *Minnesanteckningar*.

42. Eidenström; Norin; and Boström, *Den organiserade miljörörelsen*, 20.

43. Désirée Haraldsson, *Skydda vår natur! Svenska Naturskyddsföreningens famväxt och tidiga utveckling* (Lund: Lund University Press, 1987); and Micheletti, 105 f.

44. SNF, *Verksamhetsriktlinjer 1999–2000* (Stockholm: SNF, 2000), 16.
45. Friström, interview.
46. Norin.
47. Friström, interview.
48. Anders Biel et al., "Köpbeteendets psykologi—Miljömedvetenhet och vanor," i Ekström and Forsberg, eds., 1999, 135–6.
49. Bo Thunberg, "Lagom är bäst—eller?" *Sveriges Natur*, No. 1 (1996): 4. Editorial by SNF's President; and SNF, *Lagom är bäst. På spaning efter en hållbar livsstil* (Stockholm: SNF, Årsbok, 1998). Surveys on the proportion of everyday-making green citizen-consumers tend to vary, and it is difficult to sort out which statistics should be given priority. A Nordic study showed that a little over 10% of Swedish shoppers stated that the environment was the most important consideration when they choose what to buy. See Nordic Council of Ministers, *Nordiska konsumenter om Svanen. Livstil, kännedom, attityd och förtroende* (Copenhagen: Nordiskt Ministerråd, 1999), 35. A Swedish study shows that everyday-making green consumerism needs to be broken down into different activities. More people sort their trash (26% in 1992 and 55% in 2002) while fewer green shop today (22% in 1992, 30% in 1996, and 17% in 2002) and about the same proportion walk instead of taking a motor-driven vehicle (21% in 1992 and 23% in 2001). See Sverker C. Jagers and Jerker Thorsell, "Media – ett hot mot miljön," in Holmberg and Weibull eds., *Fåfängans marknad. SOM-undersökningen* (Gothenburg: Gothenburg University, 2003), 136. A third study commissioned by the Swedish Consumer Agency (*Konsumentverket*) show that 91% of all Swedes between the ages of 15 and 75 state that they shop for green products at least occasionally, 51% do it often or always. More women than men are green shoppers, though more men buy green products than in the past. The study also shows that routine green consuming has increased between 1993 and 1997—from a little over 30% to 51%. See Konsumentverket, *Allmänhetens kunskaper, attityder och agerande i miljöfrågor* (Stockholm: Konsumentverket, 1998), 9 f.
50. Sverker Sörlin, "Konsumenterna kan inte rädda miljön," *Sveriges Natur* No. 3 (1999): 29.
51. Friström, interview.
52. Vaste.
53. See "Livsstilen avgörande för miljön," *Sveriges Natur* No. 2 (1989): 49.
54. "Välj rätt pensionsfond," *Sveriges Natur* No. 5 (2000): unnumbered page, my translation.
55. "Lågenergi-politik och handla miljövänligt," *Sveriges Natur* No. 4 (1989): 22.
56. "Vi lyssnar på medlemmarna," *Sveriges Natur* No. 2 (1992): 15.
57. For example, see the following articles: "Barnens natur. Tänk på miljön hemma! Det här kan du själv göra," *Sveriges Natur* No. 1 (1989): 53; "Barnens natur. Tänk på miljön hemma! Bäst med läsk i glas!" *Sveriges*

Natur No. 2 (1989): 82–3; "Barnens natur. Tänk på miljön hemma. Miljöbäst att inte slösa med papperet," *Sveriges Natur* No. 6 (1989): 32–3.

58. SNF, www.snf.se/bmv/varfor/varfor-3.htm; and Eva Eiderström, E-mail correspondence, December 2, 2002.

59. See Ulf von Sydow, "Ett anständigt liv," *Sveriges Natur* No. 3 (1992): 11; von Sydow was the SNF President in 1992. There are many examples of how the SNF attempts to promote sustainable thinking and the responsibility that each person has for such common pool resources as air and water quality and global natural resources. A poignant one reflects the footprint metaphor by declaring "You can eat 250 grams of pork a day or fly to Mallorca every other year. Then your gas ration has been used up." See Hanna Zetterberg, "Rättvist miljöutrymme—ett användbart begrepp," *Sveriges Natur* No. 5 (1998), my translation. The SNF has also given considerable attention to the number of environmentally dangerous chemicals that are used at homes, the environmental quality of the food we buy at supermarkets, what we clean our clothes in, how product packages affect the environment, and how we can learn to drive our cars in an environmentally friendly way.

60. "Miljömärkt el räddar uttern," *Sveriges Natur* No. 3 (1998): 24.

61. "Bra Miljöval räddar skogens liv," *Sveriges Natur* No. 4 (1999): 55.

62. SNF, *Verksamhetsberättelse 1998* (Stockholm: SNF, 1998), 2.

63. SNF, *Sveriges miljöbästa butik 1993. Resultat av Naturskyddsföreningens butiksundersökning* (Gothenburgh: Good Environmental Choice Unit, 1993), 4.

64. Statistics from Good Environmental Choice show that 224 supermarkets were eco-audited in 1990, roughly 600 in 1991, and 900 in 1992. See the newspaper *Handla Miljövänligt* No. 2, 1993.

65. See the newspaper *Handla Miljövänligt* Nos. 2–3, 1993.

66. "Spana efter bra butiker. Miljövänliga veckan," *Sveriges Natur* No. 4 (1992): 25.

67. "Butiker som slutat sälja klorin" and "KF lanserar klorinersättare," *Sveriges Natur* No. 4 (1993): 32; "Succé för miljövänliga veckan," *Sveriges Natur* No. 5 (1993): 38–9; "Klorinfax ökade trycket," *Sveriges Natur* No. 6 (1993): 30; and "Klorinbarometer i taket. Butiker som slutat sälja klorin," *Sveriges Natur* No. 1 (1994): 22.

68. The publicity given to green political consumerist actions is seen to lead to a competitive advantage. An example is a complaint registered by two large manufacturers at the Swedish Broadcasting Commission against unfair coverage of a storeowner who allowed journalists from a television program on the environment to film him as he cleared his shelves of environmentally dangerous household chemicals produced by the manufacturers. See "Miljöbästa butik anmäld för radionämnden," *Sveriges Natur* No. 3 (1994): 57.

69. This new more encompassing scheme includes as criteria that the store include the following items in its assortment: KRAV-labeled eggs, fruit, vegetables, bread, potting soil, and other KRAV products, and Good

Environmental Choice eco-labeled washing detergents. It cannot sell giant or tiger shrimp, chlorine, postcards that play tunes because they include environmentally harmful batteries in them, and detergents not labeled by the unit. It must only use green electricity that has been labeled by Good Environmental Choice. See the newspaper *Bra Miljöval* No. 1 (1999): 16. See also *Handla Miljövänligt* No. 2 (1995) and 1 (1997).

70. SNF, *Verksamhetsriktlinjer 1999–2000* (Stockholm: SNF, 2000), 22; and the Good Environmental Choice website, www.snf.se/hmv/bmv.

71. An example of the impact of the week on everyday life is the 1992 campaign. One hundred local chapters of roughly 250 had some kind of activity, and daily newspapers printed 350 articles on the week. After the yearly week ended, the unit sends out evaluation forms to the local chapters to receive feedback on its theme and organization. For the year 1992, 107 chapters answered; only three believed that the week should be discontinued. See *Handla Miljövänligt* 3 (1992) as well as other years; Eva Eiderström, head of Good Environmental Choice Unit and editor of the unit's magazine "Bra Miljöval," interview, January 12, 2000; and Norin. In 1993, the number of participating local chapters was 178; 46,000 people signed a petition for milk in returnable bottles, and almost 2,000 supermarkets were surveyed. See "KlorinBarometern: Nu 206 Butiker!" *Sveriges Natur* No. 5 (1993): 32; and the advertisement "Ditt bidrag har gjort dig rikare," *Sveriges Natur* No. 3 (1994).

72. "Nu miljömärks vårt resande," *Sveriges Natur* No. 5 (1994): 16.

73. "Rusning efter miljömärkt el," *Sveriges Natur* No. 2 (1998): 50–3; and SNF, *Rekordstor försäljning av miljömärkt el. June 31, 2002.* Press release (Stockholm: SNF, 2002).

74. Eiderström, E-mail correspondence.

75. SNF, *Verksamhetsriktlinjer,* 22 f.

76. Ds 1998: 49, *Jämställdhetsmärkning. Konsumentmakt för ett jämställt samhälle* (Stockholm: Fritzes kundtjänst, 1998); and SOU 2001: 9, *Reglerna kring och inställningen till frivillig jämställdhetsmärkning av produkter och tjänster. Delbetänkande av FRIJA. Utredningen om frivillig jämställdhetsmärkning av produkter och tjänster* (Stockholm, Fritizes kundtjänst, 2001).

77. For more information on Forest Stewardship Certification in Sweden see Minna Gillberg, "Green Image or Green Practice—Towards a New Paradigm? A Case Study of the Impact of the Biodiversity Convention in Relation to the Forest Industry in Finland and Sweden," in *Nordic Research Project on the Effectiveness of Multilateral Environmental Agreements. Workshop Proceedings and Study Reports* (Copenhagen: Nordic Council of Ministers, Nord No. 18, 1996); and Boström, *Den organiserade miljörörelsen,* 13–18.

78. SNF, *Verksamhetsriktlinjer;* SNF, *FSC—skogens märkning* [online], www.snf.se.

79. European Environmental Bureau, Swedish Evidence Proves: Ecolabels Can Work! Soap Industry Forced to Reduce Pressure on Environment.

Press   Release   March   25,   1999   (Brussels: EEB),
www.eeb.org/press/soap_industry_forced_to_reduce_p.htm."

80. See e.g., "Svenskt papper inte klorfritt," *Sveriges Natur* No. 6 (1987): 55.

81. Eidenström, interview and E-mail, 2000, 2002; and "Låt inte EU avväpna miljämärkningen," *Sveriges Natur* No. 3 (1998): 12–13.

82. European Environmental Bureau, *Position of the EEB on the Commission's Proposal for the Revision of the EMAS Regulation* [online], www.eeb.org/activities/position_of_the_ebb_on_proposal_htm, 1999.

83. Compare with Robert D. Putnam, *Bowling Alone. The Collapse and Revival of American Community* (New York: Simon and Schuster, 2000), 22–24.

84. The survey was conducted by a Swedish polling institute, SIFO. Eight hundred members (200 members with a post in the Society and 600 other members) were selected to answer a questionnaire that was sent to them. It was answered by 74%. One question asked whether they considered learning about green consumerism as a reason for membership. The people interviewed were given a scale from not at all important to very important to answer the question. Significant results show that twice as many women as men considered it very important (52 and 23% respectively) as a reason for membership and that more members who had joined the Society in 1985 or later considered it very important when compared to members who joined before 1985 (42 and 29%). It may also be the case that members who never have held a post in the society find it more important as a reason for membership than those who have held posts. Members lacking university education would appear to find it more important than those with university education. Among the group of members without any post in the society, it is the ones who joined the Society in 1985 or later who consider learning about green consumerism a very important reason for membership. Members who joined earlier see green consumerism as important but not to the same extent (34 and 44%). Finally, more women without posts than men without posts consider green consumerism as a very important reason for membership (54 and 27%). Statistical information on the survey is from the SNF.

85. Vaste.

86. Statistics show that about 80% of all regional contact people for the network are women. The statistics have been taken from the newsletter *Handla Miljövänligt* No. 4 (1997) and No. 3 (1999). Another group of statistics concerns the contact people for the Environmentally Friendly Week. The only statistics available are from 1993. They show the proportion of women to be at about 75%. See *Handla miljövänligt* No. 3 (1993). A third set of statistics over the contact person for the network in the local chapters shows: 69% were women in 1997 and 71% in 1999. See Good Environmental Choice, *Kretskontaktpersoner Handla Miljövänligt 1997, 1999* (Gothenburg: Good Environmental Choice, 2000).

87. Norin.
88. Per Selle, "The Norwegian Voluntary Sector and Civil Society in Transition. Women as Catalysts for Deep-Seated Change," in Rueschemeyer et al., 1998, 159–63; and Dag Wollebæck and Per Selle, *Det nye organisajonssamfunnet. Demokrati i omforming* (Bergen: Fagbokforlaget, 2002), chs. 7 and 9.
89. Norin; Eidenström, interview; and Friström, interview.
90. A focused group interview conducted with 15 members representing different age groups, genders, and different generations of members (a group who had been members for two years and another one with membership for at least three years) was conducted by the Swedish polling institute Testologen AB in 1995. The people interviewed generally believed that the SNF stands on the side of the consumer and successfully makes the public conscious of green consuming issues. One interviewed member stated that the Society reached out to her/him more as a consumer and "...I have in any case always been a person who enjoys being out in nature" ("...och jag har ändå alltid varit friluftsmänniska"). See SNF, *Information from a focused group interview survey of members conducted by Testologen AB* (Stockholm: SNF, 1995), 17, my translation.
91. Eidenström; Norin, 2000; and see SNF survey reported in endnote 84.
92. Norin.
93. SNF, *List of employees* [online], www.snf.se/om/kansli.htm, 2000; and Eiderström.
94. Jordan et al. 163–74; and information on the listed labeling schemes in Frieder Rubik and Gerd Scholl, eds., *Eco-labelling Practices in Europe. An Overview of Environmental Product Information Schemes* (Berlin: IÖW, 2002).
95. Olof Petersson et al., *Demokrati och medborgarskap. Demokratirådets rapport 1998* (Stockholm: SNS Förlag, 1998), 55.
96. Bo Rothstein, *Corporatism and Reformism: The Social Democratic Institutionalization of Class Conflict* (Uppsala: Study of Power and Democracy in Sweden, 1987); Bo Rothstein, *Den korporativa staten: Intresseorganisationer och statsförvaltning i svensk politik* (Stockholm: Norstedts juridik, 1992); and Micheletti, ch. 5.
97. Andrew Schonfield, *Modern Capitalism. The Changing Balance of Public and Private Power* (London: Oxford University Press, 1965), 199; and Micheletti, 73 ff.
98. Micheletti, 73 ff.
99. Svante Axelsson, former secretary general of SNF, discussion about Good Environmental Choice, no date.
100. Jordan et al., 163–74; and Rubik and Scholl, eds.
101. Micheletti, 120–7.

5   SHOPPING WITH AND FOR VIRTUES

1. Patrik Aspers and Emil Uddhammar, eds., *Framtidens dygder—om etik i praktiken* (Stockholm: City University Press, 1998); and Alasdair MacIntyre, *After Virtue. A Study in Moral Theory* (London: Duckworth, 1993).
2. Göran Möller, "Den dygdiga människan," in Aspers and Uddhammar, eds., 1998, 25–33.
3. A catalogue of virtues includes elementary character ones (courage, patience, good physical condition, presence of mind, self-confidence, energy), social character ones (social skills, justice, friendliness, empathy, gentleness, loyalty, respect for authority, civility, group loyalty, generosity, ability to compromise, sense of responsibility, involvement, cooperative attitude, ability to communicate, honesty, humor, and charisma), and intellectual character ones (phronesis, ability to think abstractly, aesthetic judgment, ability to understand others, openness, and self-understanding). See Anders Tolland, "Dygder för alla tider," in Aspers and Uddhammar, eds., 1998, 65.
4. Ibid., 59–61.
5. Benjamin Cashore et al., "Legitimizing Political Consumerism: The Case of Forest Certification in North America and Europe," in Micheletti *et al.*, eds., *Politics, Products, and Markets. Exploring Political Consumerism Past and Present* (New Brunswick, NJ: Transaction Publishers, 2003).
6. Robert D. Putnam, *Bowling Alone. The Collapse and Revival of American Community* (New York: Simon and Schuster, 2000), ch. 1.
7. Dietlind Stolle, *Communities of Trust: Social Capital and Public Action in a Three Country Comparison in Sweden, Germany and the United States* (Ph.D. diss., Princeton: Princeton University, Department of Political Science, 2000).
8. For instance, Putnam, in particular chs. 2, 3, and 9
9. Patrick François, *Social Capital and Economic Development* (London: Routledge, 2002); and Saguaro Seminar in Civic Engagement in America, *Bettertogether* (Harvard, MA: John F. Kennedy School of Government, Harvard University, 2001), 4.
10. Bob Edwards and Michael W. Foley, eds., *Social Capital, Civil Society and Contemporary Democracy* (Thousand Oaks, CA: Sage, 1997).
11. Frieder Rubik and Gerd Scholl, eds., *Eco-Labelling Practices in Europe. An Overview of Environmental Product Information Schemes* (Berlin: Institut für ökologische Wirtschaftsforschung (IÖW), 2002), 319, 324.
12. See Putnam ch. 16; and Dietlind Stolle and Marc Hooghe, "Consumers as Political Participants? Shifts in Political Action Repertoires in Western Societies," in Micheletti et al., eds., 2003, 265–9.
13. Dag Wollebæck and Per Selle, *Det nye organisasjonssamfunnet. Demokrati i omforming* (Bergen: Fagbokforlaget, 2002), chs. 7 and 9.
14. Janet A. Flammang, *Women's Political Voice: How Women are Transforming the Practice and Study of Politics* (Philadelphia: Temple University Press, 1997), ch. 4.

15. Annette Baier, "Trust and Antitrust," *Ethics* 96 (1986), 245–7, 252–60; and Stolle.
16. Michele Micheletti, "Why More Women? Issues of Gender and Political Consumerism," in Micheletti et al., eds., *Politics, Products, and Markets. Exploring Political Consumerism Past and Present* (New Brunswick, NJ: Transaction Publishers), 255–58.
17. Carole Pateman, "Feminist Critiques of the Public/Private Dichotomy," in Carole Pateman, ed., 1989; and Mathis Wackernagel and William Rees, *Our Ecological Footprint. Reducing Human Impact on the Earth* (Gabriola Island, BC, Canada: New Society Publishers, 1986).
18. Norman Barry, *Respectable Trade. The Dangerous Delusions of Corporate Social Responsibility and Business Ethics* (London: Adam Smith Institute, 2000), 35.
19. David Vogel, *Kindred Strangers. The Uneasy Relationship between Politics and Business in America* (Princeton: Princeton University Press, 1996), 160.
20. This criticism is raised in the book *Can We Put an End to Sweatshops?* by Archon Fung et al. (Boston: Beacon Press, 1001), 47–8, 65–9; and in the report from International Council of Human Rights Policy, *Beyond Voluntarianism. Human Rights and the Developing International Legal Obligations of Companies* (Geneva: International Council of Human Rights Policy, 2002), 7–20.
21. Göran Ahrne, "A Labour Theory of Consumption," in Per Otnes, ed., *The Sociology of Consumption* (Oslo: Solum Forlag, 1988).
22. Compare with Richard Sennett, *The Fall of Public Man* (Cambridge: Cambridge University Press, 1977).
23. See Putnam.
24. I want to thank my good friend and colleague Dietlind Stolle (McGill) for this expression.
25. The expression "civilize capitalism" comes from Landon R. Y. Storrs, *Civilizing Capitalism. The National Consumers' League, Women's Activism, and Labor Standards in the New Deal Era* (Chapel Hill: The University of North Carolina Press, 2000).
26. Dana Frank, *Purchasing Power. Consumer Organizing, Gender, and the Seattle Labor Movement 1919–1929* (Cambridge: Cambridge University Press, 1994); and Lizabeth Cohen, *Making a New Deal. Industrial Workers in Chicago, 1919–1939* (Cambridge: Cambridge University Press, 1990).
27. Third World Traveler, *Shell Oil in Nigeria* [online], http://www.thirdworldtraveler.com/Boycotts/ShellNigeria_boycott.html, 2002.
28. See Jørgen Goul Andersen and Mette Tobiasen, *Politisk forbrug og politiske forbrugere. Globalisering og politik i hverdagslivet* (Aarhus: Magtudredning), 55–6; Olof Petersson et al., *Demokrati och medborgarskap. Demokratirådets rapport 1998* (Stockholm: SNS Förlag, 1998), 80 as well as descriptive statistics from the study provided by Jan Teorell, and Olof Petersson et al., *Medborgarnas makt* (Stockholm: Carlssons,

1989), 139 as well as descriptive statistics from the study available in the report by Göran Blomberg et al., *Medborgarundersökningen. Råtabeller* (Stockholm: Maktutredningen, 1989), 131, 165.

29. Andreas Follesdal, "Political Consumerism as Chance and Challenge," in Micheletti et al., eds., 2003, 17–18.

30. Follesdal, 4.

31. Fung et al., 3–40. *Can We Put An End to Sweatshops?* (Boston: Beacon Press, 2001).

32. Naomi Klein, *No Logo. No Space, No Choice, No Jobs* (London: Flamingo, 2000), 30ff.; and Christer Sanne, "Willing Consumers—or Locked-in? Policies for a Sustainable Consumption," *Ecological Economics* 42 (2002), 280–6.

33. Ralph Nader, "Corporations and the UN: Nike and Others 'Bluewash' their Images," *San Francisco Bay Guardian*, September 18, 2000.

34. CorpWatch, *Campaigns: Greenwash Award* [online], http:/www. corpwatch.org.

35. Jed Greer and Kenny Bruno, *Greenwash. The Reality behind Corporate Environmentalism* (Penang, Malaysia: Third World Network, 1996); and Nader.

36. For a discussion of effectiveness see Margaret E. Keck and Kathryn Sikkink, "Transnational Advocacy Networks in International and Regional Politics," *International Social Science Journal* No. 159 (March 1999): 95 ff.

37. Pierre Bourdieu, "Uniting to Better Dominance," *Items and Issues* 2 (3–4) (Winter 2001): 1.

38. Klein, ch. 9; and Fung et al., vii–xi.

39. Benjamin Barber, "Globalizing Democracy," *The American Prospect* 11 (20) (September 2000): 2.

40. Mary Kaldor, "'Civilizing' Globalization? The Implications of the 'Battle in Seattle'" [online], http://www.lse.ac.uk/Depts/global/MarySeattle.htm, 2000, 8.

41. Paul Kennedy, "Capitalist Enterprise as a Moral or Political Crusade: Opportunities, Constraints and Contradictions," in O'Connor and Wynne, eds., *From the Margins to the Centre. Cultural Production and Consumption in the Post-Industrial City* (Aldershot: Arena, Ashgate Publishing Limited, 1996), 227.

42. Ibid., 235.

43. Mads P. Sørensen, *Den politiske forbruger—en analyse af ideen og fænomenet* (Ph.D. diss., Aarhus: Department of the History of Ideas, Aarhus University), chs. 3–5.

44. Ward Morehouse, "Consumption, Civil Action and Corporate Power: Lessons from the Past, Strategies for the Future," *Development. Journal of the Society for International Development* 41 (1) (1998), 51.

45. Simon Zadek, "Consumer Works!" *Development. Journal of the Society for International Development* 41 (1) (1998): 7.

46. See for instance ibid.; Minna Gillberg, *From Green Image to Green*

Practice. Normative Action and Self-Regulation (Lund: Lund Studies in Sociology of Law, 1999), 194–208; Fung et al.; and Debora L. Spar, "The Spotlight and the Bottom Line. How Multinationals Export Human Rights," *Foreign Affairs* 77 (2) (1998).

APPENDIX

1. Laura Westra and Patricia H. Werhane, eds., *The Business of Consumption: Environmental Ethics and the Global Economy* (Lanham, MD: Rowman & Littlefield, 1998).
2. Naomi Klein, *No Logo* (London: Flamingo, 2000), ch. 17.
3. Roger Cowe and Simon Williams, *Who are the Ethical Consumers?* (London: The Co-operative Bank, no date), 13.
4. Jørgen Goul Andersen and Mette Tobiasen, *Politisk forbrug og politiske forbrugere. Globalisering og politik i hverdagslivet* (Aarhus: Magtudredningen, Aarhus Universitet, 2001), 55–6.
5. Ds 1998: 49. Jämställdhetsmärkning. Konsumentmakt för ett jämställt samhälle (Stockholm: Fritzes kundtjänst).
6. Benjamin Cashore et al., "Legitimizing Political Consumerism: The Case of Forest Certification in North America and Europe," in Micheletti *et al.*, eds., *Politics, Products, and Markets. Exploring Political Consumerism Past and Present* (New Brunswick, NJ: Transaction Publishers, 2003); Andrew Jordan et al., "Consumer Responsibility-Taking and Eco Labeling Schemes in Europe," in same edited volume; and Frieder Rubik and Gerd Scholl, *Eco-Labelling Practices in Europe. An Overview of Environmental Product Information Schemes* (Berlin: Institut für ökologische Wirtschaftsforschung (IÖW), 2002).
7. For forest certification, fragmented ownership has been shown as not being conducive for certification. For eco-labeling, competition in markets with high environmental awareness is an incentive for seeking eco-labeling approval. See Cashore et al. In the Swedish case, the presence of only three supermarket retailers facilitated the development of Good Environmental Choice. See chapter 4 in this volume.
8. Assessing the influence of global actors is acknowledged as an importance research task. See Margaret E. Keck and Kathryn Sikkink, *Activists Beyond Borders: Advocacy Networks in International Politics* (Ithaca: Cornell University Press, 1998), 25–6 and "Transnational Advocacy Networks in International and Regional Politics," *International Social Science Journal* No. 159 (March 1999): 98–9. Their ideas have been used for the five aspects.

BIBLIOGRAPHY

SECONDARY SOURCES

Ahrne, Göran. 1988. "A Labour Theory of Consumption." In *The Sociology of Consumption*, edited by Per Otnes, Per. Oslo: Solum Forlag.

Åkerman, Brita, Yvonne Hirdman, and Kajsa Pehrsson. 1983. *Vi kan, vi behövs! Kvinnorna går samman i egna föreningar*. Stockholm: Akademilitteratur AB.

Aléx, Peter. 1994. *Den rationella konsumenten. KF som folkuppfostrare 1899–1939*. Stockholm: Brutus Östlings Bokförlag Symposion.

Alinsky, Saul. 1971. *Rules for Radicals. A Practical Primer for Realistic Radicals*. New York: Vintage Books.

Alinsky, Saul. 1971. "Proxies for People. A Vehicle for Involvement. An Interview with Saul Alinsky," *Yale Review of Law and Social Action* 1 (Spring): 64–9.

Anderson, C. W. 1990. *Pragmatic Liberalism*. Chicago: University of Chicago Press.

Andersson, Monica. 1976. *Sacco Vanzetti—en politisk rättegång*. Förening BHS Småskrifter No. 6. Borås: Föreningen BHS publicerar.

Annan, Kofi. 2001. *Dag Hammarskjöld and the 21st Century. The Fourth Dag Hammarskjöld Lecture*. Uppsala: Dag Hammarskjöld Minnesfond.

Appleton, Arthur Edmond. 1997. *Environmental Labelling Programmes. International Trade Law Implications*. London: Kluwer Law International.

Aronsson, Peter, Patrik Aspers, Ludvig Beckman, Fredrik Erixon, Michele Micheletti, Göran Möller, Kenneth Strömberg, and Emil Uddhammar. 2001. *Dygder som drivkraft och föredöme*. Stockholm: City University Press.

Aspers, Patrik and Emil Uddhammar eds. 1998. *Framtidens dygder—om etik i praktiken*. Stockholm: City University Press.

Ayres, Edith. 1934. "Private Organizations Working for the Consumer," *The Annals of the American Academy of Political and Social Science* 173 (May): 158–65.

Baier, Annette. 1986. "Trust and Antitrust," *Ethics* 96: 231–60.

Bang, Henrik P. and Eva Sørensen. 1999. "The Everyday Maker: A New Challenge to Democratic Governance," *Administrative Theory and Praxis* 21 (3): 325–41.

Barber, Benjamin. 2000. "Globalizing Democracy," *The American Prospect* 11 (20, September): 1–6.

Barry, Norman. 2000. *Respectable Trade. The Dangerous Delusions of Corporate Social Responsibility and Business Ethics.* London: Adam Smith Institute.

Bar Yam, Naomi Bromberg. 1995. "The Nestlé Boycott. The Story of the Who/UNICEF Code for Marketing Breastmilk Substitutes," *Mothering* (Winter): 56–63.

Bauman, Zygmunt. 1995. *Life in Fragments.* Oxford: Blackwell.

Baumgartner, Frank R. and Bryan D. Jones. 1991. "Agenda Dynamics and Policy Subsystems," *The Journal of Politics* 53 (4): 1044–74.

Beck, Ulrich. 1994. "The Reinvention of Politics: Towards a Theory of Reflexive Modernization." In *Reflexive Modernization. Politics, Tradition and Aesthetics in the Modern Social Order*, edited by Ulrich Beck, Anthony Giddens, and Scott Lash. Oxford: Polity Press.

Beck, Ulrich. 1997. *The Reinvention of Politics. Rethinking Modernity in the Global Social Order.* Oxford: Polity Press.

Beck, Ulrick and Elisabeth Beck-Gernsheim. 2001. *Individualization.* London: Sage Publications.

Benford, Robert D. and Danny L. Valadez. 1998. *From Blood on the Grapes to Poison on the Grapes: Strategic Frame Changes and Resource Mobilization in the Farm Worker Movement.* Paper for the Annual Meeting of the American Sociological Association, San Francisco, CA, August 21.

Bennett, W. Lance. 2003. "Branded Political Communication: Lifestyle Politics, Logo Campaigns, and the Rise of Global Citizenship." In *Politics, Products, and Markets. Exploring Political Consumerism Past and Present*, edited by Michele Micheletti, Andreas Follesdal, and Dietlind Stolle. New Brunswick, NJ: Transaction Publishers, 2003.

Bernstein, Steven and Benjamin Cashore. 2000. "Globalization, Four Paths of Internationalization and Domestic Policy Change: The Case of Eco-forestry Policy Change in British Columbia, Canada," *Canadian Journal of Political Science* 33 (1): 67–99.

Bernstein, Steven and Benjamin Cashore. 2001. "The International–Domestic Nexus: The Effects of International Trade and Environmental Politics on the Canadian Forest Sector." In *Canadian Forest Policy: Regimes, Policy Dynamics and Institutional Adaptations*, edited by M. Howlett. Toronto: University of Toronto Press.

Biel, Anders, Maria Larsson, and Tommy Gärling. 1999. "Köpbeteendets psykologi—Miljömedvetenhet och vanor." In *Den flerdimensionella konsumenten—en antologi om svenska konsumenter*, edited by Karin M. Ekström and Håkan Forsberg. Gothenburg: Tre Böcker.

Bierman, John. 1982. *Raoul Wallenberg. En hjälte i vår tid. Biografi om "mannen som räddare 100 000 judar," hans liv, kamp och försvinnande.* Stockholm: AWE/Geber.

Black, David. 1999. "The Long and Winding Road: International Norms and Domestic Political Change in South Africa." In *The Power of Human*

Rights. International Norms and Domestic Change, edited by Thomas Risse, Stephen C. Ropp, and Kathryn Sikkink. Cambridge: Cambridge University Press.

Blaikie, Norman. 2000. *Designing Social Research. The Logic of Anticipation*. Cambridge: Polity Press.

Blomberg, Göran, Olof Petersson, and Anders Westholm. 1989. *Medborgarundersökningen. Råtabeller*. Stockholm: Maktutredningen.

Bloom, Paul N. and Ruth Belk Smith, eds. 1986. *The Future of Consumerism*. Lexington, MA: Lexington Books.

Blowfield, Mick and Keith Jones. N.d. *Ethical Trade and Agricultural Standards–Getting People to Talk*. Greenwich: Natural Resources Institute. (www.nri.org/NRET/IFASpapr.htm).

Bohstedt, John. 1988. "Gender, Household and Community Politics. Women in English Riots 1790–1810," *Past and Present* 120 (August): 88–122.

Bose, Subhas Chandra. 1931. *Swadeshi and Boycott*. Calcutta: Liberty Newspapers Limited.

Boström, Magnus. 1999. *Den organiserade miljörörelsen. Fallstudier av Svenska Naturskyddsföreningen, Världsnaturfonden, WWF, Miljöförbundet Jordens Vänner, Greenpeace och Det Naturliga Steget*. Stockholm: Score, Stockholm University.

Boström, Magnus. 2001. *Miljörörelsens mångfald*. Lund: Arkiv förlag.

Bourdieu, Pierre. 2001. "Uniting to Better Dominance," *Items and Issues* 2 (3–4) (Winter): 1–4.

Brainerd, J. G., ed. 1934. "The Ultimate Consumer. A Study in Economic Illiteracy," *The Annals of the American Academy of Political and Social Science* 173 (May): ix–xiv.

Branting, Georg. 1927. "Ansvaret. Slutkapitel i SACO-Vanzettidramat." In *Festskrift tillägnad Georg Branting uttgiven vid hans 60-årsdag 21 september 1947*, edited by Zeth Höglund and Hjalmar Mehr. Stockholm: Saxon & Lindström.

Breen, T. H. 1988. " 'Baubles of Britain': The American and Consumer Revolutions of the Eighteenth Century," *Past & Present* No. 119 (May): 73–104.

Breen, T. H. 1999. "Narrative of Commercial Life: Consumption, Ideology, and Community on the Eve of the American Revolution." In *Consumer Society in American History. A Reader*, edited by Lawrence B. Glickman. Ithaca, NY: Cornell University Press.

Brennan, William J. 1990. *Dissenting Opinion, FTC v. Superior Court Trial Lawyers' Association*. 493 U.S. 411, 436.

Briggs, Lyman J. 1934. "Services of the National Bureau of Standards to Consumers," *The Annals of the American Academy of Political and Social Science* 173 (May): 153–7.

Brill, Hal. 2000. *Investing with Your Values. Making Money and Making a Difference*. Gabriola Island, BC: New Society Publishers.

Brown, Judith, M. 1972. *Gandhi's Rise to Power. Indian Politics 1915–1922.* Cambridge: Cambridge University Press.

Brown, Judith, M. 1985. *Modern India. The Origins of an Asian Democracy.* Delhi: Oxford University Press.

Brunsson, Nils and Bengt Jacobsson, eds. 2000. *The World of Standards.* Oxford: Oxford University Press.

Bryans, Alex. 1995. "Boycott to Protest French Nuclear Testing," *Peace and Environmental News,* September. (http://perc.ca/PEN).

Burns, Maggie and Mick Blowfield. N.d. *Approaches to Ethical Trade: Impact and Lessons Learned.* Unpublished report. University of Greenwich: National Resources and Ethical Trade Programme, Natural Resources Institute.

Burns, Nancy, Key Lehman Schlozman, and Sidney Verba. 2001. *The Private Roots of Public Action. Gender, Equality, and Political Participation.* Cambridge, MA: Harvard University Press.

Burtt, Shelley. 1993. "The Politics of Virtue Today: A Critique and a Proposal," *American Political Science Review* 87: 360–8.

Caldwell, D. J. 1998. *Ecolabeling and the Regulatory Framework: A Survey of Domestic and International Fora.* Washington, D.C.: Consumer's Choice Council.

Case, Samuel. 1996. *The Socially Responsible Guide to Smart Investing. Improve Your Portfolio as You Improve the Environment.* Rocklin, CA: Prisma Books.

Cashore, Benjamin, Graeme Auld, and Deanna Newson. 2003. "Legitimizing Political Consumerism: The Case of Forest Certification in North America and Europe." In *Politics, Products, and Markets. Exploring Political Consumerism Past and Present,* edited by Michele Micheletti, Andreas Follesdal, and Dietlind Stolle. New Brunswick, NJ: Transaction Publishers.

Castells, Manuel. 1997. *The Rise of the Network Society.* Oxford: Blackwell.

Chwe, Michael Suk-Young.1999. "Structure and Strategy in Collective Action," *American Journal of Sociology* 105 (1): 128–56.

Cochoy, Franck. 2003. "Industrial Roots of Contemporary Political Consumerism: The Case of the French Standardization Movement." In *Politics, Products, and Markets. Exploring Political Consumerism Past and Present,* edited by Michele Micheletti, Andreas Follesdal, and Dietlind Stolle. New Brunswick, NJ: Transaction Publishers.

Cohen, Lizabeth. 1990. *Making a New Deal. Industrial Workers in Chicago, 1919–1939.* Cambridge: Cambridge University Press.

Cook, Gary, David Downes, Brennan Van Dyke, and John B. Weiner. 1997. *Applying Trade Rules to Timber Ecolabeling. A Review of Timber Ecolabeling and the WTO Agreement on Technical Barriers to Trade.* Geneva: Center for International Environmental Law (CIEL).

Cowe, Roger and Simon Williams. N.d. *Who are the Ethical Consumers?* London: The Cooperative Bank.

Crossley, Rachael. 1996. *A Review of Global Forest Management Certification Initiatives: Political and Institutional Aspects.* Paper for the Conference on

Economic, Social, and Political Issues in Certification of Forest Management. Malaysia, May 12–16. (http//:www.forestry.ubc.ca/concert/crossley.html).

Dekker, Eduard Douwes. 1917. *Max Havelaar of de koffijveilingen der Nederlandsche handelmaatschappij*. Amsterdam: Publisher information not available.

Delanty, Gerald. 2000. *Citizenship in a Global Age. Society, Culture, Politics*. Buckingham: Open University Press.

Domini, Amy. 2001. *Socially Responsible Investing. Making a Difference in Making Money*. Chicago: Dearborn Trade.

Downs, Anthony. 1957. *An Economic Theory of Democracy*. New York: Harper & Row.

Damjanov, Tobias. 1995. "Stopping the Tests," *PeaceNews*. (http://www.peacenews.info/ issues/ 2394/pn239402.htm).

DiMaggio, Paul J. and Walter W. Powell. 1983. "The Iron Cage Revisited: Institutional Isomorphism and Collective Rationality in Organizational Fields," *American Sociological Review* 48 (1983): 147–60.

Duit, Andreas. 2002. *Tragedins institutioner. Svenskt offentligt miljöskydd under trettio år*. Stockholm: Stockholm Studies in Politics, No. 89, Department of Political Science, Stockholm University.

Easton, David. 1965. *A Framework for Political Analysis*. Englewood Cliffs, NJ: Prentice Hall.

Edwards, Bob and Michael W. Foley, eds. 1997. *Social Capital, Civil Society and Contemporary Democracy*. Thousand Oaks, CA: Sage.

Ekström, Karin M. and Håkan Forsberg, eds. 1999. *Den flerdimensionella konsumenten—en antologi om svenska konsumenter*. Gothenburg: Tre Böcker.

Eliasoph, Nina. 1998. *Avoiding Politics. How Americans Produce Apathy in Everyday Life*. Cambridge: Cambridge University Press.

Elkington, John and Julia Hailes. 1989. *The Green Consumer's Supermarket Guide. Shelf by Shelf Recommendations for Products Which Don't Cost the Earth*. London: Gollancz.

Esaiasson, Peter. 1990. *Svenska valkampanjer 1866–1988*. Gothenburg: Gothenburg Studies in Politics No. 22, Department of Political Science, Gothenburg University.

Ewen, Stuart. 1988. *All Consuming Images*. New York: Basic Books.

Featherstone, Liza. 2000. "The Student Movement Comes of Age," *The Nation* October 16.

Featherstone, Lisa and United Students Against Sweatshops. 2002. *Students Against Sweatshops*. London: Verso.

Fehrenbacher, Scott. 2001. *Put Your Money Where Your Morals Are. A Guide to Values-Based Investing*. Nashville: Broadman and Holman Publishers.

Fernstrom, Meredith M. 1986. "Corporate Public Responsibility: A Marketing Opportunity?" In *The Future of Consumerism*, edited by Paul N. Bloom and Ruth Belk Smith. Lexington, MA: Lexington Books.

216 BIBLIOGRAPHY

Flammang, Janet A. 1997. *Women's Political Voice: How Women are Transforming the Practice and Study of Politics.* Philadelphia: Temple University Press.

Follesdal, Andreas. 2003. "Political Consumerism as Chance and Challenge." In *Politics, Products, and Markets. Exploring Political Consumerism Past and Present,* edited by Michele Micheletti, Andreas Follesdal, and Dietlind Stolle. New Brunswick, NJ: Transaction Publishers.

Follesdal, Andreas, Michele Micheletti, and Dietlind Stolle. 2003. "Conclusion." In *Politics, Products, and Markets. Exploring Political Consumerism Past and Present,* edited by Michele Micheletti, Andreas Follesdal, and Dietlind Stolle. New Brunswick, NJ: Transaction Publishers.

Forsberg, Annika. 1995. *Meet Sweden.* Stockholm: ISAK.

François, Patrick. 2002. *Social Capital and Economic Development.* London: Routledge.

Frank, Dana. 1994. *Purchasing Power. Consumer Organizing, Gender, and the Seattle Labor Movement 1919–1929.* Cambridge: Cambridge University Press.

Friedan, Betty. 1965. *The Feminine Mystique.* Harmondsworth: Penguin.

Friedman, Monroe. 1995. "On Promoting a Sustainable Future Through Consumer Activism," *Journal of Social Issues* 51 (4): 197–215.

Friedman, Monroe. 1999. *Consumer Boycotts. Effecting Change Through the Marketplace and the Media.* New York: Routledge.

Friedman, Monroe. 2003. "Using Consumer Boycotts to Stimulate Corporate Policy Changes: Marketplace, Media, and Moral Considerations." In *Politics, Products, and Markets. Exploring Political Consumerism Past and Present,* edited by Michele Micheletti, Andreas Follesdal, and Dietlind Stolle. New Brunswick, NJ: Transaction Publishers.

Fritzell, Johan and Joakim Palme, eds. 2001. *Välfärdens finansiering och fördelning.* SOU 2001: 57. Stockholm: Fritzes Kundtjänst.

Fung, Archon, Dara O'Rourke, and Charles Sabel. 2001. *Can We Put An End to Sweatshops?* Boston: Beacon Press.

Giertz, Eric and Bengt U. Strömberg. 1999. *Samverkan till egen nytta. Boken om konsumentkooperativ idé och verklighet i Sverige.* Stockholm: Prisma.

Gillberg, Minna. 1996. "Green Image or Green Practice—Towards a New Paradigm? A Case Study of the Impact of the Biodiversity Convention in Relation to the Forest Industry in Finland and Sweden." In *Nordic Research Project on the Effectiveness of Multilateral Environmental Agreements. Workshop Proceedings and Study Reports.* Copenhagen: Nordic Council of Ministers, 18.

Gillberg, Minna. 1999. *From Green Image to Green Practice. Normative Action and Self-Regulation.* Lund: Lund Studies in Sociology of Law.

Glickman, Lawrence B. 1997. *A Living Wage. American Workers and the Making of Consumer Society.* Ithaca, NY: Cornell University Press.

Glickman, Lawrence B. 1999. "Born to Shop? Consumer History and American History." In *Consumer Society in American History. A Reader*, edited by Lawrence B. Glickman.

Glickman, Lawrence B., ed. 1999. *Consumer Society in American History. A Reader*. Ithaca, NY: Cornell University Press.

Glickman, Lawrence B. 2001. "The Strike in the Temple of Consumption: Consumer Activism and Twentieth-Century American Political Culture," *The Journal of American History* 88 (1): 99–128.

Goldberg, Cheryl. 1999. "Don't Buy Where You Can't Work." In *Consumer Society in American History. A Reader*, edited by Lawrence B. Glickman. Ithaca, NY: Cornell University Press.

Goldberg, Cheryl. 2003. "Political Consumer Action: Some Cautionary Notes from African American History." In *Politics, Products, and Markets. Exploring Political Consumerism Past and Present*, edited by Michele Micheletti, Andreas Follesdal, and Dietlind Stolle. New Brunswick, NJ: Transaction Publishers.

Goul Andersen, Jørgen. 1993. *Politik og samfund i forandring*. Copenhagen: Förlaget Columbus.

Goul Andersen, Jørgen. 1999. *Hvad folket magter. Demokrati, magt og afmagt*. Köpenhamn: Jurist- og Økonomforbundts Forlag.

Goul Andersen, Jørgen and Mette Tobiasen. 2001. *Politisk forbrug og politiske forbrugere. Globalisering og politik i hverdagslivet*. Aarhus: Magtudredningen, Aarhus Universitet.

Goul Andersen, Jørgen and Mette Tobiasen. 2003. "Who are these Political Consumers Anyway? Survey Evidence from Denmark." In *Politics, Products, and Markets. Exploring Political Consumerism Past and Present*, edited by Michele Micheletti, Andreas Follesdal, and Dietlind Stolle. New Brunswick, NJ: Transaction Publishers.

Granovetter, Mark. 1978. "Threshold Models of Collective Behavior," *American Journal of Sociology* 83 (6): 1420–43.

Greer, Jed and Kenny Bruno. 1996. *Greenwash. The Reality Behind Corporate Environmentalism*. Penang, Malaysai: Third World Network.

Gustafson, Per E. 1998. "Gender Differences in Risk Perception: Theoretical and Methodological Perspectives," *Risk Analysis* 18 (6): 805–11.

Halkier, Bente. 1999. "Consequences of the Politization of Consumption: The Example of Environmentally Friendly Consumption Practices," *Journal of Environmental Policy and Planning* 1: 25–41.

Halkier, Bente, Lotte Holm and Terkel Møhl. 2002. *Institutional Determinants of Consumer Trust in Food: Six Country Studies*. Working paper for the workshop in the EU project "Trust in Food" in Copenhagen, June.

Halme, Minna. 1995. "Environmental Issues in Product Development Processes: Paradigm Shift in a Finnish Packaging Company," *Business Ethics Quarterly* 5 (4): 713–33.

Halme, Minna. 1997. *Environmental Management Paradigms Shifts in Business Enterprises: Organizational Learning Relating to Recycling and*

Forest Management Issues in Two Finnish Paper Companies. Tampare: University of Tampare.

Haraldsson, Désirée. 1987. *Skydda vår natur! Svenska Naturskyddsföreningens famväxt och tidiga utveckling.* Lund: Lund University Press.

Harrington, John C. 1992. *Investing with Your Conscience. How to Achieve High Return Using Socially Responsible Investing.* New York: Wiley.

Harrison, Kathryn. 2000. *Too Close to Home: Dioxin Contamination of Breast Milk and the Political Agenda.* Paper for the ECPR Workshop on "The Politics of Food," Copenhagen, April 14–19.

Hedström, Peter. 1994. "Contagious Collectivities: On the Spatial Diffusion of Swedish Trade Unions, 1890–1940," *American Journal of Sociology* 99 (5): 1157–79.

Henderson, Hazel. 1991. "New Markets, New Commons, New Ethics: A Guest Essay," *Accounting, Auditing & Accountability Journal* 4 (3): 72–80.

Hirdman, Yvonne. 1983. *Magfrågan. Mat som mål och medel. Stockholm 1870–1920.* Stockholm: Rabén & Sjögren.

Hirdman, Yvonne. 1983. "Den socialistiska hemmafrun." In *Vi kan, vi behövs! Kvinnorna går samman i egna föreningar,* edited by Brita Åkerman, Yvonne Hirdman, and Kajsa Pehrsson. Stockholm: Akademilitteratur AB.

Hirschman, Albert O. 1970. *Exit, Voice, and Loyalty Responses to Deline in Firms, Organizations, and States.* Cambridge, MA: Harvard University Press.

Hirschman, Albert O. 1982. *Shifting Involvements. Private Interest and Public Action.* Princeton, NJ: Princeton University Press.

Höglund, Zeta and Hjalmar Mehr, eds. 1927. *Fest skrift tillägnad Georg Branting uttgiven vid hans 60-årsdag 21 september 1947.* Stockholm: Saxon & Lindström.

Holmberg, Hans-E. 1999. *Konsumentundersökning om ekologiska produkter/ KRAV.* (http://www.krav.se).

Holmberg, Sören. 1999. "Down and Down We Go: Political Trust in Sweden." In *Critical Citizens. Global Support for Democratic Government,* edited by Pippa Norris. Oxford: Oxford University Press.

Holmberg, Sören and Kent Asp. 1984. *Kampen om kärnkraften: en bok om väljare, massmedier och folkomröstningen.* Stockholm: Liber.

Holmberg, Sören and Lennart Weibull, eds. 2003. *Fåfängens marknad. SOM-undersökningen,* SOM-report No. 33. Gothenburg: Gothenburg University.

Holzer, Boris and Mads Sørensen. 2001. *Subpolitics and Subpoliticians.* Arbeitspapier 4 des SBF 536 Reflexive Modernisierung. Munchen: University of Munich.

Howlett, M., ed. 2001. *Canadian Forest Policy: Regimes, Policy Dynamics and Institutional Adaptations.* Toronto: University of Toronto Press.

Inglehart, Ronald. 1997. *Modernization and Postmodernization. Cultural, Economic, and Political Change in 43 Societies.* Princeton: Princeton University Press.

Jacobs, Meg. 1999. " 'Democracy's Third Estate': New Deal Politics and the Construction of a 'Consuming Public,' " *International Labor and Working-Class History*. Special issue on Class and Consumption 55 (Spring): 27–51.

Jagers, Sverker C. and Jerker Thorsell. 2003. "Media – ett hot mot miljön." In Sören Holmberg and Lennart Weibull, eds., *Fåfängans marknad. SOU-undersökningen 2003*. SOM-report No. 33. Gothenburg: Gothenburg University.

Jeffcott, Bob and Lynda Yanz. 2000. *Codes · of Conduct, Government Regulation and Worker Organizing*. ETAG (Ethical Trading Action Group) Discussion Paper 1. Toronto: ETAG.

Jordan, Andrew, Rüdiger K. W. Wurzel, Anthony R. Zito, and Lars Brückner. 2003. "Consumer Responsibility-Taking and Eco Labeling Schemes in Europe." In *Politics, Products, and Markets. Exploring Political Consumerism Past and Present*, edited by Michele Micheletti, Andreas Follesdal, and Dietlind Stolle. New Brunswick, NJ: Transaction Publishers.

Jordan, Grant. 2001. *Shell, Greenpeace and the Brent Spar*. Basingstoke: Palgrave.

Kaldor, Mary. 2000. " 'Civilizing' Globalization? The Implications of the 'Battle in Seattle,' " *Millennium: Journal of International Studies* 29 (1): 105–14.

Keck, Margaret E. and Kathryn Sikkink. 1998. *Activists Beyond Borders. Advocacy Networks in International Politics*. Ithaca: Cornell University Press.

Keck, Margaret E. and Kathryn Sikkink. 1999. "Transnational Advocacy Networks in International and Regional Politics," *International Social Science Journal* (No. 159, March): 89–101.

Kennedy, Paul. 1996. "Capitalist Enterprise as a Moral or Political Crusade: Opportunities, Constraints and Contraditions." In *From the Margins to the Centre. Cultural Production and Consumption in the Post-Industrial City*, edited by Justin O'Connor and Derek Wynne. Aldershot: Arena, Ashgate Publishing Limited.

Kennedy, Paul. 2003. "Selling Virtue: Political and Economic Contradictions of Green/Ethical Marketing in the U.K." In *Politics, Products, and Markets. Exploring Political Consumerism Past and Present*, edited by Michele Micheletti, Andreas Follesdal, and Dietlind Stolle. New Brunswick, NJ: Transaction Publishers.

King, Mary. 1999. *Mahatma Gandhi and Martin Luther King Jr. The Power of Nonviolent Action*. Paris: UNESCO Publishing.

Klein, Naomi. 2000. *No Logo. No Space. No Choice. No Jobs*. London: Flamingo.

Klint, Jakob. 1997. *Max Havelaar-mærkede produkter—en undersøgelse af forbrugeren og storkunden*. Copenhagen: CASA.

Kolk, Ans and Rob van Tulder. 2002. "Child Labor and Multinational Conduct: A Comparison of International business and Stakeholder Codes," *Journal of Business Ethics* 36: 291–301.

Kollman, Kelly and Aseem Prakash. 2001. "Green by Choice?: Cross-National Variation in Firms' Responses to EMS-based Environmental Regimes," *World Politics* 53 (April): 399–430.

Kooiman, Jan. 1993. "Governance and Governability: Using Complexity, Dynamics and Diversity." In *Modern Governance. New Government–Society Interactions*, edited by Jan Kooiman. London: Sage Publications.

Kotler, P. 1972. "What Consumerism Means for Markets," *Harvard Business Review* May–June: 48–57.

Kristensen, Niels Nørgaard. 1999. "Brugerindflydelse, politisk identitet og offentlig styring," *Nordisk Administrativt Tidsskrift* No. 1: 42–62.

Kuhre, W. Lee. 1997. *ISO 14020s. Environmental Labelling-Marketing. Efficient and Accurate Environmental Marketing Procedures.* Upper Saddle River, NJ: Prentice Hall.

Lash, Scott. 2001. "Individualization in a Non-Linear Mode," foreword to Ulrick Beck and Elisabeth BeckGernsheim, *Individualization.* London: Sage Publications.

Liljedahl, Elisabeth. 1975. *Stumfilmen i Sverige—kritik och debatt. Hur samtiden värderade den nya konstarten.* Stockholm: Skrifter från dokumentationsavdelningen nr. 18, Svenska Filminstitutet.

Linton, Magnus. 2000. *Veganerna—en bok om dom som stör.* Stockholm: Atlas.

Los Angeles Times. 1995. "British to Boycott French Wine Until Weapons Testing Stops." Also published in *The Tech* 155 (39): 3. (http://wwwtech.mit.edu/V115/N39/ brit.39w.html).

Lowndes, Vivien. 2000. "Women and Social Capital: A Comment on Hall's 'Social Capital in Britain,'" *British Journal of Political Science* 30 (3): 533–7.

Lynd, Robert S. 1933. "The People as Consumers," *Recent Social Trends in the U.S. Report of the President's Research Committee on Social Trends. Volume II.* New York: McGraw-Hills Book Company, Inc.

Lynd, Robert S. 1934. "The Consumer Becomes a 'Problem,' The Ultimate Consumer. A Study in Economic Illiteracy," *The Annals of the American Academy of Political and Social Science* 173 (May): 1–6.

Lynd, Robert S. 1936. "Democracy's Third Estate: The Consumer," *Political Science Quarterly* 51: 481–515.

MacIntyre, Alasdair. 1993. *After Virtue. A Study in Moral Theory.* Second Edition. London: Duckworth.

Magnusson, Åke. 1974. *Konsumentbojkott—ett användbart vapen? Om kooperationen och Sydafrikafrågan.* Kooperativ Information No. 5. Stockholm: KF.

Majumdar, R. C., H. C. Raychaudhuri, and Kalikinkar Datta. 1960. *An Advanced History of India.* London: Macmillan & Co.

March, James G. and Johan P. Olsen. 1995. *Democratic Governance.* New York: The Free Press.

Marcuse, Herbert. 1964. *One Dimensional Man.* London: Sphere.

Mayntz, Renate. 1993. "Governing Failures and the Problem of Governability: Some Comments on a Theoretical Paradigm." In *Modern*

Governance. New Government-Society Interactions, edited by Jan Kooiman. London: Sage Publications.

McClosky, Herbert. 1968. "Political Participation." In *International Encyclopedia of the Social Sciences Vol. 12,* edited by David L. Sills. New York: Macmillan Co. & Free Press.

Michelman, Frank I. 1999. *Brennan and Democracy.* Princeton: Princeton University Press.

Micheletti, Michele. 1985. *Organizing Interest and Organized Protest. Difficulties of Member Representation for the Swedish Central Organization of Salaried Employees (TCO).* Stockholm: Stockholm Studies in Politics No. 29, Department of Political Science, Stockholm University.

Micheletti, Michele. 1995. *Civil Society and State Relations in Sweden.* Aldershot: Avebury.

Micheletti, Michele. 2003. "Why More Women? Issues of Gender and Political Consumerism." In *Politics, Products, and Markets. Exploring Political Consumerism Past and Present,* edited by Michele Micheletti, Andreas Follesdal, and Dietlind Stolle. New Brunswick, NJ: Transaction Publishers.

Micheletti, Michele and Dietlind Stolle. 2001. *Political Consumption. Politics in a New Era and Arena.* Research Project funded by the Swedish Council of Research, Stockholm, Sweden.

Micheletti, Michele, Andreas Follesdal, and Dietlind Stolle. 2003. *Politics, Products, and Markets. Exploring Political Consumerism Past and Present.* New Brunswick, NJ: Transaction Publishers.

Miller, Alan J. 1991. *Socially Responsible Investing. How to Invest with Your Conscience.* New York: New York Institute of Finance.

Miller, Daniel. 1995. "Consumption as the Vanguard of History. A Polemic by Way of an Introduction." In *Acknowledging Consumption. A Review of New Studies,* edited by Daniel Miller. New York: Routledge.

Möller, Göran. 1998. "Den dygdiga människan." In *Framtidens dygder—om etik i praktiken,* edited by Patrik Aspers and Emil Uddhammar. Stockholm: City University Press.

Morehouse, Ward. 1998. "Consumption, Civil Action and Corporate Power: Lessons from the Past, Strategies for the Future," *Development. Journal of the Society for International Development* 41 (1): 48–53.

Mouffe, Chantal. 1993. *The Return of the Political.* London: Verso.

Nader, Ralph. 2000. "Corporations and the UN: Nike and Others 'Bluewash' their Images," *San Francisco Bay Guardian,* September 18.

Nader, Ralph, Eleanor J. Lewis, and Eric Weltman. 1992. "Shopping for Innovation. The Government as Smart Consumer," *The American Prospect* 11 (Fall): 71–92.

Nava, Mica. 1991. "Consumerism Reconsidered. Buying and Power," *Cultural Studies* 5 (2): 157–73.

Nava, Mica, Andrew Blake, Iain MacRury, and Barry Richards, eds. 1997. *Buy this Book. Studies in Advertising and Consumption.* London: Routledge, 1997.

Norris, Pippa, ed. 1999. *Critical Citizens. Global Support for Democratic Government.* Oxford: Oxford University Press.

Norris, Pippa. 2002. *Democratic Phoenix. Reinventing Political Activism.* Cambridge: Cambridge University Press.

Olson, Mancur. 1975. *The Logic of Collective Action. Public Goods and the Theory of Groups.* Harvard: Harvard University Press.

Örbrink, Mats. 1973. *FNL-rörelsen i Sverige: en historik.* Stockholm: DFFGs skriftserie.

Orleck, Annelise. 1993. " 'Who are that Mythical Thing Called the Public': Militant Housewives during the Great Depression," *Feminist Studies* 19: 147–72.

Ostrom, Elinor. 1990. *Governing the Commons. The Evolution of Institutions for Collective Action.* Cambridge: Cambridge University Press.

Ostrom, Elinor. 1999. *Self-Governance and Forest Resources.* Jakarta, Indonesia: Center for International Forestry Research (CIFOR). Occasional Paper No. 20. (http://www. cgiar.org/cifor).

Otnes, Per, ed. 1988. *The Sociology of Consumption.* Oslo: Solum Forlag.

Ottman, Jacquelyn. 1998. *The Debate over Eco-Seals: Is Self-Certification Enough?* J. Ottman Consulting. (http://www.greenmarketing.com/articles/ama_Mar-2-98.html).

Packard, Vance. 1981. *The Hidden Persuaders.* Harmondsworth: Penguin.

Pateman, Carole. 1989. "Feminist Critiques of the Public/Private Dichotomy." In *The Disorder of Women: Democracy, Feminism and Political Theory*, edited by Carole Pateman. Oxford: Polity Press.

Pateman, Carole, ed. 1989. *The Disorder of Women: Democracy, Feminism and Political Theory.* Oxford: Polity Press.

Peacey, Jonathan. N.d. "The Marine Stewardship Council Fisheries Certification Program: Progress and Challenges" (www.msc.org).

Peretti, Jonah with Michele Micheletti. 2003. "The Nike Sweatshop Email: Political Consumerism, Internet, and Culture Jamming." In *Politics, Products, and Markets. Exploring Political Consumerism Past and Present*, edited by Michele Micheletti, Andreas Follesdal, and Dietlind Stolle. New Brunswick, NJ: Transaction Publishers.

Peters, B. Guy and Donald J. Savoie, eds. 1995. *Governance in a Changing Environment.* Montreal and Kingston: McGill-Queen's University Press.

Petersson, Olof, Anders Westholm, and Göran Blomberg. 1989. *Medborgarnas makt.* Stockholm: Carlssons.

Petersson, Olof, Jörgen Hermansson, Michele Micheletti, Jan Teorell, and Anders Westholm. 1998. *Demokrati och medborgarskap. Demokratirådets rapport 1998.* Stockholm: SNS Förlag.

Power, Michael. 1992. "The Politics of Brand Accounting in the United Kingdom," *European Accounting Review* 1: 39–68.

Power, Michael. 1997. *The Audit Society. Rituals of Verification.* Oxford: Oxford University Press.

Prakash, Aseem. 1999. "A New-Institutionalist Perspective on ISO 14000 and Responsible Care," *Business Strategy and the Environment* 8: 322–35.

Prittie, Terence and Walter Henry Nelson. 1978. *The Economic War Against the Jews*. London: Secker & Warburg.

Purkis, Jonathan. 1996. "The City as a Site of Ethical Consumption and Resistance." In *From the Margins to the Centre. Cultural Production and Consumption in the Post-Industrial City*, edited by Justin O'Connor and Derek Wynne. Aldershot: Arena, Ashgate Publishing Limited.

Putnam, Robert D. 2000. *Bowling Alone. The Collapse and Revival of American Community*. New York: Simon and Schuster.

Rees, William E. 1998. "Reducing the Ecological Footprint of Consumption." In *The Business of Consumption: Environmental Ethics and the Global Economy*, edited by Laura Westra and Patricia H. Werhane. Lanham, MD: Rowman & Littlefield.

Rice, Paul D. and Jennifer McLean. 1999. *Sustainable Coffee at the Crossroads*. Washington D.C.: Consumer's Choice Council.

Ross, Andrew, ed. 1999. *No Sweat. Fashion, Free Trade, and the Rights of Garment Workers*. New York: Verso.

Rothstein, Bo. 1987. *Corporatism and Reformism: The Social Democratic Institutionalization of Class Conflict*. Uppsala: Study of Power and Democracy in Sweden.

Rothstein, Bo. 1992. *Den korporativa staten: Intresseorganisationer och statsförvaltning i svensk politik*. Stockholm: Norstedts juridik.

Rothstein, Bo. 1998. *Just Institutions Matter. The Moral and Political Logic of the Universal Welfare State*. Cambridge: Cambridge University Press.

Rothstein, Bo, ed. 1995. *Demokrati som dialog. SNS-demokratiråds 1995 års rapport*. Together with Peter Esaiasson, Jörgen Hermansson, Michele Micheletti, and Olof Petersson. Stockholm: SNS Förlag.

Rubik, Frieder and Gerd Scholl. 2002. *Eco-Labelling Practices in Europe. An Overview of Environmental Product Information Schemes*. Berlin: Institut für ökologische Wirtschaftsforschung (IÖW), Report IÖW-SR 162/02.

Rueschemeyer, Dietrich, Marily Rueschemeyer, and Björn Wittrock, eds. 1998. *Participation and Democracy. East and West. Comparisons and Interpretations*. London: M. E. Sharpe.

Russel, Trevor, ed. 1998. *Greener Purchasing. Opportunities and Innovations*. Sheffield: Greenleaf Publishing.

Sahlin-Andersson, Kerstin. 1996. "Imitating by Editing Success. The Construction of Organizational Fields." In *Translating Organizational Change*, edited by Barbara Czarniawska and Guje Sevón. Berlin: Walter de Gruyter.

Sainsbury, Diane. 1996. *Gender, Equality, and Welfare States*. Cambridge: Cambridge University Press.

Salomon, Kim 1996. *Rebeller i takt med tiden. FNL-rörelsen och 60-talets politiska ritualer*. Stockholm: Rában Prisma.

Sanne, Christer. 2002. "Willing Consumers—or Locked-in? Policies for a Sustainable Consumption," *Ecological Economics* 42: 273–87.

Scammell, Margaret. 2000. "The Internet and Civic Engagments: The Age of the Citizen-Consumer," *Political Communication* 17: 351–5.

Schonfield, Andrew. 1965. *Modern Capitalism. The Changing Balance of Public and Private Power*. London: Oxford University Press.

Selle, Per. 1998. "The Norwegian Voluntary Sector and Civil Society in Transition. Women as Catalysts for Deep-Seated Change." In *Participation and Democracy. East and West. Comparisons and Interpretations*, edited by Dietrich Rueschemeyer, Marily Rueschemeyer and Björn Wittrock. London: M. E. Sharpe.

Sennett, Richard. 1977. *The Fall of Public Man*. Cambridge: Cambridge University Press.

Sikkink, Kathryn. 1986. "Codes of Conduct for Transnational Corporations: The Case of the WHO/UNICEF Code," *International Organization* 40: 815–40.

Sklar, Kathryn Kish. 1998. "The Consumers' While Label Campaign of the National Consumers' League 1898–1919." In *Getting and Spending. European and American Consumer Socities in the 20th Century*, edited by Susan Strasser, Charles McGovern, and Matthias Judt. Cambridge: Cambridge University Press.

Slater, Don. 1997. "Consumer Culture and the Politics of Need." In *Buy This Book. Studies in Advertising and Consumption*, edited by Mica Nava, Andrew Blake, Iain MacRury, and Barry Richards. London: Routledge.

Smith, N. Craig. 1990. *Morality and the Market. Consumer Pressure for Corporate Accountability*. London: Routledge.

Smith, Paul. 1997. "Tommy Hilfiger in the Age of Mass Customization." In *No Sweat. Fashion, Free Trade, and the Rights of Garment Workers*, edited by A. Ross. New York: Verso.

Solér, Cecilia. 1997. *Att köpa miljövänliga dagligvaror*. Stockholm: Nerenius & Santérus Förlag.

Sołtan, Karol Edward. 1999. "Civic Competence, Atrractiveness, and Maturity." In *Citizen Competence and Democratic Institutions*, edited by Stephen L. Elkin, and Karol Edward Solltan. University Park, PA: Pennsylvania State University Press.

Sörbom, Adrienne. 2002. *Vart tar politiken vägen? Om individualisering, reflexivitet och görbarhet i det politiska engagemanget*. Stockholm: Almqvist & Wiksell International.

Sørensen, Eva. 1997. "Brugeren og demokratiet," *Grus* 53: 81–96.

Sørensen, Mads P. 2002. *Den politiske forbruger—en analyse af ideen og fænomenet*. Aarhus: Department of the History of Ideas, Aarhus University. Doctoral dissertation.

Sörlin, Sverker. 1999. "Konsumenterna kan inte rädda miljön," *Sveriges Natur* No. 3: 29.

Spaargaren, Gert. 1997. *The Ecological Modernization of Production and Consumption*. Landbouw: Landbouw Universiteit Wageningen. Doctoral dissertation.

Spar, Debora L. 1998. "The Spotlight and the Bottom Line. How Multinationals Export Human Rights," *Foreign Affairs* 77 (2) (1998): 7–12.

Sparkes, Russell. 2000. "Social Responsible Investment Comes of Age," *Professional Investor* June. (http://www.uksif.org/publications/article-2000–06/contents.shtml).

Stevens, Georgia L. 1994. "Linking Consumer Rights with Citizen Roles: An Opportunity for Consumer Educators," *The Journal of Consumer Education* 12: 1–8.

Stolle, Dietlind. 2000. *Communities of Trust: Social Capital and Public Action in a Three Country Comparison in Sweden, Germany and the United States.* Princeton: Princeton University, Department of Political Science. Doctoral dissertation.

Stolle, Dietlind and Marc Hooghe. 2003. "Consumers as Political Participants?" Shifts in Political Action Repertoires in Western Societies. In *Politics, Products, and Markets. Exploring Political Consumerism Past and Present*, edited by Michele Micheletti, Andreas Follesdal, and Dietlind Stolle. New Brunswick, NJ: Transaction Publishers.

Storrs, Landon R. Y. 2000. *Civilizing Capitalism. The National Consumers' League, Women's Activism, and Labor Standards in the New Deal Era.* Chapel Hill: The University of North Carolina Press.

Strasser, Susan, Charles McGovern, and Matthias Judt, eds. 1998. *Getting and Spending. European and American Consumer Societies in the 20th Century.* Cambridge: Cambridge University Press.

Sulkanen, Pekka. 1997. "Introduction." In *Constructing the New Consumer Society*, edited by Pekka Sulkanen, John Holmwood, Hilary Radner, and Gerhard Schulze. New York: St. Martin's Press.

Svallfors, Stefan. 2001. "Kan man lita på välfärdsstaten? Risk, tilltro och betalningsvilja i den svenska välfärdsopinionen 1997–2000." In *Välfärdens finansiering och fördelning*, edited by Johan Fritzell and Joakim Palme. SOU 2001: 57. Stockholm: Fritzens Kundtjänst.

Sverrisson, Árni. 2001. "Translation Networks, Knowledge Brokers and Novelty Construction: Pragmatic Environmentalism in Sweden," *Acta Sociologica* 44 (4): 313–27.

Szrompk, Piotr. 1991. *Society in Action. The Theory of Social Becoming.* Cambridge: Polity Press.

Tamm Hallström, Kristina. 2000. *Kampen för auktoritet: standardiseringsorganisationer i arbete.* Stockholm: School of Business, Ekonomiska Forskningsinstitutet (EFI).

Tarrow, Sidney. 1998. *Power in Movement: Social Movements and Contentious Politics.* Cambridge: Cambridge University Press.

Teorell, Jan. 2001. *Political Participation and the Theories of Democracy. A Research Agenda.* Paper for the Annual Meeting of the American Political Science Association, San Francisco, CA.

The Economist. 2000. "How Green is Your Market?" January 8, 76.

Titus, Philip A. and Jeffrey L. Bradford. 1996. "Reflections on Consumer Sophistication and Its Impact on Ethical Business Practice," *The Journal of Consumer Affairs* 30 (1): 170–94.

Tolland, Anders 1998. "Dygder för alla tider." In *Framtidens dygder—om etik i praktiken*, edited by Patrik Aspers and Emil Uddhammar. Stockholm: City University Press.

Trend, David. 1996. "Democracy's Crisis of Meaning." In *Identity, Citizenship, and the State*, edited by David Trend. New York: Routledge.

Van Gunsteren, Herman R. 1998. *A Theory of Citizenship. Organizing Plurality in Contemporary Democracies.* Bolder, CO: Westview Press.

Vivekanandan, B. 1997. *International Concerns of European Social Democrats.* Basingstoke: Macmillan.

Vogel, David. 1975. "The Corporation as Government. Challenges and Dilemmas," *Polity* 8: 5–37.

Vogel, David. 1996. *Kindred Strangers. The Uneasy Relationship between Politics and Business in America.* Princeton: Princeton University Press.

Vogel, David. 2003. "Tracing the Roots of the Contemporary Political Consumerist Movement: Marketized Political Activism in the U.S. in the 1960s." In *Politics, Products, and Markets. Exploring Political Consumerism Past and Present*, edited by Michele Micheletti, Andreas Follesdal, and Dietlind Stolle. New Brunswick, NJ: Transaction Publishers.

Wackernagel, Mathis and William Rees. 1996. *Our Ecological Footprint. Reducing Human Impact on the Earth.* Gabriola Island, BC, Canada: New Society Publishers.

Wallensteen, Peter. 2000. *A Century of Economic Sanctions: A Field Revisited.* Uppsala: Department of Peace and Conflict Research, Uppsala University.

Patricia H. Werhane. 1991. *Adam Smith and His Legacy for Modern Capitalism.* Oxford: Oxford University Press.

Wessells, Cathy, Holger Donath, and Robert J. Johnston. 1999. *U.S. Consumer Preferences for Ecolabeled Seafood: Results of a Consumer Survey*, unpublished report. Rhode Island: Department of Environmental and Natural Resource Economics, University of Rhode Island.

Westra, Laura and Patricia H. Werhane, eds. 1998. *The Business of Consumption: Environmental Ethics and the Global Economy.* Lanham, MD: Rowman & Littlefield.

Wollebæck, Dag and Per Selle. 2002. *Det nye organisajonssamfunnet. Demokrati i omforming.* Bergen: Fagbokforlaget.

Wuthnow, Robert. 1998. *Loose Connections. Joining Together in America's Fragmented Communities.* Cambridge: Harvard University Press.

Young, Iris Marion. 1994. "Gender as Seriality: Thinking about Women as a Social Collective," *Signs: Journal of Women in Culture and Society* 19: 713–38.

Zadek, Simon. N.d. *Trade Fair.* (http:/www.zadek.net/tradefair.pdf).

Zadek, Simon. 1998. "Consumer Works!" *Development. Journal of the Society for International Development* 41 (1): 7–14.

Zadek, Simon and Pauline Tiffen. 1996. " 'Fair Trade': Business or Campaign?" *Development. Journal the Society for International Development* 3: 48–53.

Zadek, Simon and Pauline Tiffen. 1998. *Dealing with and in the Global Economy: Fairer Trade in Latin America. Sustainable Agricultural and Development Experiences.* TNI On-Line Archives. (http://www.tni.org/achives/tiffen/tiffzad.htm).
Zadek, Simon, Peter Puzan, and Richard Evans, ed. 1997. *Building Corporate Accountability. Emerging Practices in Social and Ethical Accounting, Auditing and Reporting.* London: Earthscan Publications Ltd.
Zhao, Dingwix. 1998. "Ecologies of Social Movements: Student Mobilization During the 1989 Prodemocracy Movement in Beijing," *American Journal of Sociology* 103 (6): 1493–529.

PRINTED PRIMARY SOURCES

Aschehong og Syldendals Stora Norske Leksikon. 1986. Vol. 2. Oslo: Kunskapsforlaget.
Axelsson, Svante. 1999. "Miljömärkning—ett tecken på misslyckande," *Bra Miljöval Magasin* No. 1: 10–14. Svante Axelsson was secretary general of the Society for Nature Conservation.
Bra Miljöval Magasin. Newspaper for Environmental Choice. Gothenburg: Good Environmental.
Bryntse, Göran, Birgitta Johansson, and Gunilla Johansson. 1987. *Oblekt papper—för miljöns skull.* Stockholm: Svenska Naturskyddsföreningen.
Council on Economic Priorities (CEP). 1988. *Shopping for a Better World.* New York: Council on Economic Priorities.
CEP. 1998. *The Corporate Report Card. Rating 250 of America's Corporations for the Socially Responsible Investor.* New York: Dutton Book, Penguin Putnam Inc.
Directorate-General for Agriculture, European Commission. 1997. *The Common Agricultural Policy. Attitudes of EU Consumers to Fair Trade Bananas.* Brussels: European Commission.
Ds 1998: 49. *Jämställdhetsmärkning. Konsumentmakt för ett jämställt samhälle.* Government publication from Ministry of Labor. Stockholm: Fritzes kundtjänst.
Encyclopædia Judaica Jerusalem. 1971. "Boycott, Anti-Jewish." Band 4. Jerusalem: Keter Publishing House, 1278–80.
Environics International. 1999. *The Environmental Monitor. Global Public Opinion on the Environment. 1999 International Report.* Toronto: Environics International. (www.environics.net/eil/articles/green.)
Environics International. 2000. *How Green is Your Market and the Environmental Monitor. Global Public Opinion on the Environment, 1999 International Report.* (http:// www.environics.net/eil/articles/green/) and (www.environics. net/eil/iemnew/IEM99.highlights.pdf).
European Commission. 1996. *Public Procurement in the European Union: Exploring the Way Forward.* Communication adopted by the Commission

on November 27, 1996 on the proposal of Mr. Monti. Brussels: European Union.

European Commission (Commission of the European Communities). 2001. *Green Paper. Promoting a European Framework for Corporate Social Responsibility.* Brussels: COM (2001) 416 final.

Friström, Anders. 1989. *PM om marknadsorienterat miljöarbete.* February 6. Unpublished material. Stockholm: SNF.

Friström, Anders. 1989. *Anteckningar från uppvaktning hos Margot Wallström angående ett svenskt miljömärkningssystem.* August 21. Unpublished material. Stockholm: SNF.

Gahrton, Per. 1972. "Aktuella frågor: Feldt, Helén och matpriserna." *Sydsvenska Dagbladet (Snällposten).* March 2.

Good Environmental Choice. 2000. *Kretskontaktpersoner Handla Miljövänligt 1997, 1999.* Unpublished material. Gothenburg: Good Environmental Choice.

Handla miljövänligt! Vardagshandbok för en bättre miljö 1998. Stockholm: SNF.

Handla miljövänligt. Nyhetsbrev för Naturskyddsföreningens Projekt Handla Miljövänligt. Newsletter for the Act and Buy Environmentally network within the Society for Nature Conservation. Gothenburg: Good Environmental Choice.

Holm, Fredrik. 1989. *Förslag till aktiviteter med anledning av diskussionen på TEM.* April 10. Unpublished material. Stockholm: SNF.

Holm, Fredrik. 1989. *Minnesanteckningar från seminarium om miljömärkning mm på TEM-gården i Sjöbo April 6–7.* April 10. Unpublished material. Stockholm: SNF.

Instituttet for Fremtidsforsning and Elsam. 1996. *Den politiske forbruger.* Copenhagen: Elsam.

International Council of Human Rights Policy. 2002. *Beyond Voluntarianism. Human Rights and the Developing International Legal Obligations of Companies.* Geneva: International Council of Human Rights Policy.

Konsumentverket. 1998. *Allmänhetens kunskaper, attityder och agerande i miljöfrågor.* Report No. 7. Stockholm: Konsumentverket.

Kvällsposten (local Swedish newspaper). 1972. "Husmödrarnas mjölkkrig blir ett politiskt hot." February 27.

Liber (large Swedish publisher). 1988. Two press releases. One dated March 8 invited journalists to a press conference entitled "*4 miljoner Liber-böcker på miljövänligt paper.*" The other one is dated March 14 and entitled "*Miljövänliga Liber-böcker minska klorutsläpp i våra sjöar.*" Stockholm: Liber Publications.

LUI Marknadsinformation AB. 1999. *Konsumentundersökning om ekologiska produkter/KRAV.* Unpublished report. Stockholm: LUI.

LRF and Ekologiska Lantbrukarna. 2001. *Vägen till marknaden. Ekologiska produkter. En underlag för kommunikation om ekologiska produkter med konsumenternas önskemål och kunskaper som grund.* Unpublished report. Stockholm: LRF.

Miljömärkt. 1998. "Sveriges mest kända miljömärke." Magazine for the Nordic White Swan Eco-Label. No. 3.

Nordic Council of Ministers. 1999. *Nordiska konsumenter om Svanen. Livstil, kännedom, attityd och förtroende.* TemaNord: Miljö/konsument. No. 592. Copenhagen. Nordiskt Ministerråd.

Oblekt papper för miljöns skull! 1983. Gothenburgh: Förlaget Bokskogen.

Our Common Future. 1987. United Nations: World Commission on Environment and Development. Oxford: Oxford University Press.

Raphael, Axel and Eliel Löfgren. 1908. *Blockad, bojkott och svarta listor. Två mötesuttalanden i andledning af hr Hilderbrands motion om ändring af 3§ 11:0 Tryckfrihetsförordningen.* Stockholm: A. B. Nordiska Bokhandeln.

Roth, Ann-Katrine. 1998. *EQ 2000. Kvalitetssäkring av jämställdhetsarbete.* Stockholm: Jamställdhetskonsult/E(uro)Quality.

SIFO. 2001. *Vad händer med Sverige.* SIFO telephone survey, 1000 persons, May 29–31, 2001. Stockholm: SIFO.

SNF. 1988. *Information från Svenska Naturskyddsföreningen.* Press release on Finnish chlorine-bleached paper. Exact date not included in the press release. Stockholm: SNF.

SNF. 1989. *Yttrande över betänkandet "miljömärkning av produkter" (SOU 1988:61).* SNF's official comments to the report, vårt nr 31/90 AF 890321. Stockholm: SNF.

SNF. 1989. *Anteckningar från uppvaktning hos Margot Wallström angående ett svenskt miljömärkningsystem.* August 21. Margot Wallström was Minister of Environment. Unpublished material. Stockholm: SNF.

SNF. 1993. *Sveriges miljöbästa butik 1993. Resultat av Naturskyddsföreningens butiksundersökning.* Gothenburgh: Good Environmental Choice Unit.

SNF. 1995. *Information from a Focused Group Interview Survey of Members Conducted by Testologen AB.* Unpublished material. Stockholm: SNF.

SNF. 1997. *Det märks. Naturskyddsföreningen om miljömärkning.* Stockholm: SNF.

SNF. 1997. *Alla bra miljöval märkta produkter.* Stockholm: SNF.

SNF. 1998. *Lagom är bäst. På spaning efter en hållbar livsstil.* Stockholm: SNF. Årsbok.

SNF. 1998. *Verksamhetsberättelse 1998.* Stockholm: SNF.

SNF. 2000. *Protokoll fört vid Svenska Naturskyddsföreningens riksstämma i Karlshamn den 17–18 juni 2000.* Unpublished material. Stockholm: SNF.

SNF. 2000. *Verksamhetsriktlinjer 1999–2000.* Unpublished material. Stockholm: SNF.

SNF. 2000. *List of employees.* (www.snf.se/om/ kansli.htm).

SNF. 2002. *Historien om Bra Miljöval.* (www.snf.se).

SNF. 2002. *Rekordstor försäljning av miljömärkt el. June 31, 2002.* Press release. Stockholm: SNF.

SNF. 2002. *FSC—skogens märkning.* (www.snf.se).

230 BIBLIOGRAPHY

SOU. 1988: 61. *Miljömärkning av produkter. Betänkande av Utredning om miljömärkning av produkter.* Government report. Stockholm, Fritizes kundtjänst.

SOU. 2001: 9. *Reglerna kring och inställningen till frivillig jämställd-hetsmärkning av produkter och tjänster. Delbetänkande av FRIJA. Utredningen om frivillig jämställdhetsmärkning av produkter och tjänster.* Government report. Stockholm, Fritizes kundtjänst.

Svenska Sacco-Vanzetti Försvarskommittén. 1928. *Sacco-Vanzetti rörelsen i Sverge. Redogörelse för Svenska Sacco-Vanzetti försvarskommittens verksamhet.* Stockholm: Svenska Sacco-Vanzetti försvarskommittén.

Sveriges Natur. The SNF newspaper.

Thunberg, Bo. 1996. "Lagom är bäst—eller?" *Sveriges Natur,* No. 1: 4. Editorial by SNF's president.

Tinnacher, Walter. 1987. Letter to Svenska Naturskyddsföreningen, "Angående: Tidskriften 'Sveriges Natur' " February 21, 1987. Unpublished material. Stockholm: SNF.

Vi. 1988. "Miljövänlig vi!" No. 10: 27. Magazine for the KF.

von Sydow, Ulf. 1992. "Ett anständigt liv," *Sveriges Natur* No. 3: 11. von Sydow was the SNF president in 1992.

Zetterberg, Hanna. 1998. "Rättvist miljöutrymme—ett användbart begrepp," *Sveriges Natur* No. 5.

INTERNET SOURCES

African-Americans Boycott Disney. 2002. www.laker.net/webpage/African.htm.

Association of European Consumers. 2001. *Responsible Consumption.* Position Paper October. www.consumer-aec.org.

AFL-CIO. 2001. *"The AFL-CIO Investment Program."* www.aflcio.org/publ/estatements/feb2001/investmentprogram.htm.

AFL-CIO. 2002. *AFL-CIO National Boycott List.* Union Label and Service Trades Department. www.unionlabel.org/donotbuy/ Default.htm.

Amnesty International. 2000. *Socially Responsible Investment Campaign.* www.amnesty.org.uk/business/campaigns/sri.shtml.

Angelfire. 2002. *Labor Law Breakers and Their Crimes. Abuser List.* www.angelfire.com/nd/NoahWeb/labor.html.

Banco. 2001. *Ethical Guidelines for Banco Socially Responsible and Charity Funds.* www.banco.se.

Biological Farmers Association. 2002. *The Australian Certified Organic.* www.bfa.com.au.

Bio-Gro New Zealand. 2002. *About Bio-Gro.* www.bio-gro.co.nz/docs/about.htm.

Boycott Crown Oil. 2000. www.boycottcrownoil.

Bra Miljöval. 2003. *Bra Miljöval-registret.* www.snf.se/bmv/bmv-register/index.cfm.

CAFE (Consumers Against Food Engineering). 2000. www.cafemd.org/cafe.htm.

Center for Economic Justice. 2002. *World Bank Bonds Boycott.* www.econjust.net/wbbb/index.html.

CERES (Coalition for Environmentally Responsible Economics) 2002. www.ceres.org.

Christian Aid. 2000. *A Sporting Chance. Tackling Child Labour in India's Sport Goods Industry.* www.christian-aid.org.uk/reports/sporting.htm.

Consumer's Choice Council. 2000. www.consumerscouncil.org.

Council of Institutional Investors. 2002. www.cii.org.

Codes of Conduct. 2002. www.codesofconduct.org.

Co-op America. 2002. *Co-op America's Boycott Action News.* www.boycotts.org.

Co-op America. 2002. *Co-op America's Boycott Organizers' Guide.* www.coopamerica.org.

Co-op America. 2002. *Invest Responsibly.* www.coopamerica.org.

CorpWatch. 2002. *CorpWatch Bulletin Board.* (http://www.corpwatch.org/bulletins/PAM.jsp).

CorpWatch. 2002. *Campaigns: Greenwash Awards.* http:/www.corpwatch.org.

Disney Boycott. 2002. *Your Official Disney Boycott Site!* http://www.laker.net/webpage/boycott.htm.

Disney's Child Labor and Union Busting. 2002. www.laker.net/webpage/aadisneylabor.htm.

Divest Now. 2002. *Divest from Israel.* www.princetondivest.org, harvardmitdivest.org, ucdivest.org.

Ecocert Belgium. 2002. www.ecocert.be/ecopresenteng.html.

Eco Mark. 2002. *The Eco Mark Program.* www.jeas.or.jp/ecomark/english/tebiki.html.

European Environmental Bureau (EEB). 1999. *Swedish Evidence Proves: Ecolabels Can Work! Soap Industry Forced to Reduce Pressure on Environment.* Press Release, March 25. Brussels: EEB. www.eeb.org/press/soap_industry_forced_to_reduce_pohtm.

EEB. 1999. *Position of the EEB on the Commission's Proposal for the Revision of the EMAS Regulation.* www.eeb.org/activities/position_of_the_ebb_on_proposal_htm.

EFTA. 2002. *Fair Trade: Let's Go Fair. Fair Trade—History, Principles and Practices.* www.eftafairtrade.org/Document.asp?DocID=33&tod=152942.

EFTA. 2002a. *Fair Trade Networks.* www.eftafairtrade.org/Document.asp?DocID=78&tod=9106.

Ethical Investment Research Service (EIRIS). 2000. *About EIRIS.* www.eiris.u-net.com.

Elster, Jospeh K. 1996. *Letter to Disney.* www.geocities.com/CapitolHill/1555/Disney1.html.

Ethical Consumer. 2002. *Welcome to Ethical Consumer.* www.ethical consumer.org

Ethical Consumer. 2002. *Why Buy Ethically? An Introduction to the Philosophy Behind Ethical Purchasing.* ww.ethicalconsumer.org/aboutetc/why_buy_ethically.htm.

Ethical Consumer. 2002. *Links.* www.ethicalconsumer.org/links.htm.

ETI (Ethical Trading Initiative). 2002. www.ethicaltrade.org.

Ethical Funds. 2002. *About Us.* www.ethicalfunds.com.

Ethical Investors. 2002. *Services for Charities. Retirement Planning.* www.ethicalinvestors.co.uk/charity_retire.htm.

EU-Flower. N.d. http://europa.edu.int/comm/environment/ecolabel.

EU-Flower. 2002. *EU Eco-label.* http://europa.eu.int/comm/environment/ecolabel.

EUROSIF (European Sustainable and Responsible Investment Forum). 2002. *EUROSIF.* www.eurosif.info.

Fairtrade Center. 2000a. www.fairtradecenter.a.se/but_v.phtml.

Fairtrade Center. 2000b. *Fondsparande.* www.fairtradecenter.a.se/p_fond.html.

Fairtrade Labeling Organization (FLO). 2002. *Fairtrade: a better deal.* www.fairtrade.net/better_deal.html.

Fairtrade Labeling Organization International (FLO-I). 2000. www.faitrade.net.

FLO News Bulletin. 2002. "International Fairtrade Certification Mark," No. 6 (April): 3–4. www.fairtrade.net.

Friends of the Earth (FOE). 2000. www.foe.org.uk/campaigns/food_and_biotechnology.

FOE. 2001. *FOE Calls for Ethical Pension Information.* Press Release, March 28. www.foel.org/uk.

FOE. 2002. *Real Food. Campaign.* www.foe.org.uk/campaigns/real_food/issues/food_for_all.

Friends of Al-Aqsa. 2002. *Urgent Action: Campaign 2. Disney Promotes Israeli Occupation.* www.aqsa.org.uk/activities/campaign2.html.

Friends Provident. 2000. *Friends Provident. Stewardship Newsletter,* No. 8 (Winter) 1999/2000. www.friendsprovident.co.uk/portal/aboutus.html.

Friends Provident. 2002. *Welcome to the Socially Responsible Investment Web Site.* www.friendsprovident.co.uk/stewardship/bottom.jhtml?jsessionid=CS04WY4Z.

Forest Stewardship Certification (FSC). 2000. *Welcome to the Forest Stewardship Council.* www.fscoax.org/index.html.

FSC. 2000. *FSC Process Guidelines for Developing Regional Certification Standards.* FSC A.C. document 4.2. www.fscoax.org/html/4-2.html.

FSC. 2000. *Forest Stewardship Council A.C. By-Laws.* Document 1.1. www.fscax.org/html/1-1.html.

FSC. 2002. *Frequently Asked Questions.* www.fscoax.org/principal.htm.

GAP. 2000. *Code of Vendor Conduct.* www.gapinc.com/community/sourcing/vendor_conduct.htm.

GEN (Global Ecolabelling Network). www.gen.gr.jp.

Gene Watch. 2002. *Food Labelling*. www.genewatch.org/News/labeling.htm.

Genetics Forum. 2002. *Food Briefing Paper*. www.geneticsforum.org.uk/foodfact.htm.

Global Compact. 2002. *The Global Compact*. unglobalcompact.org.

Greenpeace. 2002. *Shopper's Guide to GM*. www.greenpeace.org.uk.

Green Seal. 2002. *About Green Seal*. www.greenseal.org/about.html.

High Moral Grounds. 2002. *Say No To Monopolies. Boycott Microsoft*. www.vcnet.com/bms.

Hollbrook, Leah. 1997. *Disney, Inc., Feeling the Wrath of Southern Baptist*. www.siue.edu/ALESTLE/library/summer1997/jun.25.97/Disney.hml.

International Baby Food Action Network (IBFAN). 2002. *Don't Be a Mug—Give Nescafé The Boot. Stop Bottle Baby Deaths—Boycott Nestlé*. www.babymilkaction.org/pages/boycott.html.

In Defense of Animals (IDA). 2002. *P & G Kills*. www.idausa.org/index.shtml and www.pandgkills.com.

International Federation for Alternative Trade (IFAT). 2002. *IFAT the Global Network for Fair Trade*. www.ifat.org/dwr/home.hml.

International Federation of Organic Agricultural Movements (IFOAM). 2002. *Information about IFOAM*. www.ifoam.org/whoisifoam/general.html.

International Forest Industry Roundtable (IFIR). 2001. *Proposing an International Mutual Recognition Framework*. IFRI report, edited by James Griffiths. www.sfms.com/recognition.htm.

International Peace Bureau (IPB). 1995. "IPB Calls for Boycott of French Goods," *Wise News Communique*, June 30. www.antenna.nl/wise/435/4293-4.html.

International Organization of Standardization (ISO). 2000. *What are standards*. www.iso.ch/infoe/intro.htm.

International Tropical Timber Organization. 2002. *What is the International Tropical Timber Agreement?* www.itto.or.jp/inside/about.html.

Kenworthy, Eldon. 1997. *Responsible Coffee Campaign: Organic, Sustainable, Fair-Traded Issues*. www.planeta.com/ecotravel/ag/coffee/campaign/campaignb.html.

KRAV (Kontrolförening för ekologisk odling). 2000. *Året 1999*. www.krav.se.

KRAV, 2002. *Foreign Certification Bodies Recognized by KRAV*. www.krav.se.

Kuida, Jenni "Emiko." 1997. "Why You Should Boycott Disney," *The Rafu Shimpo*, June 24. www.kuidaosumi.com/JKwriting/Disney.html.

LO (Landsorganisationen i Sverige, Swedish Trade Union Council). 2002. "Rättvist kaffe på Metall." *LO Globalt*, November 4. www.lo.se

Max Havelaar Foundation. N.d. www.maxhavellar.nl/eng.

Miljömärkarna. 2000. www.miljomarkarna.org.

Miller, David. 1997. "The Case Against Disney: Twenty-Three Reasons (and Counting) to Beware of the 'Magic Kingdom,'" *The Ethics and Religious Liberty Community*. www.erlc.com/Culture/Disney/1997/case.htm.

Mother Earth. 1995. *News Conference and Action Launches FME's International Boycott Against French Nuclear Testing.* Press Release, November 18. www.motherearth.org/archive/archive/boycot/pr01.html.

Marine Stewardship Certification (MSC). 2000a. www.msc.org/homeage.html.

MSC. 2000. *Chain of Custody Certification. Questions and Answers.* www.msc.org.

Maquila Solidarity Network. 2002. *Is it a Boycott?* www.maquilasolidarity.org/tools/campaign/boycott.htm.

NAACP. www.naacp.org.

National Resources Defense Council. 2002. *North Atlantic Swordfish. NRDS's Give Swordfish a Break Campaign Nets Victory for Recovery Efforts.* www.nrdc.org/wildlife/fish/nswordbr.asp.

Native Forest Network. 2002. *Boycott Woodchipping Campaign.* www.green.net.au/boycott/bwcintro.htm.

New Economics Foundation. 2001. *The Naked Consumer. Why Shoppers Deserve Honest Product Labelling.* Report January. London: New Economics Foundation. www.neweconomics.org.

New Economics Foundation. 2002. *About New Economics Foundation.* www.neweconomics.org

Network of European World Shops (NEWS). 2002. www.worldsshops.org.

Network of European World Shops. 2002. *European Commission Communication on Fair Trade.* www.worldshops.org/fairtrade/communication4.htm.

NikeWatch Campaign. 2002. *Just Stop It.* www.caa.org.au/campaigns/nike.

Organic Consumers Association. 2002. *Campaigning for Food Safety, Organic Agriculture, Fair Trade and Sustainability.* www.organicconsumers.org.

Office of Consumer Affairs, Industry Canada. 2000. *An Evaluative Framework for Voluntary Codes.* http://strategis.ic.gc.ca/SSg/ca01227e.html.

Ø-Label. 2002. *The Ø-Label—The State-Controlled Guarantee Symbol.* Denmark. www.fvm.dk/oko_uk/high_final_okouk.asp?page_id=290.

Organic Consumers Association. 2002. *Starbucks/Fair Trade Campaign.* www.organicconsumers.org/starbucks/index.htm.

Organic Consumers Association. 2002. *Call to Action for Global Boycott.* www.organicconsumers.org/callAction.html.

Organic Food Federation. 2002. *About Us and Frequently Asked Questions.* www.orgfoodfed.com.

Organic Trust. 2002. *The Organic Trust Symbol.* www.iol.ie/~organic/trust.html.

Organic Trade Association. 2002. *Organic Consumer Trends 2001.* www.ota.con/consumer_trends_2001.htm.

Oxfam. 2000. *Oxfam's Clothes Code Campaign.* www.oxfam.org.uk/campaign/clothes/clocodh.htm.

Oxfam. 2003. *Join thte Big Noise. Make Trade Fair.* www.maketradefair.org.

Oxfam. N.d. www.oxfam.org.uk/fairtrad/whyft.htm.

Oxfam Canada. 2000. *See the Label, Feel the Pain.* http://novanewsnet.
ukings.nf.ca.stories/99-00/000211/swetshop.htm.
Pesticide Action Network International. 2002. *PAN International
Campaigns.* www.pan-international.org/campaignsEn.html.
PAX World Funds. 2002. *The History of Pax.* www.paxfund.com/matures.htm.
PeaceNet. 1995a. *Campaign Against Nuclear Testing.* July 12.
http://nativenet.uthscsa.edu/archive/nl/9507/0415.html.
PeaceNet. 1995b. *Physicians Condemn French Nuclear Testing.* September 6.
http://nativenet.uthscsa.edu/archive/nl/9507/0415.html.
PEFC (The Pan European Forest Certification). 2000. www.pefc.org.
PEFC. 2002. *Statues of PEFC.* 222.pefc.org/statutes3.htm.
Rättvisemärkt. 2000a. www.raettvist.se.
Rättvisemärkt. 1998. *Samarbete för etiska placeringar!* Press release,
November 23. www.raettvist.se/press63.htm.
Responsible Coffee Campaign. 2002. *Wake Up and Smell the Coffee.* www.plan-
eta.com/ecotravel/ag/coffee/campaign/campaignb.html.
Right Livelihood Award. 2002. *Award Recipients 1980–2000.* www.
rightlivelihood.se.
Salam, Muna. 1997. *Disney's Unholy War on African Americans and Muslims.*
www.arabmedia.com.
Saguaro Seminar in Civic Engagement in America. 2001. *Bettertogether.*
(Harvard, MA: John F. Kennedy School of Government, Harvard
University.
Shareholder Action Network (SAN). 2002. *Shareholder Activity as a Tool
for Corporate Transparency and Democracy.* www.foe.org/international/
shareholder/toolsfordemocracy.html.
SAN. 2002. *Take Action.* www.shareholderaction.org/action.cfm.
Seaweb. 2002. *Give Swordfish a Break.* www.seaweb.org/campaigns/
swordfish/swordpr2.html.
Smithsonian Migratory Bird Center. 2002. *Shade Grown Coffee.*
http://natzoo.si.edu/smbc/Research/Coffee/coffee.htm.
Social Accountability International. 2000. *A General Introduction.*
www.cepaa.org.
Social Investment Forum. 2000. *What is the Social Investment Forum?*
www.socialinvest.org.
Statskontoret. 2000. "Översyn av offentlig upphandling." Välkommen till
Dagens Förvaltning www.statskontoret.se/dagensforvaltning/nyheterna/
artiklar/199.shtml.
Stop E$$O. 2002. *Don't Buy E$$O.* www.stopesso.com.
Swan (Nordic Swan eco-label). 2002. www.svanen.nu.
TCO Development. 2002. *This is TCO Development.* www.tcodevelopmentl.
com/i/omtcodevelopment/index.html.
Third World Traveller. 1998. *Ongoing Boycotts—1998!* www.thirdworld
traveler.com/Boycotts/Ongoing.
Third World Traveller. 2002. *Shell Oil in Nigeria.* www.third
worldtraveler.com/Boycotts/ShellNigeria_ boycott.html.

TransFair USA. 2002. *History.* www.transfairusa.org/about/history.html.
Transport Salaried Staff Association. 1999. *TSSA Ethical Investment Charter.* www.tssa.org.uk/news/jnl/9912/ethics.htm.
Uncaged. 2002. *Uncaged Campaigns. Boycott Procter and Gamble.* www.uncaged.co.uk/news/2002/boycott.htm.
UK Social Investment Forum. 2000. *Welcome to the UK Social Investment Forum Website.* www.uksif.org/home/welcome/content.shtml.
USDA Organic. 2002. *The National Organic Program. Organic Food Standards and Labels: The Facts.* www.ams.usda.gov/nop/Consumers/brochure.html.
Woodchip Watch. 1999. "About the Boycott Woodchipping Campaign," A Quarterly Publication of the Boycott Woodchipping Campaign. www.green.net.au/woodchip/watch.html.
WWF (World Wildlife Foundation). 2000. *Schweiziskt tryckeri först i världen med FSC-certifikat.* Press release, No. 7 (August). www.wwf.se.
WWF (World Wildlife Foundation U.K.). 2002. *Wildlife Benefits from Organic Farming.* www.wwf.org.uk.
WRC (Worker Rights Consortium). 2000. *WRC Companion Document.* www.workersrights.org/.
Young, Rick. 2002. "Green Coffee," *Fault Line* June 10. www.faultline.org/news/2002/07/coffee.html.

Talks

Andersson, Renée. 2002. "Enfrågerörelser." Conference ("Politikens nya villkor") held by the Budget Unit at the Ministry of Finance. May.

Interviews

Axelsson, Svante. N.d. General secretary of the SNF. Discussion about Good Environmental Choice.
Dobson, Chad. 2000. Head of Consumer's Choice Council, Washington D.C. Interview. February 22.
Eiderström, Eva. 2000. Head of Good Environmental Choice Unit and editor of the unit's magazine "Bra Miljöval." Interview. January 12.
Eiderström, Eva. 2002. E-mail correspondence. December 2.
Friström, Anders. 2001. Staff member of the Swedish Society for Nature Conservation and one of the people who started the Good Environmental Choice process in the 1980s. Interview. January 16.
Norin, Helena. 2000. Handling officer, Good Environmental Choice. Interview. January 12.
Vaste, Lars. 2000. Information head at the Swedish Society for Nature Conservation. Conversation on chlorine-bleached paper in connection with his willingness to let me read his archival material. Interview. December 13.

INDEX